THINK FAST: THE ADD EXPERIENCE
Edited by Thom Hartmann & Janie Bowman

This book gathers expert inform~~~~~~~~~ ~~ ~~~~~~~t and
presents ever~~~~~~~ ~~~~~~~~~~~~ ~~~~ ~~~~ ~~ ~~~~~~~ ~~~~ nat that
can be read f~~~~~~~~
specific topics

"A delightful s~~~~~~~~
—Jane B. Shu~~~~~~~~

$12.95, Trade p~~~~~, ISBN 1-887424-08-3
256pp, 6 1/4 x 9 1/4

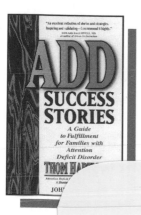

ADD SUCCESS STORIES
*A Guide to Fulfillment for Families with
Attention Deficit Disorder*
Thom Hartmann
Introduction by John J. Ratey, M.D.
Inspiring real-life stories that show how people
with ADD can succeed in school, at work,
and in relationships.

"Inspiring and validating—I recommend it highly"
—Edward Hallowell, M.D.,

3 1/2

D!
R

-4,

R

Ramundo

-9,

Contra Costa Child Care Council
1035 Detroit Ave., Ste. 200
Concord, CA 94518

UN~~~~~~   945
A~~~~~~   RS
QUANTITY   00) 788-3123

Beyond ADD

*Hunting For Reasons In
The Past & Present*

Thom Hartmann

Thom Hartmann is a pioneer in ADD research. His previous books have shown how individuals with ADD are not just "hyperactive" or "easily distracted," but actually possess highly adaptive, entrepreneurial skills–traits which served ancient hunters but meet with resistance in modern agrarian societies.

In *Beyond ADD* Thom Hartmann explores possible genetic origins and discusses how ADD-related traits may have served to further human evolution. He spotlights how modern life contributes to ADD, including a toxic environment that neurologically damages fetuses, nutritional deficiencies, quick-fix consumer culture, television and overpopulation. Hartmann documents the difficulty gifted children encounter in an educational system that does not stimulate them, and the hardships for visual learners in an auditory environment. As he discusses brain chemistry and physiology, he examines the pros and cons of the controversial drug Ritalin.

Hartmann urges people with ADD to resist society's stigmatization of them as victims and to realize that the more we understand about ADD, the easier it will be to change our lives.

$12.95, Trade paper, 224pp, ISBN 1-887424-12-1

*Available at bookstores everywhere
Bulk discounts for ADD groups are available at (800) 788-3123*

Survival Strategies For Parenting Your ADD Child

Dealing With Obsessions, Compulsions, Depression, Explosive Behavior, and Rage

Survival Strategies For Parenting Your ADD Child

Dealing With Obsessions, Compulsions, Depression, Explosive Behavior, and Rage

George T. Lynn, M.A., C.M.H.C.

Underwood Books, Inc.
Grass Valley, California

Survival Strategies
ISBN 1-887424-19-9

An Underwood Books title by arrangement with the author. No part of this book may be reproduced in any form or by any electronic or mechanical means including information storage and retrieval systems without explicit permission from the author or the author's agent, except by a reviewer who may quote brief passages. For information address the publisher: Underwood Books, Box 1609, Grass Valley, California 95945.

Distributed by Publishers Group West
Manufactured in the United States of America
Cover design by Nora Wertz/Nora Wertz Design

FIRST EDITION
10 9 8 7 6 5 4 3

The ideas in this book are based on the author's personal experience with ADD, and as such are not to be considered medical advice. This book is not intended as a substitute for psychotherapy or the medical treatment of Attention-deficit Hyperactivity Disorder and the various medications described herein can only be prescribed by a physician. The reader should consult a qualified health care professional in matters relating to health and particularly with respect to any symptoms which may require diagnosis or medical attention.

Library of Congress Cataloging-in-Publication-Data:
Lynn, George T. 1945-
    Survival strategeis for parenting your ADD child : dealing with obsessions, compulsions, depression, explosive behavior and rage / by George T. Lynn. -- 1st ed.
        p.   cm.
    Includes bibliographical references (p.   ).
    ISBN 1-887424-19-9
    1. Attention deficit-hyperactivity disorder--Popular works.
I. Title.
RJ506.H9L96   1996
618.92'8589--DC20   96-30751
                                                                    CIP

Acknowledgements

First, I thank my clients who have shared their strategies, stresses, and triumphs with me, enabling me to pass these tools along to others. I thank all the parents, single adults, and kids who have taught me what it's like to live with Attention Differences and thrive. I find delight in being a "conduit" for the kind of practical parenting genius that my clients have brought to my life.

And thanks to my wife, Joanne Barrie Lynn, conceptual collaborator and extraordinary poet and writer. Her brilliance and creativity are seen in the best parts of this book.

To Thom Hartmann, my on-line colleague and idea tester. I first met Thom in the Compuserve A.D.D. Forum and have greatly benefited since from his encouragement and creative mentoring. And to Tim Underwood, publisher of this book, for guiding me on my maiden voyage as an author and assigning Carol LaRusso to me to edit the work. Carol's patience in teaching me the craft of book writing and her artistry in helping me clarify and articulate my message has been invaluable.

I am indebted to a whole line of conceptual mentors whose original insights form the backbone of theory behind my approach to helping A.D. kids: Fritz Perls, father of Gestalt Therapy, who is my inspiration for understanding individual perception. To Jean Piaget for his brilliant insights into the impact of experience on cognition and perception. To Dr. David Comings for explaining, in terms we all can understand, what is happening on a biochemical level when our kids do the strange things that they do.

To Suzanne Kobasa and Salvatore Maddi whose research on

stress hardiness gave me a vision of how to stay psychologically healthy despite the stress. And to Connirae and Steve Andreas, master practitioners of Neurolinguistic Programming (NLP), whose work has refined and educated my understanding of how the way A.D. children *see* things impacts their feelings and behavior.

Closer to my home are my friends, colleagues, and teachers: Man With Ravens, a Seneca medicine man whose perspective on Native American spirituality has been of invaluable assistance to my son Gregory (with whom he did a traditional Native American healing) and in my work with the wild-spirited children that come to my counseling practice.

Finally, I honor Lou Cenname, Gregory's principal at John Muir Elementary School in our home town of Kirkland, Washington, and David St. Antoine, his teacher there. David and Lou have demonstrated such trustworthiness, talent, matter-of-fact acceptance of Gregory, and interest in him that he couldn't help but learn. Joanne and I are deeply indebted to these two dedicated educators.

Contents

Acknowledgments   ix

Introduction: **What Grows in the Garden?
Varieties of Attention Difference**   xiii

Part One: **Understand the Nature of the
Challenge**   1

Chapter One: **Seeing Is Behaving—How a
Child's Perceptual Style Causes Behavior
Problems**   3

Chapter Two: **A Wellness Model for Parenting
Attention Different Children**   29

Chapter Three: **How Stress Cycles Make
Problems Worse**   43

Chapter Four: **How to Take Care of Yourself So
You Can Take Care of Your Child**   55

Part Two: **Strategies for Successful
Management of Individual Problems**   65

Chapter Five: **Calming Hyperactivity**   67

Chapter Six: **Cooling Oppositionality**   83

Chapter Seven: **Overcoming Self-Righteousness
and Making Friends**   91

Chapter Eight: **Educating Emotional Wildness**   99

Contents

Chapter Nine: **Confronting Dangerous, Destructive, and Risky Behavior** 109

Chapter Ten: **Transcending Depression** 121

Chapter Eleven: **Healing Rage** 133

Chapter Twelve: **Meeting the Challenge of Obsessions and Compulsions** 145

Part Three: **Strategies for Changing Family Distress Cycles to Family Eustress Cycles** 159

Introduction to Part Three 161

Chapter Thirteen: **Moving Through the Grief Cycle** 165

Chapter Fourteen: **Taming "Uproar" to Revitalize Your Marriage** 175

Chapter Fifteen: **Meeting the Challenge of School-Caused Stress** 185

Chapter Sixteen: **Mastering the Stressors of Single Parenting** 211

Chapter Seventeen: **Dealing with the Blended Family Blues** 223

Conclusion: **Creating Community to Contain Our Kids' "Wyrd" Gifts** 235

Part Four: **Appendix** 241

Article by Walter J. Crinnion, N.D.: **Nutritional Alternatives to Ritalin—Treating the Causes as Well as the Symptoms** 243

Chapter Notes and Bibliography 253

About the Author 263

Index 265

Varieties of Attention Difference

The Garden

I recently spoke with a remarkable woman who came to me to set up counseling for her ten-year-old son, diagnosed with severe Attention Deficit Hyperactivity Disorder (A.D.H.D.) The boy had a twelve-year-old brother who was diagnosed with Bipolar Mood Disorder (BMD).

This woman, a single mom, was under a lot of stress dealing with her two sons. I know how temperamental, depressed, and oppositional kids with the A.D.H.D. diagnosis can get and the frequent rages seen in Bipolar Disorder can disturb the harmony and comfort of the most expertly parented families. I asked her how she dealt with her stress.

"What stress?" she said. "Look, I figure we're all plants in a garden. Some plants need a lot of sunshine, some need shade. Some you have to water all the time, others seek the very dry places. I just happen to have three wild varieties that you don't see too often, but I love them the more for their distinctiveness."

As our conversation proceeded it became clear that she was not into Pollyanna denial of her situation and talked about the toll that her job as a parent had taken Yet her attitude of acceptance toward her sons was as smart as it was inspiring. She was not into moping or melodramatics about her situation even though she could well have been. As the boys' mother, she saw her job as a challenge to be managed with ingenuity and perseverance. She was a dedicated gardener of her boys' spirits, and I knew those boys would thrive.

The eustress attitude: key to effective parenting

The attitude that this woman has is what pioneering researcher Dr. Hans Selye called the "eustress" attitude, essential to surviving the experience of parenting difficult children. Selye said that eustress (the "eu" prefix means "good" in Latin) keeps people healthy despite the stress that they face because these people see stressors as challenges, not blessings or curses.

Eustress begins with the labels that we use. Call a kid "deficit" and you create a reality of helplessness. Call him "different" and you open up his potential to realize all the gifts that come with being extraordinary. This is why I use the terms "Attention Different" or "A.D." to describe kids like my own son, Gregory, who has "severe Attention Deficit Hyperactivity Disorder" and "mild Tourette Syndrome with tics and obsessions." He is indeed different but he brings with his difference special gifts: his emotional presence, his joy, his creativity, his talent for white-hot focus on something until he masters it.

Getting to eustress is difficult if you're in the dark about what's happening with your child. That's why the most successful parents never stop exploring the quality of their child's experience and never stop looking at options for doing things differently. In fact, if you look closely enough, you will see that Attention Different patterns connect your child with other A.D. kids in certain ways. Each child is idiosyncratic, but all Attention Different children share patterns of hypersensitivity in the way they focus on things and handle stress. Once you understand these patterns, you are in a position to help your child, to give him what he needs. In Chapter One, I describe how to fine-tune your exploration of the way your child focuses and what you can do to help.

This book was written primarily for parents of Attention Different children in the pre-adolescent years who show symptoms of A.D.H.D., Attention Deficit Disorder with Hyperactivity (A.D.D. is a term coming into common parlance but is not a medical diagnosis), Tourette Syndrome (T.S.), and Bipolar Mood

Disorder diagnoses. Attention Different children in this age range face different issues than teen-agers and other parenting strategies are necessary.

The liabilities of being Attention Different—the organizational problems, learning problems, temper control, and other issues weigh heavily on the self-esteem of the elementary school-age child. The techniques found in the following chapters will help you get your A.D. child through this span of years with his self-confidence and optimism about the world intact.

The distress and eustress tie-in

Early in his life, it became clear to me that my son Gregory's behavior would become most problematic when he was under stress. This is a truism for any parent who has a child with attention differences.

My partner Joanne Barrie Lynn and I taught stress management to adults many years before I started working as a counselor with Attention Different children. The models of wellness I learned from my stress management work have greatly assisted my understanding of my young clients. In fact most of the problematic behaviors associated with Attention Different kids—the temper, the oppositionality, the silliness and "emotional delays," and the obsessiveness—mimic the "fight or flight" reaction that humans have to stressors. If problems happen when a kid is under stress, decrease his stress and build his strength. Smart parents do the same for themselves. This is the eustress parenting attitude in a nutshell.

Help your child by taking care of yourself

There is another aspect of eustress that you may forget in the day-to-day crisis of managing your child; you can only help him to the degree that you take care of yourself. Your job is one of most stressful that anyone can have and you are not immune to burnout. My intention here is to provide strategies to create a sense of harmony, wellness, and joy in your own life.

The guidelines for self-care in Chapter Four are gleaned from the sweat and tears of many of my clients and from my own experience. These guidelines are offered knowing that taking care of your difficult child will always end up "on your plate." The hard reality is that no one—no school counselor, teacher, psychiatrist, attorney, or physician, can shoulder the responsibility that is yours. The buck stops with you.

He will need your shoulder to scream and cry on hundreds of times in his growing up. He will need you to stand there and take his rage and not hit him. He will need you to provide a "container" for the energies that spill out of him and gobble up the peace of mind in your home. You will be able to provide him with this kind of presence if, and only if, your psychological batteries are charged and your confidence is up. Because this is a project in stress management, achieving greater wellness in your relationship with your child is the central focus of this book.

The issue of medication

Psychoactive drugs are widely used to control hyperactivity and enable children to keep focus at school. These drugs do not correct A.D. challenges but normalize brain function while in the child's system so as to reduce problematic behavior.

The use of Ritalin, the primary brand name stimulant used for control of hyperactivity, is growing by geometric proportions in this country. The drug helps Attention Different children to focus and stay calm. It is also occasionally over-prescribed by doctors who do so at the urging of parents who are attempting to respond to pressure from their child's school district to get him "under control."

The fact that when both parents work and need a reliable child-care setting often pushes them to get their child on stimulants. Off the medication, the child may do just fine until he hits stress overload. Once this happens, he makes a scene which upsets the flow of work in his large, overcrowded classroom. The school then calls you to come and get him. This distress cycle is maintained by the school's inability to teach the child, and the pressure comes down on you.

Giving the child Ritalin takes the responsibility off the school district (and district taxpayers) and puts it on you and your child. The child may or may not be able to get along without it. Some kids are inappropriately medicated. But most likely he's on the medication because when he's not he needs more extensive one-to-one attention in class.

I do not discuss the use of Ritalin to a great extent. Instead I have more to offer as a coach for dealing with the public school bureaucracy, the kingpins in the distress cycle that make Ritalin a necessity. That topic, covered in Chapter Fifteen, is one of the longest ones in this book for good reason. Schools put enormous stress on parents of Attention Different kids. The cycle ends when the system becomes more skilled in responding to the child's special needs.

I do deal with the issue of using anti-depressant drugs to treat depression and obsessive compulsive problems in Chapters Ten and Twelve respectively. These conditions are potentially health—and life—threatening, and the use of medication is probably the quickest way to stabilize a child's life.

The organization of this book

In Chapters One through Four, which make up Part I of the book, I show how your child's way of seeing the world puts pressure on him, and what you can do to relieve these pressures and build his strength of personality. In Chapter Four are techniques for you to take care of yourself so that you can take care of him.

Part II contains eight chapters which deal with helping your child manage aspects of his A.D. that I have seen to be among the most problematic for my client families. Chapter Five shows you ways to calm your child's hyperactivity. The succeeding chapters show how to manage oppositionality, self-righteousness, emotional wildness, dangerous behavior, depression, rage, and obsessions.

In the five chapters that form Part III, I talk about patterns of distress that occur in families with A.D. kids and what you can do to change these patterns. These are the essential predicaments of people like you and me who are forced to deal with stress that most parents can't comprehend.

Part III begins with Chapter Thirteen and the grief process that families experience after diagnosis. In Chapter Fourteen I describe how a family can turn into a battleground around an Attention Different child and how to prevent this dynamic.

Chapter Fifteen deals with school-caused stress, a major problem for most families with special-needs kids. Chapter Sixteen shows how to survive the challenges of parenting an A.D. child on your own. Single-parenting an A.D. kid is a true test of personal resourcefulness.

Chapter Seventeen discusses the myriad of stressors that come to bear on blended families—those with adopted A.D. kids or non-A.D. step-parents in the household. In this chapter are ideas for building a positive and happy blended family environment.

Part IV, the Appendix, contains an article by Dr. Walter J. Crinnion, a leading naturopathic physician who discusses the tie-in between diet, allergies, and problematic behavior. Many "urban legends" abound about alternative approaches so I was very pleased to get Dr. Crinnion's insights on the research about dietary factors that actually make a difference.

I enjoyed returning to the metaphor of the garden in the concluding chapter. The experience of writing this book has reminded me that our kids are "different good" in so many ways. Wild-spirited as they are (and I hold the word "wild" in a positive light), they have an enormous contribution to make for the well-being of all of us. If our children are going to make it, we have to create parenting strategies, a family structure, and a community that accepts them for who they are. This book is written to assist you in meeting this challenge.

Survival Strategies For Parenting Your ADD Child

Dealing With Obsessions, Compulsions, Depression, Explosive Behavior, and Rage

PART ONE

Understand the Nature of the Challenge

CHAPTER ONE

Seeing Is Behaving:
How a Child's Perceptual Style
Causes Behavior Problems

"Our brains are constantly in flux, adapting to serve our lives."

—Robert Ornstein, *The Roots of Self*

The great developmental psychologist Jean Piaget observed that children grow in mental ability through a process of assimilation and accommodation. The child first lets in, or assimilates, his experience. Then, he noted, the child's ability to comprehend more complex material moves to a new plateau: an accommodation of the new information occurs that results in a growth of the brain itself.

Accommodation can be seen in the child's greater understanding of events in his environment and in the growth of his ability to understand the complexity of things. An actual change in brain structure was later documented by medical researchers who found that the protective coating around neural pathways in the brain called the myelin sheathe had grown in areas of the brain specific to the learning process.

This assimilation and accommodation process is the way intelligence develops. Step by step the child's intelligence becomes more capable of handling complexity. The heart of this process is his ability to focus on something—to pick it out from its environment, its background, and highlight it in consciousness, as a figure against its background.

Forming figure from ground in this way is like breathing: Breath in, Breath out, pause. He concentrates on one figure. Something else attracts him. He works to understand it. Breath in; he takes it in. New ground forms around the figure. He takes it in deeper, now accommodating to it. Breath out. Pause. If the rhythm is right, the child will move from one figure to the next. Growth will be natural and marked by development in intellectual and sensory capacity.

This process is neurologically driven by the release of endorphins, the brain's natural opiates. When the child completes the process he is rewarded by a little endorphin squirt. Stimulus satisfaction occurs. Since all new learning is powered by this process, this is why mastering a task, getting better at it, is so satisfying. This brings the child back for more. Stimulus satisfaction energizes and rewards the child, like a good deep breath.

External stimulation comes to the child through all his sensory modes—sight, hearing, smell, touch, and taste.

Internal stimulation comes from brain centers that contain stored thoughts and images. Cognitive input is received as images. These are images he remembers or that he anticipates in the future. Cognitive input is also received as verbal word strings that form thoughts (the auditory process). Some people are more apt to cognitively process their experience with images and mind pictures, whereas others will process it more auditorily.

Emotional stimulation comes to the child from brain centers concerned with organizing his response to his environment. The four basic emotion groups are mad, glad, sad, scared. A variety of mood states made up of combinations of these four emotional groupings are experienced as emotional stimulation.

Kinesthetic stimulation comes as sensations of movement, position, or tension in the body. Kinesthetic sensation is experienced as our overall sense of body well-being, our sense of being relaxed or of being "uptight." For many Attention Different children, the kinesthetic domain contains feelings of undifferentiated tension in the body. This is often expressed as a sense of being driven or pressured on an overall body/mind level.

Finally, internal stimulation may come as *proprioceptive sensation*. Proprioceptive feelings originate in body tissues and musculature and are sensed by receptors called proprioceptors. Tics, the semi-voluntary muscle and vocal movements seen in Tourette Syndrome are preceded by the premonitory sensation which is experienced as "a psychic itch."

External Stimulation	**Internal Stimulation**
• Sight	• Cognitive: visual and auditory input
• Hearing	• Emotional: mad, glad, sad, scared
• Vision	• Kinesthetic: sense of overall well-being
• Taste	• Proprioceptive: sense of muscle tension
• Smell	

Types of Stimulation: The Nine Sensory Domains

The normal child has a high degree of sensory integration

If figure/ground interaction is smooth, a child can move from one of these sensory modalities to another quite easily. His external senses process smoothly with his internal senses and he is able to communicate his reactions, demands, and delights and come to closure on events. If functioning normally, his neurologic figure and ground "shifter" makes about ten shifts a second to process new information, new sensation, and assimilates it.

This child is able to see clearly what is going on around him in both his social and natural environments, and respond to people and events appropriately. He makes focus in such a way that the cycle of contact, of finding the figure and the organization ground around it, proceeds smoothly. This results in completed contact and learning.

"Attention Different" (A.D.) children have problems keeping their focus in one sensory domain "uncontaminated" by another sensory domain

Some children have difficulty focusing on a specific figure against its background in order to assimilate it. I call these children "Attention Different" to illustrate the idea that though they have significant problems in information processing and human interaction in the crowded modern cultural environment, they are not deficit. In fact, they possess unique gifts (described in the next chapter) that compensate for their abnormal perceptual styles.

Attention Different children focus on things around them differently, having a different perceptual style than normal kids. Unlike other children who seem able to screen stimuli out, to let in just enough to digest, A.D. children appear to be unshielded or hypersensitive to external and/or internal stimulation. This unshielded quality leaves them open to stress that normal children do not experience, and gives their lives a sense of unusual intensity, of stimulus flooding.

They experience what might be termed "sensory contamination." This denotes a condition in which one sense modality influences another modality, leading to an ineffective response. A good example of this is the "driven," hyperactive behavior of children and adults with the diagnosis of Attention Deficit Hyperactivity Disorder. In "A.D.H.D.," pressure from kinesthetic sensors (body tension) contaminates the cognitive dimension. This results in the inability of the child to think clearly (cognate) about one thing.

Another A.D. child may not be able to retain the meaning or thread of what people say to him because of some distraction from his visual senses. He can't keep his mind on his plan for the day because his consciousness is contaminated with intrusive worries or obsessions from the cognitive domain.

The severity of this problematic behavior is directly related to the degree of pressure the A.D. child experiences from his openness to a particular source of stimulation as well as to the intensity of the stimulation. A child with a mild case of A.D.H.D. may be able to compensate for the contamination of kinesthetic stimulation and cognitive stimulation by deliberately focusing on his thinking process and blocking his sense of restlessness. A child who is more profoundly A.D.H.D. may not be able to exert this control. He may feel hopelessly swept away by distracting stimuli from the kinesthetic domain.

The Attention Different child has problems shifting from one sensory domain to another

Another defining characteristic of the Attention Different child is his lack of figure/ground flexibility. It is difficult for him to shift from the internal to external sensory domains and also to focus on things when in one domain or the other. For example, it is hard for him to move his fixed attention from a task to pay attention to his mother who wants him to go to the store with her. It is also difficult for him to shift internal mood states—from feeling sad to feeling glad. A child can get "stuck" in one place or the other.

Another example of this phenomenon would be the difficulty that an Attention Different child experiences in a classroom situation requiring him to make transitions from one activity to another. A normal kid can go through the change of focus required easily; "I was doing "x" and now I'm doing "y." The Attention Different child's figure/ground shifter locks up and he continues to do "x," becoming greatly distressed if his teacher tries to "grind his gears" to shift him to "y."

. . .

Why it is important to know your child's medical diagnosis

The practical intention of this book is to help you manage your child's behavior and your own stress. Though we won't achieve this by a detailed discussion of the various diagnoses assigned to Attention Different children by the Diagnostic and Statistical Manual (DSM IV) published by the American Psychiatric Association, it still is useful to know how Attention Different children are categorized.

Though the Manual gives no hint about how to change behavior in children it does describe patterns of behavior and feeling that give a clue to the severity of impairment of function. The "excessive talking" of a child diagnosed as A.D.H.D. is not the same as the "pressured speech" of a child with Bipolar challenges (see below). It is important to see patterns, how "symptoms" may group together. The DSM IV gives something of a standard of comparison, a checklist to begin assessing the day-to-day reality of your child's life.

In addition, it is useful to understand how the medical establishment sees the problem. You need to be able to differentiate one condition from another in advocating for your child with his doctor and school officials. It helps also to have a clear picture of what the DSM IV misses in its description of our kids. The wild, disinhibited behavior seen in a majority of children with Tourette Syndrome is not mentioned. Neither is the tendency for obsessions and compulsions commonly found in T.S., Bipolar Disorder, and in the A.D.H.D. condition. To have a say in your child's diagnosis it is necessary to have a good understanding of the limitations of the official "labels" that are assigned to him.

Four diagnostic categories are included here under my umbrella term of "Attention Different." These diagnostic groups are described below. The first two diagnostic categories—Attention Deficit/Hyperactivity Disorder with inattention, and Attention Deficit/Hyperactivity Disorder with impulsivity, are commonly referred to as "Attention Deficit Disorder" or A.D.D. I prefer this moniker to the DSM label but stay true to the Manual in this chapter to achieve a greater descriptive precision. In fact, the perceptual style of an A.D.H.D. child with hyperactivity may be quite different from one without this behavior.

Attention Deficit /Hyperactivity Disorder Predominantly Inattentive Type (314.00) Six or more of the following symptoms must be present. Some symptoms must be present before age 7, with impairment present in two or more settings (school and home).

-poor attention to details

-doesn't listen

-poor follow-through

-poor organization

-trouble keeping attention in task and at play

-avoids tasks requiring sustained mental effort

-easily distracted

-forgetful

Attention Deficit/Hyperactivity Disorder with impulsivity (314.01) Six or more or the following symptoms:

-fidgets

-leaves classroom desk

-runs excessively

-blurts answers

-interrupts or intrudes on others

-unable to play quietly

-acts "driven"

-talks excessively

-difficulty awaiting his turn

These diagnoses describe different perceptual styles

The DSM IV provides only a static and partial description of your A.D. child. Its descriptions can be compared to stop-action snapshots taken by doctors whose aims are to identify the child, pigeon-hole him, and medicate him.

Your child acts the way he does because he has a specific way

Tourette's Disorder (307.23)

-motor and vocal tics   -onset before 18

-tics occur over a year   -condition not due to other causes

-distress and social impairment

Bipolar (Manic-Depressive) Disorder (296.7)

For a diagnosis of *depression* five or more symptoms from the left hand
column must be present. For *mania,* abnormally elevated or irritable
mood and at least three of the symptoms listed in the right hand column
must be present.

-depressed mood   -inflated self-esteem

-loss of pleasure   -decreased need for sleep

-significant weight loss   -pressured speech

-sleep problems   -flight of ideas

-moves and acts slowly   -distractible

-fatigue   -increase in goal direction

-feelings of worthlessness   -compulsive pursuit of pleasure

-recurrent thoughts of death

-poor concentration

-clinically significant distress

Diagnosis also requires that "marked impairment" of occupational or
social function occurs.

of focusing and handling stimulation; this gives you a way to work
with him. The term Attention Different describes the reality of the
situation. Because your child pays attention differently than other
kids, it is important to identify how he processes and integrates
sensory information.

The three defining factors of Attention Different children are analyzed below for each of the above diagnoses. These factors are: 1. Sensory mode contamination, 2. Strength of hypersensitivity to a particular mode, and 3. Ability of the child to make figure/ground shift from one mode to another.

Attention Deficit Hyperactivity Disorder (primarily inattentive type)

1. *Sensory mode contamination.* The A.D.H.D. child without hyperactivity may be hypersensitive in all five external senses, with a particular sensitivity to visual stimulation. Oftentimes there is also a strong sensitivity to the internal emotional input with a predilection for the "sad" dimension. This child may show evidence of "depression," a problem described in greater detail in Chapter Ten.

2. *Strength of hypersensitivity.* Visual stimulation may be overpowering to the inattentive A.D.H.D. child, resulting in the tendency to get stuck in a daydream that lasts for hours. In this state, he may have a difficult time understanding any auditory input delivered to him. This inability to listen may set up a powerful failure experience at school. The result is an increased vulnerability to the incursion of sad emotions into his consciousness.

3. *Figure/ground shift ability.* The child may have a strong preference for introversion, for living in his own little world, as if he possessed a powerful psychological "coiled spring" that pulls him inside whenever he faces stress or unpleasantness. Moving into vigorous contact with the outside world is difficult.

Attention Deficit Hyperactive Disorder with impulsivity

1. *Sensory mode contamination*: all five external domains. He may be painfully sensitive to the feeling of certain types of fabric on his skin. He may have peculiar aversions to certain smells or be markedly overstimulated by florescent lights. Certain sounds, such as the crunching of potato chips or a high-pitched voice may drive him up the wall.

In the internal dimension, he is sensitive to emotional, cognitive, and kinesthetic stimuli, which gives him a "driven" appearance. Drivenness occurs as a result of over-sensitivity to all three internal stimuli wrapped up together.

2. *Strength of hypersensitivity.* Most A.D.H.D. children are powerfully overstimulated from kinesthetic stimuli as a separate domain. The degree of hyperstimulation in all other modalities varies child to child on a "bell curve." Some have fairly mild oversensitivity and others experience such powerful hypersensitivity that they become frantic in highly stimulating environments.

3. *Figure/ground shift ability.* The A.D.H.D. child will often seem "beside himself" or "out of body," totally lost in the external world. He may experience great difficulty in taking in information received from his senses to focus on it. He has trouble forming figure/ground in such a way to perceive meaning and learn from what is going on around him.

A good way to describe this process is to use the metaphor of a clutch in a car. The car has power in potential at all times and the clutch is used to distribute and regulate this instantly available power. The A.D.H.D. child, like all children, has a continual bank of emotional and kinesthetic power available but lacks the ability to smoothly regulate this power; his clutch is always "slipping." Feeling kinesthetically over-pressured and unable to achieve focus, his energy discharges itself in a series of frantic starts and endless running, which eventually results in exhaustion.

Tourette Syndrome (T.S.)

1. *Sensory mode contamination.* The Tourettic child experiences contamination from all five external senses and four "internal" sense modalities to include proprioceptive sensation. This gives rise to the "tics" or semi-voluntary vocal or motor muscle movements which are symptomatic of the disorder. He is especially vulnerable to emotional stimulation from the limbic brain (see Chapter Three for a description of limbic brain function).

2. *Strength of hypersensitivity.* Tourettic children tend to be powerfully and profoundly hypersensitive in all domains, with

specific extremes in the proprioceptive, emotional, and cognitive domains. These children tend to be at the extreme ends of the range of emotional expression—call it "A.D.H.D. to the tenth power."

This combination of emotional and cognitive overload can lead to the experience of obsessions. These obsessions manifest as overcharged "worry thoughts:" the fear of contamination, or ritualistic behavior such as hand washing, meant to make the child safe from the danger message contained in the obsession.

3. *Figure/ground shift ability.* Kids with T.S. have the ability to shift from the internal to the external domain and also within domains, but often get stuck in one place or the other. They may cycle rapidly between states without taking a breath. The Tourette child may cycle from a fairly normal state of consciousness to obsessing furiously about something—then move from an over-charged rageful emotional state to a almost ecstatically happy state. Very little actual figure/ground completion is seen in these rapid visits to the nine sensory domains.

Bipolar Mood Disorder

1. *Sensory mode contamination.* Typically, the child with this diagnosis experiences contamination from all his internal and external senses and may even show the tics seen in Tourette Syndrome. The dominant and sometimes disabling cross-contamination of emotional stimulation, especially of rage and sadness, with kinesthetic pressure, results in misery and depression

2. *Strength of hypersensitivity.* Intense, over-pressured stimulation from the emotional and kinesthetic domains are experienced in the Bipolar condition. In the manic phase a child may express his sense of pressure by incessant talking that darts from one subject to another. The child may have rage attacks (rage that lasts in excess of 30 minutes is diagnostic of Bipolar) or he may be continually depressed, irritable, obsessional, or frightened.

3. *Figure/ground shift ability.* The Bipolar child is most likely to become trapped in depressive emotional energy and not know how to get out of this painfully dark funk. Unlike depression that

occurs as a side condition of other attention differences, the child feels walled off from relief, from sunlight, from any sense of joy in his life. Thus his depression may be expressed as rage at anyone and anything around him, and he is vulnerable to suicidal thinking. This is the most profound Attention Different condition.

Attention Different children may carry elements of each of these diagnoses

Many A.D. kids carry a little piece of all of these diagnoses, and therefore definitive categorization is difficult. In reality, each child is distinguished more by the individual way he focuses on things and processes information than by his diagnostic category. You should be able to define his style of focus with some precision, and not rely on a simple definition of his disorder. Once you understand how his perceptions result in the actions he takes, you can help him.

A child may be diagnosed as "comorbid" (multi-symptoms)— Tourette Disorder, Attention Deficit Hyperactivity Disorder, and Bipolar Disorder. The Tourette neurologist finds that the child has

Attention Different diagnoses overlap

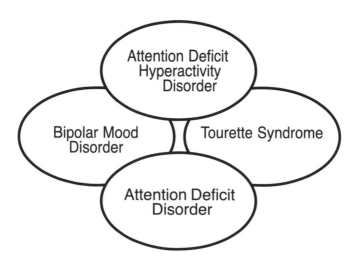

tics and diagnoses him after observing them. He also may see aspects of A.D.H.D. in the kid's silly, disinhibited mannerisms, which is very common in T.S.

Another doctor may find evidence of Bipolar Disorder, citing as evidence the severe angry depression that the boy can get into. These labels by themselves do not help us understand the particular situation in a way to help the child.

If these physicians take the time to talk with the child and observe him, to study the phenomena behind the child's behavior, they will notice that he had considerable capability for self-control when in a low stress context. (See Chapter Five for dealing with hyperactivity.) They would see that his Tourettic wildness was offset by a powerful sense of the spiritual—he might be a born mystic, a kid capable of intense wonder and with a complex understanding of his situation.

These doctors would see how his mood swing was related to intrusive stimuli from emotional centers in his brain. And they also would observe that he was powerfully visual and extremely sensitive to the emotional states of others. This knowledge would give them the ability to set up a learning environment for him that was visually stimulating. And it would point to the need to lower his overall stress in order to help him with his lack of emotional control.

Any wisdom that we have depends on the questions that we ask. Asking questions to find out how a child focuses on things will show us the problems he faces in a way that will allow us to help him.

Why not include *Autism* as an Attention Difference?

Autism is a neurologic condition in which a child will appear cut off from his surroundings, lost in his own world, and unreachable. He is a little dreamer who can sit in the corner for hours focusing on sparkles in the rug in front of him or the dust floating by in the air. Typically, Autism appears before the first three years of life and results in disturbances of physical, social, and language skills. It is primarily characterized by an abnormal response to sensations, usually an extreme hypersensitivity.

In the "high functioning" variety of Autism termed Asperger's

Disorder, the child may be capable of social interaction and classroom learning but will show a severe lack of social empathy (recognizing other feelings), He will hyperfocus on one thing to the exclusion of all others, will speak in a pressured monotone (like the character "Data" on the T.V. program *Star Trek*), and will require an extreme degree of predictability in his everyday life.

Autism *is* an attention difference. Children with Autism have the most difficult time of any kids shifting attention between sensory domains in the Attention Different spectrum. But I do not cover this condition in the following chapters because Autistic kids by and large do not comprehend emotional meanings in language and therefore would not benefit from many of the techniques in this book. They share Data's problems in knowing what love is, what humor is, or how to socially interact with people. Another book is needed to do this particular subject justice!

Autistic children have great gifts and often grow into adults who make remarkable contributions. People like Temple Grandin, the enigmatic and brilliant designer profiled in Dr. Oliver Sacks's book *An Anthropologist On Mars*, artist Vincent Van Gogh, pianist Glenn Gould, actor Peter Sellers, and many other modern luminaries show features of the quirky genius of the Autistic.

Gifted as they are, their world is a special place with a special culture and topography defined by their perceptual style. Temple Grandin in her book, *Thinking In Pictures*, describes a funny moment in her conversations with Oliver Sacks. They were talking about Shakespeare and she admitted that she "never got what Romeo and Juliet were doing." She had no concept of the romantic. This is an emotional difference that greatly changes the meaning of language for Autistics and requires that outsiders to this condition learn their language.

The Autistic child also experiences a lot of difficulty in abstracting from his experience in order to do things differently the next time. His processing is extremely concrete. He does not have the ability to generalize to new situations but will tend to follow things by absolute rote direction. If directions vary he will be lost or ineffectual.

You can teach an A.D.H.D. child to do his own laundry in the washing machine and then put it into the dryer if it is wet. This child will run the dryer until the clothes are dry. An Autistic child's way of doing laundry may involve following a list of written directions but if variance occurs he may not be able to self-correct. If the dryer isn't hot enough but just tumbling the clothes around, the Autistic child will take the wet clothes out after the prescribed time and put them away after carefully folding the garments. The Autistic child's brain processes information very much like a computer. He may be capable of complex processing tasks (this is not about I.Q.) but, like the computer, he will not typically initiate new action on his own to correct for unexpected variables.

The lack of understanding of emotional meaning and the intensely concrete thinking system of Autistic kids make them different from ninety-five percent of children in the Attention Different population. Though many of the parental self-care strategies listed throughout this book will be useful to parents of Autistic kids, especially those with a mix of Autism and A.D.H.D., Bipolar Disorder, or T.S., it is important to make clear that profound differences in perceptual style exist which require an in-depth, book-length treatment on their own.

Methods for Assessing Perceptual Style

I have mentioned that the action you take to help your child must properly accommodate his perceptual style. Kids act the way they do for reasons that are particular to the pressure that they are feeling. Before you take action, you need to have a clear idea of what is going on. The Arabic proverb says "Measure twice, cut once." This is very applicable in planning permanent change in your child's life and your own life toward greater well-being.

Observe your child's reactions and keep a log

Their are no "one size fits all" methods for getting a handle on how your child sees the world and what his internal experience of it is. Probably the best way is simply for you to get into the habit of watching him. Keep a log book to note his strengths and stressors (more on stressors in the next chapter) and reactions. Observe him especially closely for signs that he is having a problem making figure/ground focus by noting situations in which he does not pay attention and therefore cannot remember details of the situation. Note *when* he has problems. The time of day he misfires will tell you a lot about how to reduce his stress by adjusting what is happening around him. And look at internal factors such as diet and medication.

Enter into a consultancy relationship with him

I like the consultant model of helping your child. If he wants your help, offer it but do so only on his request. Your objective must be to make your child more self-supporting and less in need of your help.

1. Ask him what he is experiencing when he is having a problem, and assist him in articulating his "head space" to you. If, for example, he starts screaming at you when you require him to finish a particular project, ask "Are you mad at me because I didn't give you enough time to finish or because you didn't know what you should do next?"

2. Ask him why he does certain things. One bright nine-year-old I've worked with in counseling told me that he aggravates his teacher "to see her face turn red." This is a clue to me that he is experiencing a lack of stimulus satisfaction due to "stimulus flooding" in the crowded classroom. Another child ventured the comment that this was a way to get the teacher's attention, because his interpersonal skills were so poor he couldn't get it any other way.

3. Have him draw a picture of how he is feeling and study his drawing with him to note how it expresses a certain kind of frustration or emotion. A boy who continually fights with his older sister may not be able to explain it to you but can show you in a drawing what she does to provoke him. Other children know well how to aggravate the Attention Different child's hyper-sensitivity to certain stimuli and will do so with a vengeance. As you go

over his drawing perhaps you are able to determine his sensitivity to certain sounds: "Here she is crunching her damn potato chips," or to different kinds of "creepy touch." This would be a clue to kinesthetic tenderness.

4. Observe his sleep patterns. Many Attention Different kids have obsessions at night that can go on for hours keeping them awake but which appear like insomnia or "rebound" effects from stimulant medication. They do not like to talk about their obsessions and so the wise parent is best advised to simply practice empathy and wait. "You look like you were having a hard time getting to sleep last night. I used to get 'the worries' when I was a kid at night. Do you sometimes get dumb stuff stuck in your head you can't get rid of?"

Assessing your child's perceptual style

Use the Perceptual Style Checklist on the following page to get an idea of your child's perceptual style.

Get to know the inner world of your child by seeing how problematic behaviors balance the craving for stimulus satisfaction with the need for safety

Even the most problematic behaviors of our A.D. kids make sense if they are seen as the child's way of coping with hypersensitivity to stimulation. The child is doing what he thinks he must to deal with the stress of the situation.

The craving for stimulus satisfaction is seen in the rapid, impulsive, or high-risk behavior typical of Attention Different children. Writer Thom Hartmann describes the pursuit of stimulation for ADD'rs with the metaphor of a fish jumping out of the water to snatch a bug flying by. Hartmann points out that high stimulation gives the ADD person a feeling of aliveness! This need to feel alive is a basic motivator for everyone and it will power a kid into some intense hyperactivity. It is the great "Yes!" shouted to the universe.

A child's behavior is also pushed by the need to have a sense of order amidst the chaos of his internal experience; this is the great statement "No!" seen in his rage and defiance. He attempts

Perceptual Style Checklist

Quality of Focus	Yes	No
1. Does he lack figure/ground flexibility? This will show as difficulties making transitions and acute slowness in problem-solving (even simple problems).		
2. Does he experience internal pressure?		
• emotional		
• cognitive: flooded with ideas		
• cognitive: obsessive-compulsive		
• kinesthetic: feeling "driven"		
• proprioceptive: tics		
3. Does he experience external pressure, a feeling of being unshielded to stimuli? If so, what specific stimuli?		
• sights		
• sounds		
• smells		
• touch		
• taste		
4. If unshielded either to internal or external stimulation, under stress does he go: *Outward*--hyperactive, angry, aggressive, obnoxious, or anxious fixation? *Inward*–to become quiet, or uncommunicative, the "*inattentive A.D.H.D.*" type?		
5. Is he "under energized" at the contact boundary between his internal world and the external world -- the depressed or Bipolar child		

to establish safety, manageability, predictability, and routine. The urge to feel satisfied and the drive to create personal control over the chaos, to be safe, are two pressures constantly in battle in the child's psyche. His distinct personality will show how he handles these compelling forces in his life.

The dual pressures on Attention Different children

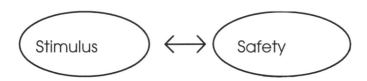

How differences in perceptual style result in different behavioral challenges

The techniques provided in this book show you how to help your child balance the powerful urges for both stimulus satisfaction and safety. As excruciating as his behavior is, it serves a purpose—it is important to get an idea, in the case of each behavioral challenge, just what purpose is served. Knowing this, you are in a position to help him achieve his purposes without the disturbing and distressing chaos that accompanies the behavior.

Hyperactivity, rage, silliness, provocative and aggressive behavior, self-righteousness (never seeing the other kid's point of view), and compulsivity are acted out quite differently for kids with different perceptual styles.

❖ *Hyperactivity* may be an attempt to gain a sense of stimulus satisfaction. The child flooded with stimuli fishes within a stream of continually arousing figures to find one that stands out from all the others and gives him satisfaction. This is a common pattern typical of children with the A.D.H.D. diagnosis.

Another child may act hyperactive for a totally different reason. This child is stuck in obsession on some internal figure and may appear hyperactive but is simply involved in a compulsive behavior that mimics hyperactivity. He must close every drawer in the room. He must clean every speck off the floor. Unlike the

A.D.H.D. child, this child's fast and furious moves are propelled by the need to complete some compulsion to still the inner chaos.

❖ *Oppositionality*, for the child who is hypersensitive to external or internal stimulation, may be a way of putting some order in the chaos. This is a way of saying "No. I will maintain order. I cannot sort the options and so take the only one that I see as right. I cannot tolerate any more ambiguity. There is too much chaos."

The *obsessing* child may be oppositional as a result of terror at having her obsession pattern interrupted. This child does not do her homework because she is not finished computing all the substances that weigh exactly two ounces or believes that touching paper is tantamount to inviting contamination and disease. Her parents do not see her suffering and interpret her resistance as a power play. This misassumption can lead to considerable distress for all concerned.

❖ *Self-Righteousness* for the A.D. child can be more pronounced than it is with other kids. Unlike non-A.D. kids, the A.D. child's judgment of other kids can be so intense that it has the feeling of paranoia to it. The child's conviction that he is always right and others always wrong is set off by the same sense of internal chaos that powers his oppositionality.

This child, so present-focused that he is unable to plan and control his social interactions, therefore seeks to freeze-frame everyone else into predictable patterns. Struggling to get a sense of focus on things, the child goes inward, losing recognition of how his social circumstances and the behavior of others change from moment to moment. He feels out of control, a "stranger in a strange land," and attempts to gain control by rigid self-definition as well as rigid judgment of others.

❖ *Emotionally immature behavior*, be it silly, aggressive, distracting, or just very annoying, may be an attempt to get a reaction out of the environment. It has sufficient "signal strength" to get through the child's flooded perceptual screen. The parent will be antagonized and attacked until he blows his cool, giving the child momentary stimulus satisfaction. It is important to assess the feel of a child's provocation to determine if it is an attempt to control you or to defend himself from you.

❖ *Dangerous, destructive, and risky behavior* is hyperactivity with an aggressive, searching focus. This behavior, more common in older pre-teens, shows that the balance in the stimulus satisfaction vs. safety debate has shifted toward gaining more stimulation. This behavior, like hyperactivity, is more pronounced when a kid is stressed. He will ride his bike too fast, stay out too late, and hang out with the most exciting (sometimes dysfunctional) kids. He may shoplift or get into petty vandalism. He is driven to test the limits of his culture to contain him.

Many A.D. children seem quite worldly, even precocious, when you speak with them seriously about their lives. At age eleven, a child may have the wisdom of a fourteen-year-old. This child may also have the same appetite for stimulation as the fourteen-year-old A.D.'r. This can be distressing to parents who are not yet psychologically prepared to raise a teen-ager.

❖ *Depression.* It is important to examine the roots of depression so that you know what kind of remedial action is necessary. The depression that is "hard wired" in a kid's brain, as is seen in Bipolar disorder involves a contamination of primitive, dark mood into consciousness. A less severe variety of depression can come about as a result of a child's failure experience, or can be a result of stimulant medication overdose.

All depressions involve a slowing of the figure/ground cycle and a loss of excitement. The apathetic look and feel of the child expresses this loss of excitement. Energy is pulled within to deal with the internal crisis of shaking the mood of darkness that has descended upon the child. He may not look it, but he is working hard at an extremely slow pace to return some joy to his life.

❖ *Rage* in the A.D. child may be an attempt to lift the sense of internal drivenness that is felt like a smothering plastic bag. Or it may be a reaction to fairly mild aggressive action from another that is perceived, in a moment of rage, as life threatening. Rage may also be a response to a parent's attempt to control a child which is perceived by the child (given his internal sense of chaos) as overwhelming. The expressed volume of the child's response is set subjectively to his experienced volume of received aggressiveness or discipline, not to the actual degree of domination by the other. The signal strength of the experience is greatly exaggerated by the child's hypersensitivity to this kind of stimulation.

Rage and aggressiveness may be used by the child as self-protective techniques that move the conflict out to a place military tacticians call "the forward edge of the battle area." If you feel sure you will be attacked and are greatly in fear of being overwhelmed, move the conflict out away from you. Throw them off. Distract them because if they really got close they would see what a "mess and a failure" you are.

Provocative and aggressive behavior may also simply be a rebound effect from medication. The mini-withdrawal that occurs every day from stimulant medication may constitute a major internal stressor for a child. This should be dealt with as such, not as an acceptable side effect of the medication.

❖ *Compulsions, obsessions, and tics* are, like Bipolar depression, "hard wired" into base brain neurology of many Attention Different children. These challenges strongly express the urge to safety of A.D. kids. Compulsions give the child a sense of relief of cognitive pressure from the intrusive personal safety messages called obsessions. In performing the compulsive behavior, the child "makes himself safe" from the threat foreshadowed in the obsessional thought.

The tic relieves proprioceptive pressure called "premonitory sensations," felt as "itchy feelings" in the musculature. Though Tourettic children can suppress tics, the proprioceptive sensation must eventually be expressed in the tic or the child will lose all control of his life, walking into walls, not being able to sleep or eat. This is an anti-stimulation impulse; stimulation itself has become the enemy. It hurts to live.

Analyzing Motivation On the "Satisfaction" vs. "Safety" Continuum

Refine your idea of your child's style of managing the dual pressures for stimulus satisfaction and safety by completing the checklist:

Problematic Behavior Gives the A.D. Child
A Sense Of Stimulus Satisfaction Or Safety

Stimulus	Satisfaction	*or* Safety
Hyperactivity		
Oppositionality		
Self-righteousness		
Emotional immaturity		
Dangerous behavior		
Depression		
Rage		
Compulsions		
Obsessions		

The question of intentionality and normalcy

The question of intentionality is highly relevant here because
a child's behavior will seem so intentional, although it will wax
and wane depending on the setting. Every parent of an Attention
Different child knows that problematic behavior is worse when

the child is under stress. If we take seriously the idea that problematic behavior is triggered by stress, we understand better why it can vary depending on the situation.

I have learned to listen past the angry pronouncements and threats made by my young clients toward their teachers, parents, and peer adversaries. Though they may seem perfectly normal and focused in their anger, other needs and impulses are driving them. These impulses show themselves in the child's unwillingness to listen to any rebuttal in their way of seeing reality. Their behavior is intentional in the same way that scratching a mosquito bite is intentional. They do it to relieve stress and irritation.

The child who has problems getting a clear focus on things around him will explode in rage if interrupted in his activity without notice. The interrupting adult is requiring him to move out of the safe space of his current focus to an unknown place that is confusing to him. He does not explode to be spiteful or out of "intention" but because this transition to him is a distressing surprise.

The child who is overstimulated by bright lights will "go ballistic" in the classroom over the slightest stressor. He doesn't do it to be oppositional or defy the teacher. He reacts this way because his environment is gradually putting enormous pressure on him that is not evident to anyone else in the classroom. Like making a dog listen to an extremely high decibel noise, it will drive him nuts.

The key to the intentionality question lies in understanding what stresses a child experiences in a particular situation. Then sort out from this analysis the degree to which he is reacting as a normal kid and the degree to which his behavior is influenced by his A.D. perceptual style. In my counseling work with Attention Different kids, I sometimes am surprised to find underneath my serious contemplation about a particular behavior the obvious fact that the child is behaving normally for his age. Sometimes a kid just feels like "flipping off" his teacher or punching his brother. This is normal behavior for kids learning to test boundaries and get a sense of themselves.

I have learned to look for the pattern in the behaviors of A.D. children. Normal children will also do uncharacteristic things but then will settle back into a fairly predictable study state. The behavior of Attention Different children is also predictable if it's seen as a natural protective response to stress that, at least for the moment, the child feels is beyond his control.

CHAPTER TWO

A Wellness Model for Parenting Attention Different Children

"But it must be said from the outset that a disease is never a mere loss or excess— that there is always a reaction, on the part of the affected organism or individual to restore, to replace, to compensate for and to preserve its identity, however strange the means may be..."

—Dr. Oliver Sacks

The spirit of A.D. children shines through when they are relaxed, happy, and comfortably focused. Problems occur when the child is experiencing stress from either internal or external sources. Once you understand how stress relates to attentional problems you can create the environmental setting that brings out the best in your child.

The General Adaptation Syndrome: A brief review

Dr. Hans Selye, a pioneering stress researcher, originated the idea that human beings react to stress in an identifiably similar pattern. He said that when people are put under either psychological or physical stress their bodies and minds go through a predictable set of reactions. Together these form what he called "The General Adaptation Syndrome" or "G.A.S." This set of reactions, which form the "fight or flight" stress response, has been hard-wired into our neurology since the beginning of human history.

Selye said that we react in three predictable stages: *a. alarm,* in which our body systems are alerted to deal with the stressor; *b.* *resistance*, in which specific organ systems are delegated to protect the body from the stressor; and *c. exhaustion*, the stage that is entered if primary organ systems cannot handle the stressor. Once the "threat" is eliminated or the disease resisted, the body returns to a state of relaxation.

Our body's reactions during the General Adaptation Syndrome include:

a. Stored sugars pour into the bloodstream for quick energy.
b. Heart and breath rate shoots up; breathing becomes shallow.
c. Muscles tense in preparation for strenuous action.
d. Digestion ceases so blood may be diverted to muscles and brain.
e. Perspiration and salivation increase.
f. We experience a state of hyper-alertness and tight perceptual focus—"big picture" thinking shuts down and a state of mental expectation of immediate danger and risk becomes operant.

The body is kicked into its stress reaction through a chain of events that begins with the reception of stimulation by the senses and the forwarding of this information to areas of the brain designated to react to it. Normal people react to stimulation with the G.A.S. if the stimulation is novel enough, strong enough, or if the person is particularly vulnerable to the type of stimulation. Everyone has a different threshold.

An example of the way two people might react to the explosion of a firecracker illustrates how this reaction works. When the explosion occurs nearby, each person goes into the stress reaction instantaneously. The noise is not expected and therefore is novel, the first criterion for a stressor. It is loud and therefore has sufficient signal strength. One person may jump a little at the noise and recover quickly. Another who is more sensitive to the noise may react violently, go through the full G.A.S., and take an hour or two to calm himself down.

This increased sensitivity to the stimulation, similar to how the second person in the example reacted, is the same thing that causes problematic behavior in Attention Different kids. Their neurological over-receptivity causes them to feel overwhelmed by stimulation which causes rapid and continual triggering of the G.A.S. This results in depletion of the neurotransmitters dopamine and serotonin in the frontal lobes. Since an adequate supply of these two neurotransmitters is required for the inhibition of behavior, depletion correlates directly with disinhibited, problematic, behavior. Low dopamine in the brain's frontal lobe, the thinking brain, is a core biochemical reality of being A.D.

Research has also documented that the stress reaction can lead to all the problematic behaviors characteristic of Attention Different children. These include: depression, hyperactivity, rage, short attention span, aggressive behavior, poor tolerance to further stress, and (in Tourette Syndrome) an increase in tics.

The individual's perceptual process is key to kicking off the stress reaction because it occurs when stimulation, either positive or negative, is perceived to be overwhelming or out of the person's control. Lack of a sense of control sets the person up for the stress reaction. Research on laboratory rats has demonstrated that all of the above behaviors are greatly reduced when the animals have some control over a stressor impinging on them.

All of the problematic behaviors of Attention Different children to include depression, anxiety, inability to focus, and combativeness are also seen in people who are distressed to the point of burnout in their lives from stressors that they cannot control.

The G.A.S. and learning problems

Living the General Adaptation Syndrome day to day can also take its toll on the child's basic ability to learn things that other children and adults take for granted. Learning takes place as a result of making contact with the environment, of good focus, and completion of the assimilation and accommodation cycle described in Chapter One. Neurologic preference for fight or flight shuts down the child's ability to relax and complete the learning cycle. Most evident delays will be seen in his social skills, as the interpersonal environment is his greatest stressor. Problem-solving delays will also be evident.

Children with the most profound attention differences also

show language delays because the formation of language requires daily practice in the give and take of social interaction and the assignment of meaning to things. The brain's neural patterning for language begins at birth and continues throughout early childhood, through the assimilation and accommodation pattern mentioned in the last chapter. If this process is slowed by the need to continually adapt to new stress, language development may be impaired. If the child is continually operating from "condition red" it is unlikely that he will have had the down time, the relaxed time, to build an intellectual repertoire of language skills.

The wellness model points the way to healing

Hans Selye made it clear that stress is a natural protective reaction and becomes threatening to the person only when stressors are not dealt with. This can result in body exhaustion, the erosion of the immune response, and disease. In the case of Attention Different children, when the child's chronic stress reaction is misunderstood or mishandled, a lifelong pattern of failure and unhappiness can result.

The beauty of this way of looking at the problematic behaviors of Attention Different children is that the stress model also points the way to what we need to do to help the child heal and achieve a life as full of joy as it is of sometimes painful intensity. The dramatic behavior of our Attention Different kids points the way to achieve wellness in their lives.

Essential ingredients of stress "hardiness"

In 1979 University of Chicago researchers Suzanne Kobasa and Salvatore Maddi built on Selye's concepts to identify the essential ingredients in the lives of people who stay healthy despite the stress that they experience. Strengthening these "hardiness factors" are key to helping the Attention Different child deal with his problems and realize all his gifts. Maddi and Kobasa's hardiness factors include:

a. The person has *support* in his life from others and has an outlet for giving and receiving love. Selye focused on the giving aspect of this interaction and called this "egoistic altruism." Other researchers have shown how important feeling loved and supported is to staying healthy. This is also an essential ingredient for the health and healing of your Attention Different Child: He must at all times feel loved and supported by you in his struggles to overcome his problematic reactions to the stresses he faces. Love keeps him afloat while he's doing the important work of re-educating himself to deal with the particular stresses of his perceptual style.

b. The person feels in *control* of his life and does not feel overwhelmed by events. He experiences a sense of personal freedom and does not see setbacks to his goals as insurmountable obstacles but as challenges.

The Attention Different child's feeling of being out of control not only of himself but of events around him is central to his distress and low self-esteem. All a parent's strategies must help him develop more self-control and focus in the way that he responds to events so that he is better able to moderate his reactions and get on top of them earlier. This takes practice and patience on your part but the returns can be remarkable and dramatic. The techniques provided in this book beginning with the next chapter will help you give your child more control over his reactions.

c. Finally, these stress hardy people have a *sense of purpose* in their lives. They have something that they can commit themselves to that makes life worth living.

The fierce sense of purpose of most Attention Different children is a parent's greatest ally. Most Attention Different children come by this sense of willfulness naturally; it is a requirement for them to be headstrong and stubborn in order to overcome the continual internal experience of being out of control, lost in chaos.

The wisest parents know that it is far better to have a stubborn fighter of a child than one whose spirit is gone or almost gone, who merely goes along, depressed and uncommitted to anything.

Natural hardy gifts of Attention Different children

Attention Different children have many natural strengths that come as by-products of their struggle to cope in their high stress day-to-day lives. Look for these strengths and bring them into your plans to help your child. Some natural "hardiness factors" of Attention Different children:

❖ Have a capability for profound connection with the animal kingdom and nature. They love animals and are staunch defenders of animal rights and the environment.

❖ Are intensely spiritual and experience awe of natural events— of starry nights, waves coming into the shore, fragrant dense forests.

❖ Are artistic. Art is at its core the expression of desire for unification with and understanding of its subject. This is the positive side of living with such open boundaries. And the A.D. child is typically very visually oriented. He may be more proficient in artistic communication than in any other form.

❖ Are natural musicians. As part of their fight or flight equipment, many Attention Different children have exceptionally good hearing as well as vision. Auditory acuity and openness to things around them gives them a natural predilection to enjoy music as an expression of the passion that they feel for things.

❖ They are very good at computers and electronics. This facility comes as a result of three factors: The computer is visual, provides memory prompts, and is fast enough to pace the child's rapid change in focus—a true mechanical friend!

❖ Have an attraction for the exploration of power in the physical world. These include an ardent curiosity about fire, chemistry, and electronics.

❖ Have natural abilities in many of the "hands on" type of occupations that include science, mechanics, and medicine. Attention Different children compensate for the feeling of being flooded by stimulation by joyfully orienting to what they can touch and experience with the senses. Because they are so sensitive to many stimuli, they are excellent "gut hunch" decision makers. They have far more practice in this facility than they do in making rational and reasoned choices.

Finally, as mentioned earlier, Attention Different Children have prodigious skills in *purposeful* action that comes as a natural result of having to apply so much will power just to get through one day after another. They can be tough, stubborn and powerfully goal-directed once they have identified what they want. This is the reason, along with their other hardy characteristics, that there are so many among the successful entrepreneurs in our economy.

Given that the Attention Different child's problematic behavior replicates the stress response and that the child is most successful when he is able to bring the full weight of his natural hardiness to the task, it makes sense that a parent's strategy should involve decreasing his stress while increasing the hardiness aspects of his personality. To do this its necessary to first understand the specific external and internal stresses that your child faces.

Potential stressors at school:

❖ Inappropriate classroom physical environment—too many other kids, crowding, florescent lights, unpleasant odors, high noise levels, allergens present, classroom bland and uninteresting (boring), inability to move around, and lack of clearly posted steps for completion of classroom routines.

❖ Inappropriate teaching methods for an Attention Different child: lots of "central task processing" work (workbooks, problem solving too abstract), emphasis on fast problem solving, emphasis on writing and fast-paced spoken instruction involving many steps with little visual input, unclear task beginning and ending points, transitions to other classes and activities frequent, no prompting for transitions, and boring classroom routines.

❖ Teacher attitude that "the child is doing it deliberately" and subsequent prompting to his classmates to ostracize him or attack him. At the extreme there is use of corporal punishment or confinement in an attempt to force compliance. Also behavior modification techniques based on the faulty assumption that a child can be "retrained" out of his attention difference also can be a major stressor.

Stressors at home:

❖   Inconsistent parenting: Mom is too lenient, Dad is too severe, or both parents fight over child-rearing methods in front of the children.

❖   Misunderstanding of the time required for task completion. Many Attention Different children take at least twice as long as "normal" children to solve problems and complete tasks.

❖   Parental attitudes and poor coping skills. There is a feeling of hopelessness that the situation is out of control; one parent stays away a lot leaving responsibility to the other. Parents are alienated from each other, "wedged" apart by the child and the stress he brings. (See Chapter Fourteen for a description of this pattern.)

❖   Unresolved sibling issues. Sibs are jealous. "Why does he get away with it when I don't/didn't?" Sibs run stealth attacks on an Attention Different child, prompting him to get angry. Then sib withdraws, leaving the Attention Different child to get the flak.

❖   Crowding, poor nutrition, allergens in home, inconsistent administration of medication, high noise levels, TV left on as baby-sitter, no place for anyone to get away and self-calm.

❖   Parental misconception that the pre-pubescent Attention Different child can be "trained" out of his behaviors. The idea that the parents must tame him, train him or otherwise domesticate him before he becomes a "wild teenager."

Internal stressors include:

❖   A feeling of being over-pressured with a continually unsatisfied hunger for stimulus satisfaction.

❖   Attentional style incompatible with the demands of school environment or parental expectations leading to chronic low self-esteem and a feeling of hopelessness.

❖   Problem-solving delays involving simple to complex tasks.

❖   Physical and psychological pain as a result of tics and/or obsessions and social isolation because of these phenomena.

❖   Perfectionist tendencies, especially with regard to laborious over-completion of written schoolwork.

❖ Loneliness and poor interpersonal skills.

❖ Biochemical related mood changes such as "morning rage" and effects of exhaustion.

❖ Side effects from medication and "rebound effects," especially the grouchiness, irritability, tearfulness, and depression associated with daily withdrawal from stimulant medication.

Increase your child's personal hardiness by reframing problems as strengths

Attention Different children are very suggestible, very open to following images around them. This knowledge has become useful in my work as a counselor, for I have seen that A.D. kids can imagine positive states for themselves to a depth far greater than normal kids. This openness to suggestion allows me to help them evoke an image of calming and cooling ("fishing with Dad last summer") and use it to temper restlessness: "When you notice that you are getting restless, remember fishing!"

High self-esteem is essential to building stress hardiness. A kid has to feel good about himself in order to take on his A.D. as a challenge. We can use his suggestibility to images to build up his sense of confidence. A certain carefulness in our language is required, but not out of a spirit of being "politically correct." The language we use expresses our confidence in his ability to grow up strong and resourceful as an A.D. person. Here are some suggested "reframes" of terms you might use to describe his behavior— this will take him out of the victim or villain roles and put him more in charge of his life.

The truth is that for every supposed negative a child shows, he also is equipped with a powerful positive. I have learned from working with these kids that the worst allegations about them are always balanced with "flip side of the coin" positives. These powerful assets are the characteristics to strengthen and bring into the change process.

Reframing to show the positive helps a kid to love himself. This is vital to feeling strong enough to change. Engaging your A.D. child in discussion about his aspirations for the environment and animals puts him in contact with things outside himself in a

Problem Behavior Reframes

From:	To:
hyperactive	explorative, a young scientist avid for knowledge
slow, delayed	detail-oriented and careful, observant
distractible	creative, the artist archetype
withdrawn	deep thinker, a careful thinker, critical-minded
oppositional	purposeful, committed
judgmental	deeply committed to fairness and justice
impulsive	open to everything around him, aware, the "hunter" archetype
emotionally fragile, "easily hurt"	spiritually aware, deeply attuned to others

positive and healing way and communicates the message, "Everything in nature grows in cycles and you will too."

Build his psychological "muscularity" by requiring him to make choices

My son, Gregory, a Tourette Syndrome child with severe A.D.D., journeyed on an airplane for the first time by himself to Phoenix, Arizona, to visit his older sister. He went down as an "Unaccompanied Minor" (escorted by the stewardess) on the flight out. But on the way back, a mix-up occurred and he had to do the whole trip by himself.

It was difficult for him to deal with sitting in one place, totally by himself, in the presence of the over-stimulating environment of the plane for two hours. He told us later that he cried briefly in sheer loneliness. But when we met him at the airport, he acted like a changed boy. He was composed and mature. He had met the challenge and was feeling a new sense of freedom and confidence.

We never would have chosen this ordeal for him, but it happened and has strengthened him enough now to continue to travel by himself. Like other Attention Different children, he has had to exercise this kind of psychological *muscularity* many times. We have found it extremely important to give him the opportunity if we possibly can. This is especially true if we are crafting some new change in his routine that requires new skill in self-inhibition and focus.

Start your child with easier tasks and move to more complex tasks ones as his focus capability and muscularity builds. If, for example, you want him to learn to cook and he is able to use the stove safely, get him started with a recipe for a simple task like making toast or out-of-the-box pancakes. Compliment his success. Before you know it, you'll be eating darn tasty stir-fry presented to you proudly by your new little chef!

Always give him choices. If you want him to finish the project he is working on say, "Would you like ten minutes or fifteen to finish your project?" If you want him to get his homework done, say "You can have your friend over if you get your homework done after school or after dinner. At what time do you want to do it?"

I am reminded of the Latin derivation of the word "educate." The Latin root is "educare," which means to "draw out." The word "instruct" is derived from a Latin root which means "to put in." Your best results will not come from "instructing" your Attention Different kid but from educating him, drawing out his strengths and reducing his stress as much as possible while he takes new behavioral risks.

Target all changes around your child's purposes

If you have some change plan in mind for your A.D. child it makes a lot of sense to get his will on your side. Given the fact of his natural oppositionality (see Chapter Six for techniques to deal with it) it makes sense that helping him achieve his most passionate desires will be your most powerful motivational strategy.

One of my clients, a nine-year-old girl with severe A.D.D., had an ardent desire to play the clarinet in her school band. "No way!" said her mom, already a veteran of too many days of having to come to school and pick up her daughter after some incident. The band class was an unsupervised and highly distracting environment. She knew that her daughter had problems being over-stimulated by crowding and noise.

The girl's crowding-related stress was especially problematic for her on the bus ride home from school. Whatever she did, some other kid would always provoke her into a passable imitation of Anne of Green Gables in a fury. The bus driver was at her wit's end and the school district was beginning to make legal-sounding threats.

Her mom decided to leverage the girl's passion for the clarinet against her problems on the bus. She told her daughter that if she would ensconce herself in a book with earphones on the bus ride home and not get into any hassles, she would agree to let her try band and rent an instrument. Lo and behold! Not only was her daughter able to succeed on her own during band practice, but she also showed an exceptional ability on the instrument. She was also able to get control of herself on the bus. The music that she chose to listen to on her earphones that kept her attention away from temptation was classical clarinet! A wise choice of program.

This girl, like most Attention Different kids, was powerfully motivated to achieve her own purposes. Token incentive systems would not have worked for her unless they got her pretty quickly in line for that clarinet. She was sensitive and receptive to the *quid pro quo*, ("You do this and I'll do that.") and quite dependable in holding up her side of the bargain.

Her mother knew that in order to succeed, she had to risk that her daughter might fail in the music class. Positioning the class as a reward, it was important enough for the girl to marshal all her resources for self-control for the hour of class time. This mom stepped up to the challenge with a creativity that is often seen in "hardy" parents. She had the ability to transform the distress of her daughter's condition to achieve a powerfully positive result. How she developed this ability is the subject of the next chapter.

Application

Take a few minutes to answer these questions to examine any parenting challenge that you are facing with your Attention Different child. Note any creative inspiration:

a. Characteristics of your child's perceptual style:
("Tendency to hyperfocus; severe problems with transitions. Blood sugar effects make these problems worse if he hasn't eaten in a while.")

b. His primary behavioral challenges:
("Temper, screaming fits, withdraws under stress, acts depressed.")

c. This behavior serves the following function for providing stimulus satisfaction or safety:
("Keeps people from putting demands on him which are experienced as distressing and scary.")

d. What internal stressors are contributing to this situation?
("Wears his heart on his sleeve. Too sensitive to criticism. Has obsessions, etc.")

e. What external stressors are involved?

("Crowding at school. Boring classroom environment. Teacher's attitude that he is doing it to annoy her.")

f. What are the child's character strengths and interests? ("Extremely willful. A loving boy. Has a best buddy. Wants to look good at school. Very interested in getting a ferret.")

The next chapter contains information on how to use your analysis of the above factors to create a stress positive lifestyle for your child.

CHAPTER THREE

How Stress Cycles Make Problems Worse

"There are few if any simple stresses in human life, because as soon as a new event occurs, the imprint of old memories becomes activated, triggering the kind of stress we anticipate. Thus stress becomes a self-fulfilling prophecy."
— Dr. Deepak Chopra

In the Introduction we mentioned that Dr. Hans Selye observed that a person deals with stressors in one of two ways. He can feel overwhelmed by them and behave maladaptively, acting from a feeling of being out of control. This reaction pattern is what he termed *distress*. Or a person instead can approach the stressor as a challenge.

Keeping a sense of confidence, he wrestles with it until the situation changes for the better. This encounter strengthens him for the next stressor. Selye called this approach "eustress." He added the "eu" prefix which means "good" in Latin to "stress," coining the word "eustress." He pointed to his own research which indicated that dealing with stressors from the eustress perspective was much less taxing on the body than distress.

These two ways of dealing with stress as diagrammed on the following page:

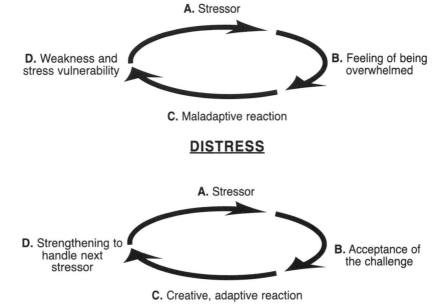

DISTRESS

EUSTRESS

The horrible homework distress cycle

Here is an example of how a distress cycle can become part of your daily life with your A.D. child.

A distress cycle occurs when a stressor "A," a request that your ten-year-old child complete his homework upon arriving home leads to "B," the child's "oppositional defiant" reaction to being told to "sit down and do your homework." This in turn leads to "C," the child's temper tantrum and your feeling of stress overload which leads to "D," a sense of weakness and vulnerability by both you and your child when it happens again.

Caught in this cycle, your child has nowhere to go and the situation just gets worse. You begin dreading your time with your son in the afternoon and the boy comes home depressed and angry, preparing himself for a bad time.

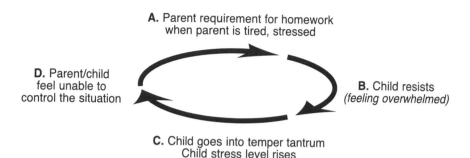

A. Parent requirement for homework
when parent is tired, stressed

D. Parent/child
feel unable to
control the situation

B. Child resists
(feeling overwhelmed)

C. Child goes into temper tantrum
Child stress level rises

The Homework Distress Cycle

Begin by taking an inventory of the stressors in the situation

The way out of this cycle is to change it so that one action does not automatically lead to the next. The first step is to inventory the internal and external stressors that are setting up your child's behavior. This analysis may reveal that his temper outbursts are related to your attempts to rush him through long homework assignments that sometimes take up to two hours. His paper and pencil problem solving skills are, like many A.D. children, very poor. He is left to do at home the reams of workbook pages he didn't finish during his school day.

Making the problem worse is your sense of guilt for your son's learning problems. "If only I were more diligent," you say to yourself. "If only I had the time to help him more, he would be fine." Your guilt fuels resentment which surfaces quickly. A child who occupies the "A.D.D." position on the attention spectrum picks up quickly on your anger and reflects it back to you as his own (sensory mode contamination).

We can correct this problem by identifying the stress that is on the child. Once this is done, the parent is in position to mobilize the child's internal hardiness resources to deal more effectively with the situation. She can change her child's routine to create a context where success is a more probable outcome than failure. This process will change the style of the child's response from distress, to what Hans Selye terms the "eustress" attitude.

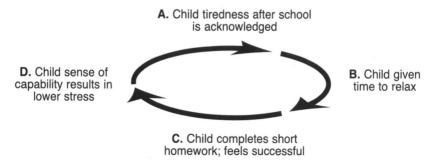

A. Child tiredness after school is acknowledged

D. Child sense of capability results in lower stress

B. Child given time to relax

C. Child completes short homework; feels successful

Going With The Flow To Get Homework Done

The Eustress cycle begins with the acknowledgment of stressor "A," which is the child's neurologic condition at three o'clock in the afternoon. He's exhausted and vulnerable to stress, along with problems in processing paper and pencil exercises. This should lead to a eustress response, "B." Give your child an hour or more to relax before getting to the homework and keep it short, no longer than a half an hour. Under these conditions, your child rapidly begins finishing the task, "C," and feels successful. This leads to "D," greater confidence and a sense of strength to take on more of this type of work during the course of the school day. No more temper tantrums occur in the afternoon. Eustress has replaced distress.

In order to implement this change, you have to let go of the idea that it is your job to make your child do the work he didn't do during the school day. Once you do so, you are moved to contact his school and put in place a series of changes to make his time at school more productive (see Chapter Fifteen for pointers in how to manage school-caused stress). To make his day productive, your son needs a lot of recharge time at home. Thus the short homework expectation.

Your creative action comes from a fresh perspective that sees the situation as a challenge with a solution. This is an example of the eustress perspective in action.

Some may be put off by what appears to be the mother's catering to the son in this example. In reality, the attitude of some parents that they have to "train him before he becomes a teenager" puts major stress on both parents and kids. One day at a time gets alcoholics through the stress of recovery, and this philosophy is just as powerful for parents of Attention Different children. One day at a time.

The eustress attitude

Your eustress attitude is essential for meeting the challenge of your child's behavior. "I can deal with this. If one thing doesn't work, I'll try something else. My child is not doing this to "get me" and he has a lot of potential to bring to the situation. Between the two of us, we'll get through." This attitude is the primary factor in success.

The view that A.D. behaviors are challenges, not set-in-concrete phenomena that doom the parent-child relationship, permits you to begin taking the proper kind of action. This leads to a strengthening of your child's psychological and perceptual muscularity for change. One step at a time—you help him strengthen his ability to screen out unwanted stimulation and focus more effectively. There is an isometric quality to this approach which has the same long-term payoff as does the patient daily muscle strengthening of an accident survivor who eventually restores himself to full health.

Limbic brain energy of Attention Different children sets up the distress reaction

Many of the structures in the brain tasked to run the stress reaction are located in an area called the "limbic brain" by neurologists, as it looks like a limb wrapped around the brain stem. This brain developed in humans hundreds of thousands of years ago and is the one we share with other animals on this planet, thus earning it the moniker of our "animal brain."

When the General Adaptation Syndrome or fight or flight response kicks in to respond to a stressor, it is the limbic brain's job to analyze the stressor and come up with an appropriate reaction. It does this by first, recalling prior memory of the stressor, then creation of an appropriate emotional response, and finally, the mobilization of the body's physical reaction as described in the last chapter.

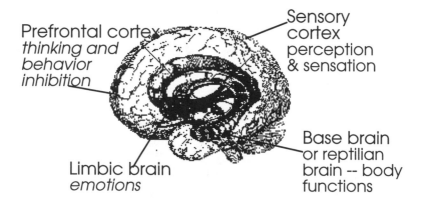

Prefrontal cortex
thinking and behavior inhibition

Sensory cortex
perception & sensation

Limbic brain
emotions

Base brain or reptilian brain -- body functions

The Cortext, Limbic, and Base Brains

The limbic brain contains a little organ called the amygdala (from the Greek word for "almond") which compares messages from the different sense organs and also the thalamus. The thalamus is responsible for integration of sensations, emotions, a sense of pain and sexual feelings and transmission of these stimuli to the motor cortex, the part of the brain tasked to movement and response. It is probably the hypersensitivity of neurons in the area of the amygdala and thalamus in Attention Different children that causes their emotional extremes and strange hypersensitivities to external sensory experience. This hypersensitivity also creates a chronic sense of internal stress, the "driven" feeling.

In Attention Different children, limbic oversensitivity causes an inappropriate excitatory reaction to stimuli. This puts continual pressure on the thinking brain, the cortex, which results in a lowering of its ability to inhibit impulsive action. The result is a natural predilection to maladaptive behavior.

The "limbic wave" effect

Much of the inappropriate behavior and feeling of Attention Different children follows a limbic wave pattern that begins slowly, and builds to a crescendo, resulting in a release of pressure from the limbic system, and a rapid drop-off of energy. This effect is most clearly seen in the child's emotional wildness reaction (see Chapter Eight) and rage reaction (see Chapter Eleven).

In rage, the child will often "announce" the beginning of this limbic wave with a change — tension in his face and clenching fists. Rage may explode quickly onto the scene or take several minutes to build to explosive potential. As the wave proceeds to its crest, the child will run around, swearing, threatening, spitting or throwing things. Limbic rage diminishes, like a seizure, once energy is discharged. After rage, the child will often express regret or behave despondently.

Enraged, some Attention Different children seem to become feral and animal-like, totally out of it. It makes sense that rage is born in the limbic brain for it is an animal reaction in the true sense of the word. Whatever the child says in rage rarely expresses his true intention. His rage, as bad as it sounds and looks, does not carry a sense of psychological malevolence. It does not express psychosis, mania, or hatred. It is simply a manifestation of his animal nature and, given the right management by his adult caregivers, can eventually be retrained to react more normally.

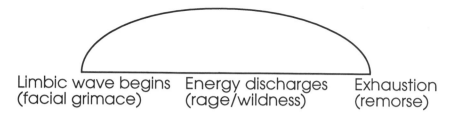

Limbic wave begins   Energy discharges   Exhaustion
(facial grimace)   (rage/wildness)   (remorse)

The limbic wave

Wrestling limbic energy to eustress

This important knowledge of the fact that your child's behavior is only partially under his control and that it will pass takes you off the hook to implement some corrective strategy. If he is far enough into the limbic state, your best action is to decrease his environmental stress as much as possible, keep your own cool, and wait for the limbic wave to pass.

Your attitude of cool patience and skill in the management of his stress will enable him to hear and use the educational strategies that you will devise once the limbic wave has run its course. This same attitude on your part will decrease the environmental stress on him so that his limbic reactivity will be less in the future.

Though you cannot command his limbic system to shut down, you can create conditions that will result in the measurable reduction in the force of the reaction each time it happens. In the following chapters you will learn how to create the psychological space for your child to begin sensing the emergence of limbic energy himself so that he can handle it more effectively.

Summary: Three steps to eustress parenting

Using the eustress attitude as a tool, we are in position to examine our child's challenges, resources and coping strategies, and come up with some creative change options. Three steps are involved in this process:

From Chapter One—Step One: Identify your child's perceptual style and personal resources. Understand how his problematic behavior provides safety and stimulus satisfaction, given the stresses of that style.

From Chapter Two—Step Two: Identify the internal and external stressors that are causing problematic behavior and stress cycles. Identify your child's internal strengths to deal with them.

From this Chapter—Step Three: Implement eustress parenting techniques by identifying and implementing changes to reduce stress as well as to strengthen the child's personal resources.

Slowly and surely derail the distress cycle, letting it transform to a eustress reaction.

Take a few minutes to apply these three steps to a parenting challenge that you are now facing with your Attention Different child.

Step One

a. Note here the characteristics of your child's perceptual style:
(Use the checklists provided in Chapter One under "Methods for assessing perceptual style.")

b. What are his primary behavioral challenges?
(Temper, screaming fits, withdraws under stress, or acts depressed.)

c. What function does this behavior serve for him? Stimulus satisfaction or safety?
(See Chapter One discussion of "Motivation behind problematic behavior.")

Step Two

d. What distress cycles are in evidence?
(Example: "The trouble begins around eleven o'clock in the morning most days. At this time, my son refuses to stop what he's doing and break for lunch. His teacher, believing he is trying to best her in a power struggle begins rushing him, thus starting a distress cycle. He loses his temper and ends up storming around the classroom pushing things over and swearing. I am then called to come and get him.")

e. What internal or external stressors are causing this situation?
(Internal: "My son's problem in making transitions, especially when he is experiencing blood sugar-related fatigue and mood shift. External: Teacher pressure to finish his work

quickly, and teacher attitude that he is doing it deliberately to get her.")

f. What strengths or resources does your child possess in order to deal with the situation?
(He is highly intelligent and creative, has friends, and likes his teacher.)

Step Three

Identify a creative action plan to shift the situation from a distress to a eustress cycle. Schedule a conference with his teacher. Let her know that a primary quality of his perceptual and problem-solving style is a tendency to hyperfocus. Explain how you prompt him to shift focus at home and ask her to double the normal problem-solving and task-completion time for him. Make sure that he gets a mid-morning snack sufficient to carry him through to lunch time.

Take a few minutes to ponder your answers to these questions for the situation that you face with your Attention Different child. See if you can craft a eustress approach that gives the child more control, builds on his natural strengths, and reduces his stress. If these three solution requirements are met, you have an excellent chance of success and establishment of a permanent eustress cycle.

The Parent's Eustress Journal

Because of the ongoing requirement for rapid change and creativity in your parenting job, you may forget what worked for you in a particular situation in the past. You may end up "re-inventing the wheel" or be at a loss for creative ingenuity in a problem you're facing. To combat this situation use the following format to build a journal of your experience and success. Take a few minutes from time to time to review what you have written. This helps you understand stress patterns in your child's life and what interventions work best.

Stress journal header descriptions

a. Behavior problem. In this column notate your child's behavioral challenge or distressing mood change.

b. Stressors. Note in this column particular stressors that may be involved in behavior worsening to include transitions, diet, medication withdrawal, environmental noise, and crowding.

c. Your eustress strategy. Record here what you did to meet the challenge of your child's behavior based on a knowledge and acceptance of his perceptual style. What action did you take to move the situation to an outcome that strengthened you and your child?

The Eustress Journal

Behavior problem	Stressors	Eustress strategy	Results

d. Results. Indicate the results of your strategy. Note how it was effective and ineffective. Note how you might change your strategy a bit in the future to meet the requirements of the situation after your latest intervention.

CHAPTER FOUR

How to Take Care of Yourself So You Can Take Care of Your Child

"You don't have to suffer continual chaos in order to grow."
—John C. Lilly

This chapter is written from the heart. I have mentioned that my twelve-year-old son, Gregory, has Tourette Syndrome (T.S.). His T.S. is seen in his hypersensitivity to stimulation in all his sense modalities to include the proprioceptive hypersensitivity that causes him to have muscle tics. A bright, handsome, compassionate boy, he can also be a temper tyrant, a rageaholic, a little tormentor, obsessive, compulsive, and totally out of it. Managing his T.S. has required that his mother, Joanne Barrie Lynn, and I hone our self-care skills to a fine edge!

The nine practices for self-care that I describe here are drawn both from our experience as parents of a very difficult child as well as the wisdom learned from the successes and struggles of my client families. These nine practices are born in the knowledge that you can help your child only if you are able to take care of yourself.

You can help your child manage his stress only if you are first able to manage your own stress. It is your shoulder that must be available for your child to cry on and scream on. No one else can do this for him. No counselor, teacher, or care-giver can replace you in his life. This challenge from your child cannot be met unless you take care of yourself. Following are nine ways to do this.

1. Accept the challenge to build your strength. There is no way to avoid the fact of your child's attention difference. No magic bullets or cures will redeem him from hyperactivity, compulsivity, oppostionality, depression, and all the other behavior challenges seen in A.D. children. Do not give up, but continually prospect for ways to improve your command of the situation. Your key to survival is to keep moving forward with as much creativity and energy as you can summon.

If one thing doesn't work, evaluate the situation and make plans to do something else. Read up on your child's condition and connect up with people to include professionals and other parents who are as explorative, and open to new and different ways to handle things as you are.

If possible, join an on-line computer service that gives you access to file and information exchange on the Internet. This is a pretty good investment, given the amount of information and support you can get on-line. CompuServe was one of the first on-line services to have a forum dedicated to exchange of information for parents of kids with attention differences.

Keep careful notes to document your child's experience with traditional medical and alternative healing approaches. A medication journal will help you track dosages and side effects. A communications journal can be used to keep in touch with your child's teacher. Get in the habit of comparing notes and planning strategy on a day-to-day basis.

And, don't take your child's attention difference *personally*. His challenging behavior is not your fault and not his fault. Your child could not eliminate these behaviors if he wanted with all his heart to do so. Don't put yourself down for not being able to change him. Feeling guilt for something you can't control is a ticket to burnout.

Realize that his aggravating behavior is not done to "get you" but because he thinks that this is the optimum self-protective strategy in the situation. Once you have a clear picture of how even his most obnoxious behavior has a positive intention behind it, you are in a position to help him realize this intention constructively, not destructively. Creative optimism is the key attitude here. It is essential for successful parenting.

2. Make sure that you have work in your life that nourishes you. Stress research demonstrates that the quality of *commitment*, of living and working for something bigger than yourself, is essential to psychological hardiness. If you are not happy in your job and must also parent a high-stress child, you are putting yourself in danger of running down your "psychic batteries" with no re-charge. Consider that it is important for you to find your Work—the capital "W" indicates your vocation, your calling, an endeavor that gives you a sense of commitment.

If financial necessity requires that you keep a job that does not nourish you, find some pastime that gives you pleasure and enables you to transcend or "big picture" your life struggles. Some parents realize this perspective through artistic pursuits. Others do it through connection with a nurturing community or a spiritual pursuit. Learn to listen to what writer Sam Keen calls the "little voice" in your ear. That's your *vocatus* that says "You are good at "x" and this is what the world needs from you." Follow this voice.

And don't make the mistake of devoting your entire life to taking care of your child. Though parenting him may be extremely demanding at times, find the time and energy to discover what you are good at, the kind of activity that gives you relaxed pleasurable focus. Make sure that some part of each day, even if it is only a small part, is available for this activity.

3. Take more *control* of your life. A primary cause of psychosomatic disease is the lack of control people have over their day-to-day lives. From the time we roll out of bed in the morning to the time we walk through the door to work, other people are calling the shots in our lives. For most people, becoming self-sufficient and totally independent is not a realistic option. But taking more control in your relationships and work lives may be easier than you think.

First, establish your priorities. Put reduction of your stress level high on the list of things that you want in your life. At work, look at your overall responsibilities, and clarify any ambiguity with your supervisors. It's important to have a sense of what you are supposed to do first and what a project or job will look like when it's done. Take the time to organize yourself, to do the important things first. Get as much control over your work plan and schedule as you can.

At work and home, try to be as *honest* as you can. Honesty is so important because it allows you to be free and in control of your life. And being in control equals stress hardiness. When you are dishonest with someone, you give them control over you. Whether it's in your relationships or work life, if you can't level with people, you are not free. Keeping up a front takes a lot of energy and moves you toward distress as a life style.

Take control in your parenting role by working out your signals with your spouse. Get clear on expectations and let your child know what they are. Attention Different children tend to be very power-oriented because of the enormous control they need to exert just to get through the day. If you are not in charge, your child *will be*, and he *shouldn't be*, for your sake and his.

4. Take control of your encounter with your local school district. Do not let professional managers in organizations mandated to help your child (schools or other service agencies) tell you what to do. As parents of a "health impaired child" (a legal definition with Special Education advantages after diagnosis) realize that the law is on your side. Let managers in charge of resource-scarce programs know that you are not going to go away or accept a level of service that does not help your child. The best way to take care of yourself is by being very assertive.

Hans Selye said that having a feeling of control over one's life is a central aspect of personal stress management. You may have to fight to keep your power with bureaucracies but the fight is worth it in terms of your child's well being and your own peace of mind. Read Chapter Fifteen to learn about keeping your power with your child's school district.

5. Attend to your physical well-being. Taking care of yourself physically is an essential aspect of maintaining your psychological well being. If you are physically run-down you will not have the energy to deal with your life and your parenting responsibilities, and you are setting yourself up for distress in many areas of your life. Stress researchers suggest the following guidelines for physical self-care:

❖ Exercise each day. Aerobic exercise (the kind that develops your breathing capacity) is best. Short walks are great. If it's difficult to do this at your workplace, try to get up and move around more in the office. Become more naturally active. You don't have to be an exercise freak or devote all your waking hours to working out. Just get in the habit of paying a little more attention to your body's internal sensations. If you feel out of breath, mind-foggy, or in a slump, recognize this as a signal to do some kind of exercise that fills your lungs with air and gets the blood circulating.

❖ Deepen your breathing. When your body is under stress, there is a tendency to take shallow breaths, from your upper chest. Get in the habit of breathing more deeply, to the diaphragm, every now and then. You'll know that you've got it right when you feel your lower abdomen expand out like a balloon filling up. This kind of breathing is relaxing in itself and provides your brain with the oxygen it needs for clear-headed problem solving. Pay attention gently to the quality of your breath.

❖ Eat more awarely. Recognize if you are eating because you are hungry or eating to fill psychological needs to soothe yourself. Eat more slowly and tune in to your body's sense of being full or not. Give yourself fifteen or twenty minutes before going back for a second helping. Cut down on your intake of unsaturated fat, red meat, and salt. Eat more vegetables, nuts, and fruit. The human intestinal tract is naturally suited for these foodstuffs and has a much harder time digesting meat and fat. Don't make your body work so hard to get the nutrition that it needs. You'll soon see the results in your sense of well-being and energy every day.

❖ Stretch. In addition to oxygenating your body with aerobic exercise, strengthen your muscle tone by getting in the habit of stretching each day. Observe how animals stretch, to get the idea. They stretch vigorously, taking themselves right up to the point of discomfort, but they do not go past this point. Stretch all your muscles with a full body, over the head, arms-up back stretch.

Incorporate stretching into your daily life; do a light runner's stretch (feet flat, pushing back on ankle and thigh tendons) when waiting in line at the grocery store. Pay attention when your body is cramping up a bit or your muscles are getting tired—stop to refresh them. Again, gentle ongoing awareness is key to knowing when to make a slight change in your routine, when to stop and relax.

6. **Cultivate an activity to release the stress of unfinished business and calm your mind every day.** One of the principle findings of stress research is that people who have a lot of "unfinished business" in their lives suffer greater health problems than those who take tasks from start to finish and see completion from their efforts. This distress pattern relates to the "control" dimension so important for distress reduction.

If your job requires you to do projects under deadline that you never see to completion (such as processing paperwork) you are vulnerable to this kind of distress. You are well advised to plan some activity in your life that is not only pleasurable but gives you a sense of completion. Some people meditate. Some do Yoga. Some go for a walk in the park. Some are gardeners or woodworkers. Some go fishing. Stress-hardy people do something each day that gives them peace of mind, predictability, and satisfaction.

Fight the temptation to dismiss yourself as "not worthy" of taking time for this kind of pursuit. Mental relaxation is as important as physical relaxation for your long-term success with the high-stress challenge of raising your Attention Different child.

7. **Choose your friends carefully, let your love out, and let go of "toxic" people.** There is no way that you can meet the challenge of raising an A.D. child alone. Welcome friends into your life who can listen with their hearts and their minds and give advice only when it's requested.

Find ways to show the love you feel. Hans Selye said that stress-hardy people show "egocentric altruism" in their lives. By this he meant that they were very giving and loving in their lives, and benefited greatly in longevity from being this way. This does not mean that you have to run out and give all your money to charity. It means that your longevity will be enhanced if you can hold both yourself and others with loving kindness. Forgive yourself and let in a sense of good will from others wherever and whenever it happens.

Be less conditional about putting out your love. You are strong enough for this and it is in your own interest to do so.

And let go of "toxic" people in your life—those who persecute you with their judgments, who give you endless streams of uninvited advice on how you should be more lenient, or less lenient, or should take advantage of the latest "cure craze." Don't allow anyone to trash you with their judgments or run your life. You've got enough on your plate as it is without having to serve as a therapeutic helper for someone else who feels under-powered in his own life and is using you to feel a sense of superiority.

8. Choose your professional helpers carefully. You will need to have a lot of professionals helping you—teachers, psychologists, educational evaluators, neurologists, and attorneys. Your primary criteria in choosing among these specialists should be the ability of the professional to listen to you and work with you. You need an ongoing relationship and shouldn't have to wait months for an appointment. Put good time up front into finding the people you want to work with long-term.

Avoid professionals who do not listen or who are enchanted with their own pet theories of "what's best for the child." You know your child better than anyone else. Be suspicious of evaluations done by professionals that lead to thousands of dollars in treatment fees that may or may not have value for your child Be suspicious of teachers, principals, and special education directors who just want you to hurry up and sign the forms so that they can do it their way.

9. Play! A good day's play every now and then is as important as a good night's sleep. Play refreshes the level of endorphin neurotransmitters in your brain, which are essential to your mood stabilization, feeling of well-being, and overall psychological fitness. Play exercises your creative side and gives you the chance to relax, to air yourself out, to come back to the natural child in yourself.

Give yourself and your kids the opportunity to play as a family. It doesn't have to be anything too expensive. Make a list of things that you all enjoy and break the list down by cost. You may find that the most pleasurable things are not necessarily the most expensive: a trip to the park on Sunday afternoon or a trip to the local video arcade to challenge your child a couple of games of his favorite diversion are options. Doing a little car camping or fishing might be perfect. Leave yourself open to inspiration.

And get away from the kids every now and then. Many parents do not allow themselves to play together as adults away from their children because they feel guilty spending time and money on themselves. Guilt can drive a wedge between partners and dry up the relationship when both people have given up the prospect of having fun together. Don't give your joy up like this. It's not good for you. Put some planning time into spending a day or two a month, at least, hanging out together or going out somewhere together, just the two of you.

The parent's self-care eustress journal

In the last chapter was a format for a daily journal to use for tracking and meeting the problematic behavior challenges of your child. Consider the use of the same type of journal to keep a record of the challenges that you face and what you are doing to take care of yourself. Use the journal as a written "memory" of your progress and an inspiration starter for new action.

a. First indicate the nature of the stressor that you are dealing with. It might be your child's behavior, or having to interact with another adult in the situation who is putting stress on you. Describe the stress a bit.

b. Note your stress reaction as a variation of *fight, flight, or hardiness.* Indicate here how you usually react to the stress your child puts on you. How do you feel after the event? How does your body react? What are your thoughts about the situation? Do you feel in control or out of control? What do you do as part of your immediate stress reaction? Did you yell, stay calm, call in another adult for support? Be specific.

c. Note your eustress strategy. Record here what you did to meet the challenge of this stressor for yourself and/or your child? If the stressor is your child's behavior, did you take action based on a knowledge and acceptance of his perceptual style? If the stressor is situational or caused by another adult, what did you do to take care of yourself and keep communications open? What action did you take to move the situation to an outcome that strengthened you and your child?

d. Results. Indicate the results of your strategy. Note how it was effective and ineffective. Note how you might change your strategy a bit in the future to meet the requirements of the situation even better.

Your Self-Care Journal

Stressor	Your reaction	Your eustress strategy	Results

Conclusion: Build a lair for yourself

Stress as a physiologic reaction draws us up into our heads out of our bodies. We get so focused on the "crisis" we see in front of us that we are unable to take a breath, to pull back, to let our creative resources kick in. Having the ability to "big picture" our situation and priorities is essential for our good health. Start this process by choosing a physical location in your home where you can seek refuge from the struggles that you face. I call this space a "lair," to indicate its similarity to a protected refuge where wild animals live and recuperate. You need this same kind of space to heal your spirit, body, and emotions after the sometimes bruising encounters you face raising your A.D. child.

Your "lair" should not be open to others unless by your invitation. I like Sam Keen's idea that people need a place to "seep" like tea—to sit with important questions and let the answers come to them. To do this, you need privacy. Consider putting an "altar" or special area in your space that contains objects that are important to you. These may be things found in nature or that represent the spiritual dimension in your life.

When you enter your space, take a moment to "build a container" of energy around you by visualizing yourself surrounded by white light, by imagining that you are breathing *in* good energy and breathing *out* unhealthy energy, or by saying a prayer that is meaningful to you. Use this time as an opportunity to relax and open yourself to the feeling of connection with a sense of your spiritual wellspring, perhaps a sense of god or goddess. Just a few minutes a day in this recharge space can yield dramatic improvement in your outlook and capability to deal with the stress of raising an A.D. child.

Acceptance of the parenting challenge without holding back, giving up, or dropping out is the primary survival requirement for parents. This is the primary path to eustress, the "survivor's attitude" that makes each stressor you face fuel your effectiveness for dealing with the next one.

PART TWO

Strategies for Successful Management of Individual Problems

CHAPTER FIVE

Calming Hyperactivity

"I'm red hot. I love this cold." (At a Jacuzzi, lying in a skiff of snow outside.)

—Gregory Barrie Lynn, age 11

You have to live with a child who literally "bounces off the walls" to understand what that expression means. I have seen hyperactive A.D. kids run back and forth from wall to wall in a room, kicking and pushing out with a foot each time they make contact with the other wall. Back and forth, back and forth.

This is a child who cannot sit still. Just can't. Just keeps moving. Exploring. Poking. Investigating. Making little noises to auditorily "confirm" some new interest. Answering your questions in monosyllabic grunts. He will not be slowed.

In Chapter One, I pointed out that hyperactivity is the result of being open to stimulation from all the five senses, coupled with a sense of body pressure, kinesthetic stimulation, the sense of drivenness. This is an energy pattern that may, later in life, become an essential part of your child's success in any profession that demands quick response—from emergency room physician to entrepreneur.

But now he drives everyone crazy. Right now the inability to stay still and communicate with adults is one of the biggest problems the child will face.

Frontal lobe dopamine and hyperactivity

Low levels of brain dopamine in the Attention Different child's frontal lobes (in his cerebral cortex) lower his ability to edit and plan his behavior. Dopamine is fuel to the inhibitory neurons that are located in the frontal lobes. Without an ample supply of it, these neurons are underpowered and ineffective to prevent reactive, reflexive, and unthinking behavior. The low dopamine levels in the brain are probably caused by hypersensitivity of the cells that take up the neurotransmitter from the space between neurons, causing the synaptic pool to be depleted. This may be a condition that is genetically transmitted.

Stress lowers brain dopamine and serotonin in the frontal lobes and can contribute to a worsening of hyperactivity. Distress gets worse as the adults around the child, driven round the bend themselves by the hyperactivity, make things worse by ineffectual yelling or inappropriate physical contact. They may try to flee the situation by ignoring him or "getting him out of the house."

Writer Thom Hartmann in his book *Attention Deficit Disorder: A Different Perspective*, argues that people with Attention Deficit Disorder are neurologically configured like expert "hunters" who figured strongly in human culture during the hunter-gatherer period of our species history. Our A.D. kids would have fit in nicely in that epoch. Today, their behavior is labeled "hyperactive." But it is the hunter qualities—the rapid movement, the searching for novelty, the delight in going into forbidden places, the sensory hypersensitivity, and the capability for rapid shift of focus that define this condition.

If he had range to roam, he would be right at home and would come to balance his energy normally. He would be raised by Hunter parents and his ability to move quickly would be valued by the whole community. But the crowding in the industrial world causes real stimulation stress to the A.D.'r. The combination of crowding and the stress of being required to respond to demands for "left brain"—rote memory and paper and pencil production tasks in the classroom—drive him and those around him to distraction.

Develop eustress by increasing your child's ability to focus—and by decreasing his internal pressure

To decrease hyperactivity you must turn down your child's experienced volume of internal pressure and power up his ability to make sharp focus on the things around him. This process replicates the way hyperactive kids naturally calm themselves when conditions are right. In this way they are able to achieve a good balance between moving and thinking.

Your child's hyperactivity is a signal that his brain needs a certain type of retraining; this can and will be accomplished with your persistence and love. My clients have taught me that hyperactivity needn't be a lifelong curse and that kids can get a pretty good handle on it as they grow toward puberty. On the positive side is the fact that once the eustress cycle is established, momentum is created for continual, day-to-day improvement in the child's ability to self-control.

It is important to realize that the eustress response to hyperactivity is an ongoing creative process. Until your child develops his own productive ways for satisfying his stimulus hunger, he will show the rapid search behavior characteristic of being Attention Different.

You will be able to help him focus in different contexts, but he will need a lot of prompting and ongoing support to generalize to other environments. It is not unusual for this training process to take his entire childhood, but the work becomes much easier as you get into the swing of it in your everyday routine. Here are nine success "secrets" for dealing with his hyperactivity:

1. Establish consistent rules, routines, and transitions. Not knowing what comes next is the factor labeled by social scientists as "ambiguity." This is a stressor that ranks along with lack of control as a major cause of distress and stress-related physical problems for people.

Attention Different children need a lot of extra help to overcome the stress that they experience related to ambiguity and loss of control, because their experience already feels chaotic. They have varying tolerance for ambiguity depending on the severity of their attention difference, but lessening this factor is important for each and every one of them.

Your A.D. child may already feel like a wild weasel rushing around without limit or boundary. He doesn't need more haphazard stimulation in his home—people coming and going, disorder, rules inconsistently enforced, meals uncertain, and events arising without warning. This environment is a prescription for gross hyperactivity.

This child will explode in an "open" crowded classroom where groups of "normal" kids happily busy themselves in activities that he finds excruciatingly over-stimulating. Create a climate conducive to positive change by using the following methods:

a. **Post your house rules in positive language** in a conspicuous place and enforce these rules in a calm, matter-of-fact manner: "In this family, we respect the property of others," or "In our family, we take pride in getting our chores done carefully and on time." Though it is probably not necessary to do so, it is important to make sure that classroom rules are also posted and followed.

b. **Establish consistent routines every day**. The establishment of routines and schedules is as important to A.D. children as it is to successful adults with attention differences. Your child needs to know what happens first and what follows next to get through his morning routine and get to school. After school he needs a good afternoon and evening routine. There should be a time set for homework. A time to do chores. And a time allocated for friends and socializing. The A.D. child without established routines is a lost A.D. child—the stress that he experiences will probably be expressed in all his challenging behaviors to include hyperactive movement and conduct problems. For this child, the old saw, "Idle time is the devil's plaything" is right on.

c. **Pay attention to unplanned events**. If unpredictable events are coming into your child's day, help him avoid "surprise stress" by clearly letting him know that his routine will be a little different: "Your dad will be picking you up after school today. I will see you later on this evening." You might help him prepare for this change by asking him to visualize himself in the new situation.

d. **Plan transitions**. Times of transition, between events, are times of especial vulnerability for A.D. kids because they do not have something to focus on at these times; it is the process of focus that allows them to organize themselves. It is very important to have daily predictability for transitions and to minimize outside stressors as he negotiates these change times.

Prompt him before transitions as needed: "I'm setting the microwave timer for ten minutes. When it goes off, close down your computer and I'll help you get dressed. O.K., the timer went off. Close your file and let's get those shoes on. We have five minutes until we have to be out the door." "Good. Now if you need to go to the bathroom, do it now. You have two minutes." At school it may be helpful for the teacher to whisper to the child to prompt him for transitions: "Start to get ready for lunch."

e. Use a daily-planner organizing system if needed. Some A.D. children will become extremely hyperactive or distressed at transition times. These kids, who are more profoundly Attention Different, need a special organizing system such as a daily calendar packaged in a three-ring binder; when they open it each morning it gives them their activity plan and schedule. Because A.D. children typically process information visually, it may be useful to have tasks represented by pictures or photographs, which are contained in insert holders in the binder.

Because A.D. children sometimes do not know when a task is finished they experience anxiety not knowing when to stop. It is important to tell them in concrete and visual terms how to determine when they are finished. They need to know what activity (such as removing a picture from an insert holder to put it in a "finished" pile) will be completed to finish the work "When you have completed your reading assignment, take your Reading Card, initial it for today, and put it on page three of your binder."

If a child has not been used to this level of consistency in his life, his initial reaction may be anger and oppositionality. This is understandable. Hear his objections respectfully and soften his resentment by telling him how you need to have predictability and routine in your life to have an organized and happy day.

f. Let go as soon as you can. At some point you may be able to loosen up in your role as schedule planner and rule enforcer. Your child may tell you, "I can do this myself. I don't need you to be on my back all the time." Give him the opportunity to control his schedule himself and see what happens. In many ways, your job is just to be persistent enough until he learns what he needs to do to take care of himself. If you give him more freedom and he succeeds, congratulate yourself! If he needs a little more help, compliment him on his readiness for more independence but tell him that you want to work with him some more to "fine-tune" his skills.

2. Find out what interests him and provide this stimulation if possible. Dr. Oliver Sacks notes that these people often lose their symptomatic behavior when they are in periods of intense focus. Dr. Sacks tells the now famous story of the Tourettic Canadian brain surgeon who, though ordinarily racked with tics and rage attacks, was calm, efficient, and gifted in the operating room. Many parents of A.D. children say the same thing: "When he's doing something that interests him, he's great. Oftentimes he is more competent, more creative, more effective than a normal kid would be."

The state of focus that A.D. children experience at these times is most probably resonated by brain activity involving the release of endorphins, the brain's home-grown pleasure substance, which in turn raises levels of the neurotransmitters dopamine and serotonin in the frontal lobe. Relaxed pleasure equals better concentration.

The things that interest these kids tend to be purposeful in some way, different from ordinary playing. They don't take to toys as much as the interesting things that adults use. Getting a "take apart" computer carcass at the local computer repair store is prized way above getting a brightly colored plastic "Masters of the Universe" toy.

Dr. Thomas Armstrong in his excellent book on dealing with hyperactivity without medication, *The Myth of the A.D.D. Child,* suggests that parents and educators need to re-vision the way that they motivate A.D. kids. Drop the emphasis on "left brain" activities and observe what these kids really like to do. He shows clearly that they are not interested in lectures, rote memory, worksheets, and boring routines. Trying to force performance in these areas is a ticket to hyperactivity.

Instead, observe your child to see what he enjoys doing and build your activity plan for him around this. Here is a sample of some of the activities on Armstrong's list:

Purposeful activity that motivates the A.D. child

- advertising
- aquariums
- the body
- biographies
- board games
- carpentry
- computers
- electronics
- the environment

- geology
- money -- investing
- Native cultures
- music
- map reading
- other cultures
- social comment
- science fiction
- writing

Armstrong tells of the teacher who built on the interest of one of his hyperactive students—interested in anything having to do with nature. He gave the boy a tape recorder, a typewriter, and a camera to go outdoors and record sights and sounds, and then to write about what he had observed back in class.

It makes sense that A.D. kids are so serious about their purposes. They have to put a lot of energy on a daily basis into keeping their focus and are able to put strong attention on activities that they know and love. Though it is important not to exploit or intrude on the child in pursuit of "hobby" interests or personal passions, these foci are opportunities for reduction of hyperactivity by organizing them into the child's daily life.

And the calmative effect of pleasant work may go on for hours after the child terminates the activity. One of nature's little gifts!

3. Watch out for food and environmental allergies. Research indicates that hyperactivity may result from allergic reactions to certain foods. Major offenders for many Attention Different children include wheat, chocolate, dairy products, refined sugar, apples, and peanuts. Consider having him evaluated for food allergies if his temper and rage problems seem associated with a particular food intake or a special time of day in which he is hungry or consumes a particular food.

The "allergic face," pasty, white, with red nose and rings under the eyes, is another clue to the possibility of an allergic reaction. Several of my clients whose children have showed this facial indication of the presence of allergies have reported significant drop-off in behavior problems once they cleared up their child's allergies.

Hyperactivity is made worse by environmental allergies. Extreme emotionality can follow allergic reactions to mold (a major offender usually worst in fall and winter) and to pollens that enter the airstream at different times of the year. This is especially problematic in early spring, when tree allergens are plentiful, and in late summer, when grass pollen is most problematic. Household dust may also cause this kind of allergic reaction.

If hyperactivity erupts all of a sudden, uncharacteristic of the child, give serious attention to the possibility that he may have been exposed to an allergen and have him checked out by an allergist. A good state-of-the-art allergy work-up with treatment might go a long way to eliminating days or months of family discord due to the hyperactivity.

Other environmental variables have also been shown to trigger the stress reaction in A.D. kids. At school, florescent lighting may be a major offender. Paint or cleaning fumes can also get them going.

The child should not be punished for his hypersensitivity to stimulation. A lot of teachers labor under the untested assumption that you curb hyperactivity by providing a bland classroom environment. It is not necessary to make his classroom environment dull. He is entitled to the same stimulation as other kids. He is not stressed by interesting things but by intrusive aspects of the setting: too many other children, too much noise, too much confusion.

4. Pay attention to the impact of television and video games. Several researchers have made a good case for the fact that television viewing can cause some degree of hyperactivity. This makes sense if you accept the assimilation/accommodation model of learning. High impact audio and visual information delivered in short blasts, sudden close-ups, pans, zooms, and bright colors are scripted into kids' T.V. because these effects stimulate the child's instinctive response to danger. The assimilated experience of this kind of visual hyperstimulation around themes involving danger may result in the brain accommodating to the stimuli by creating a mild state of fight or flight as a chronic stress effect.

To deal with this stress, the child "numbs out" his contact with the world somewhat. He is harder to reach. He needs to *sharpen* his ability to focus but has fatigued it watching T.V.

This effect is especially noticeable when kids play Nintendo games around violent themes. When the child begins playing the game he experiences a pleasant high, a little endorphin rush that comes with successfully beating the game. But as he continues to play, this high may transform into a kind of chronic agitation which is fed by his hyperfocus on the game. This agitation shows that the brain is down-regulating dopamine and serotonin in the frontal lobes to acclimate itself slightly to the "fight or flight" stimulation it is getting.

It doesn't make sense to take your kids off T.V. or video games entirely, but it is wise to observe your child's reaction to determine when enjoyment becomes stress. Take action as needed at that time. An hour of T.V. a day is probably a good standard.

And it is a good idea to get more involved in the type of

programming that he watches for the reasons stated above. You don't want all the good training you are providing to help your child calm his hyperactivity to be reversed by television programs that keep him in the hyperactive fight or flight head space. Looked at it this way, putting a limit on the amount of violent T.V. shows your child views may be important for your own psychological survival.

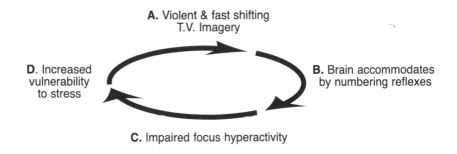

A. Violent & fast shifting
T.V. Imagery

D. Increased
vulnerability
to stress

B. Brain accommodates
by numbering reflexes

C. Impaired focus hyperactivity

T.V., Stress, and Hyperactivity

5. Make sure that he exercises regularly. The feeling of kinesthetic pressure, of drivenness, is immediately relieved by exercise. If he is into sedentary pastimes like the computer, make him get up and move around every so often. Encourage his participation in aerobic sports. Get an exercycle and a punching bag for energy discharge assistance.

Consider enrolling him in a "soft" martial arts class that emphasizes physical and emotional development over the capacity to attack others. Aikido and Tai Chi are great. Karate can also be a powerful assist in focus if training emphasizes the importance of discipline, respect, and the use of the martial art only in self-defense.

In choosing an exercise regime with him, realize that moderate exercise is best. Too strenuous exercise or that done without toning and warm-up has been shown to make kids with Bipolar characteristics more manic and giddy. This is not the outcome that you are looking for.

6. **Teach him to use breathing to relax and calm himself.** Shortness of breath occurs in the stress reaction and during the course of hyperactivity. Reverse these effects by teaching him how to breathe "down to the gut." He will know that his breath is right by the expansion of his "belly" as his diaphragm pushes up and out somewhat.

Fortunately it is impossible to be stressed and relaxed at the same time. Taking deep breaths in a relaxed and unforced way restores a more relaxed physical state quite quickly. Because he may need memory prompts to breathe, get his authorization to prompt him and enroll his teachers and other care givers at school as breathing coaches for him.

At some point teach your child the technique for letting go of pressure. This involves imagining that on the out breath he expels feelings of pressure and visualizes this as some appropriate color. On the in-breath ask him to imagine that he is filled with "a healing and calming light." Have him imagine that the light is coming in a color that suggests healing and calming, from the "ground" and the "sky above."

7. **Teach him the use of visualization to "cool" himself.** Attention Different children tend to be very visual and suggestible. To enlist this predilection for healing, think up a set of visual images that connote cooling, and pop these quickly into your conversation with him when you see he is heating up: "Remember when we went to the lake last summer, how cool and peaceful the surface of the water looked, and how cool it was to just sit there listening to the waves and watching for one of those lazy fish to come and nibble on your toes."

Use whatever cooling image comes to mind for you and talk past him so as not to encounter him too directly. Talk out the window or as if you were talking to yourself and notice when he starts to self-calm. Keep doing what you are doing until you can separate from him and then say in a matter-of-fact way "You're doing a great job of getting yourself under control. Is there anything that I can do to help you right now?"

8. **Teach him expressive and receptive communication skills.** Work to help him put into words what stress feels like in

terms of the agitation, restlessness, irritability, and body tightness that he experiences. Evolve a shorthand method for him to signal his stress level to you through the use of a range of responses on a "1" (very little stress) to "7" (extremely stressed) scale. "How're you doing, kid? You seem to be pushing a "5" on the stress scale right now. Talk to me."

Attention Different children have a difficult time articulating complex emotions. But they are reflexively kinesthetic and emotional. Reduce the barrier of language by using scaled questions to get an idea of what he is experiencing. You may be mightily surprised to find that what you thought was "rage" was really closer to "terror" for him, or what you thought was a deliberate attempt to bug people was experienced by him as crazy confusion. You must know the actual situation, what the challenge *really* is, in order to implement your change planning process. Timing him out for being a brat trying to bug people would miss the mark if what he needs is a gentle but persistent prompt to sit down, breathe down, relax, and plan his next move instead of falling into it.

9. Satisfy his need for stimulus satisfaction. In my counseling practice I have noticed that A.D. children will often have strong aversion to certain types of stimuli—certain sound tones, smells, bright lights, skin sensations, or odors. I have also noticed that they may have a particular attraction to other sensations that seem to give them a sense of stimulus satisfaction.

Some kids will rave about their enjoyment of the Scandinavian custom of dowsing in ice cold water after a hot bath or shower. Others love to spin on skates or skateboards for hours, or jump; they seem to crave the sensations of flying through space. Others may enjoy bright lights, high pitched sounds, or the mild electric shock delivered to toys and small devices with a AA batteries. A.D.'rs also tend to have powerful preferences or aversions for certain types of smells.

Once a kid satisfies his stimuli craving, he may stay calm for several hours. It is reasonable to believe that the regular delivery of certain types of stimulation may meet a need for a neural signal necessary for brain growth. This, in fact, is the basic method of practitioners of "sensory integration therapy." A typical session would include tumbling, turning, crawling, patterned movement, and relaxing "pressure therapy," where the child rests between two mats that provide a comfortably stimulating sense of contact. This is the process of assimilation and accommodation in action at the body level.

Observe what kind of stimulation seems to be sought by your child and help him get this stimulation every so often with a gentle reminder (never use a movement exercise as punishment). He may want to finish each warm shower with a cold douse or work out vigorously on a trampoline at a local indoor play center. He may love to twirl on his tire swing, or crawl about even if he is way past the age of crawling, or stretch himself in characteristic positions that are reminiscent of the stretching discipline of Yoga.

Note how he positions himself, and encourage him to do a little of his natural exercise every day. Wellness physicians like Drs. Bernie Siegel and Deepak Chopra have pointed out that the body has marvelous self-healing powers when we are able to pay attention to its needs. This powerful instinct for wellness seems to drive our A.D. kids to want physical experiences that awaken their senses in a certain way. Once we have trained ourselves to observe them, we can assist them in this process.

Daily Workout: Hyperactivity— Learning to Focus

(The Daily Workout will be a feature in Chapters Five through Twelve. The Workout builds your child's self-control and mastery over problematic behavior challenges by providing an experience that strengthens his ability to focus and manage his energy. Activities seen in this section are basic to his change process and tend to be useful for all Attention Different children whatever their perceptual style or diagnosis.)

I have earlier discussed the idea that the fundamental cause of hyperactivity is a child's inability to clearly focus on things, an ability necessary for stimulus satisfaction. Instead the child ranges from one thing to the next in "hyperactive" movement, but finds no way to settle and let ground surround figure so that the figure becomes comprehensible and can be assimilated.

One way to deal with hyperactivity at its foundation is to show your child how to make focus over his full range of possible stimuli. The activities mentioned below are a way to do this. These should be used only when he is in a fairly relaxed, open, and happy state of mind so that the doing of the exercise recalls this relaxed state and creates it on the spot.

The awareness scan

The awareness scan is a guided meditation to improve your child's sensory focus. Talk this brief meditation to him. Dots (...) indicate that you pause for a couple of seconds to "pace" his breathing and give him time to take in the experience that you are creating.

"Breathe down to your belly to relax yourself...Now imagine that you have a searchlight in your mind that you can use to focus on all the feelings in your body and let your searchlight just go to wherever you feel a little tension, tightness, warm, cold, discomfort...Just let your mind focus on the area and send a breath to it if you need to relax it...."

❖ Ask him to focus on something far away, such as the trees outside the window. Then ask him to soften his focus and let it organize around something close by such as the chair across the room. Do this with a variety of objects in your immediate environment.

❖ Suggest that he shuttle inward by asking him to put his searchlight on some internal sensation, feeling, or thought. Ask him to describe as much of his experience as he likes. Then have him move his awareness outward to describe something he sees there. "Now I am aware of a tingling feeling behind my eyes...now of the breeze of the fan on my arms" (eyes opening). "Now I see the picture on the wall, the books on the shelf." Have him focus inward again and note any thoughts he experiences. Guide him around from one sense domain to the next for a couple of minutes, and then gently bring him back to everyday consciousness.

Doing the awareness scan from time to time gives your child a memory of what it feels like to efficiently move from one stimuli to another, under conscious control. If he experiences difficulty holding an image in his mind, suggest that he turn up his internal "searchlight" a bit. This way he has to highlight the object of focus and put "into darkness just a bit" any competing stimuli around the figure that he has chosen.

Train his artist's eye

Attention Different children tend to be visual and naturally artistic if they can slow down the stream of stimuli that they experience.

When you are on outings with him, teach him to focus on objects in his environment one at a time and hold this focus as long as he can, gradually increasing his ability. As above, ask him to look at things and describe their details to you. And have him do art as a way of training his focus. If he doesn't want to draw or like to draw, appeal to his "little entrepreneur" and commission a piece of drawing with a monetary reward. Ask him to produce a good level of detail before you accept his work. The book *Drawing With Children* by Mona Brooks provides methods for him to quickly develop his skill.

Share your own methods for keeping focus on your emotions

Increase his ability to focus and identify his feeling states by discussing how you concentrate on your own emotional states of mad, glad, sad, scared. If you feel anger as a tightening in your jaws, describe this so that he can develop his own anger awareness. If you feel "scared" as tightness in your upper chest, describe this and engage him in a discussion of where and how he feels the emotion.

Remember, he has limited ability to abstract from his experience to yours so you will be most effective if you keep things concrete: "When I'm mad, my teeth grind on each other, and my jaw feels like it's in a vice. How does yours feel? When I get scared, my thinking gets real fuzzy and I feel light-headed. How do you feel when you are scared?"

If you are Attention Different yourself, make sure to share your own difficulty in focusing on things and how you have compensated for it. Tell him about the methods you use to overcome your own problems with focus and hyperactivity, for example, how you keep a notebook or put things in special places so that you will remember them. Let him know that holding focus is a problem you have and you know it requires continual exercise and practice. Say that you would like to work with him on an ongoing basis to improve the way you *both* focus. Cultivate this as a collaborative, ongoing, effort.

CHAPTER SIX

Cooling Oppositionality

"The problem is that the Big Struggle rarely achieves any constructive end. There may be short-term gains, such as getting homework done, but usually at so high a cost that it hardly seems worth it."

— Dr. Edward M. Hallowell

He's so oppositional! Why can't he just do what I ask for once? What makes him think he's Little Mister Special? His brothers and sisters think he gets away with murder and it makes it impossible for me to keep any harmony in our house!"

The legendary "No. Do it yourself, I refuse!" of Attention Different children is one of the greatest stressors that we face. Meeting the challenge of this intense oppositionality requires that we understand its particular roots in the psyche of the Attention Different child and the function that saying "No!" serves for him.

How we feel about ourselves determines how we see and evaluate critical situations around us. If we feel up, confident, in charge, we will behave competently and successfully. If we feel down on ourselves and out of control, we may adopt a "fight" or "flight" strategy to deal with it as many A.D. children do. Fortunately, most people can deal with this feeling of being overwhelmed by stepping back from the situation and taking a breath. We are able to rise above the tension of the moment and see the big picture.

Internal stress plus low self-esteem equal oppositionality

The Attention Different child has a much more difficult time shutting down intrusive stimuli; his stress is constant. Unlike "normal" kids, because his feeling of self-confidence has taken a battering, psychologically he is poorly equipped to be on top of a situation. The combination of perceptual hypersensitivity and low self-esteem causes him to experience vulnerability and distress out of proportion to the demands made on him.

Because he feels out of control he puts on the brakes to slow things down. Though he may appear focused he is not at the moment in real contact with those around him. Instead, he is tuned inward speaking the "No," to the chaos inside himself.

And he has powerful pushback. Remember what happened the last time you were in traffic and someone started tailgating you? Like many other drivers, your impulse was to slow down. Pushing back is a human reaction to warn threat away from us. This is how the A.D.D. child reacts to the typical adult strategy of "bearing down and getting tough" when faced with a child's oppositionality. Pushback. Push back hard. Never give an inch. This way of dealing with the world can become habitual.

External stress at school

Things are made worse if the child is required to do things he is incapable of. Eighty per cent of these requirements are put on him in school. Sit still. Do the paperwork. Quickly now. Is it done? Be quiet. Stand in line. Don't say "No." Cooperate and graduate.

It is important not to blame the teacher. She has thirty other kids to deal with and for her survival, a certain degree of lock-step in the classroom is required. But the teacher complicates the situation by looking at the A.D.D. child's behavior as simply intentional. "But it looks intentional!" (How many times have parents heard that assertion?) Oppositionality can look very much as though the kid is just being spiteful. But there is a reason for his behavior as we have discussed. The way he sees the situation, saying "No" gives him a tiny bit of order in his life. Without that sense of order he knows he will go crazy.

Eight Ways To Turn Oppositionality Distress To Eustress

The A.D. child experiences great frustration in solving problems—the energy it takes, the sense of inner chaos, and his low self-esteem all make him want to put on the brakes, slow the world down, and get people off his back. We can effectively deal with his reactivity by changing the way we make demands. We can avoid the "Yes, NO!" cycle by helping him develop the confidence and skill to be more in control of his life.

1. Allow more time for problem solving. Realize that it takes many A.D.D. children more time to solve left brain or "central task" learning problems given to them in the classroom or at home. Many adults quickly become impatient with the child's lack of progress and immediately restate the problem with a more urgent demand for completion. Feeling threatened and frustrated, the child will drop his problem solving activity and become engaged in the more familiar game of playing pushback with the adult.

The key is to assume a consultancy role with him in the learning process: you make your assistance available on his demand, but do not push. And it is very important to give him time and space to work the issue his own way.

2. Defuse his defensiveness with "I" statements.
Do not say: "Don't talk to me in that tone of voice."
Say: "I'll be glad to discuss this when respect is shown."

Do not say:
"Stop arguing with me."
Say: "I'll be glad to discuss this as soon as the arguing stops."

Do not say: "Pay attention."
Say: "I'll start again as soon as I know that you are with me."

Most A.D. kids are intensely sensitive to auditory stimulation and will reflexively follow the lead that you establish through your use of language. You can avoid cueing a "No...Yes" cycle by your use of positive language referents. How you act is what you'll get.

3. Use "are you not" language to set up compliance. A simple way to short-circuit opposition is to enlist your child's natural push-back to push-toward your desired outcomes. Tag your requests to him with the statement, "are you not?" "You are talking quietly, are you not?" "You will empty the waste paper basket, will you not?" You may be surprised that he will comply without a pause when you deliver the "are you not" statement in a conversational tone.

4. Use moderate consequences. Don't overwhelm him with your reaction to his misbehavior. Make consequences specific to the problem and dole them out in small increments. If he refuses to eat dinner with the family, have him get his own dinner one night a week. If time out is required, make it for 3 or 5 minutes at a time, not a half-hour or hour. Make consequences follow infractions close to real time. Short-term memory problems make delayed consequences a cause of unnecessary bitterness later on.

5. Only fight battles you can win. Don't get hooked into oppositional arguments. When you notice that you are arguing, state the desired outcome and disengage quickly. Let him have the last word and allow him to cool off. Avoid what A.D.D. expert Dr. Edward Hallowell terms "the Big Struggle" at all costs! For your own psychological survival as well as for the management of your child, you must know in your bones that you are the adult and you are in charge.

6. Attend to your timing. Remember, his oppositionality is essentially a stress response to feeling out of control. He will experience this discomfort more often when he is tired, when his meds are wearing off (especially before bedtime), when he is in social situations that demand appropriate behavior, when he is faced with the requirement for rapid problem solving, or after some "failure" experience at school.

The twelve-year-old boy you are trying to get to bed at nine-fifteen at night may have the emotional capability of a four-year-old. It is a wise parent who recognizes this reality and moves with the child toward the parent's goals softly. Settle for a little bribe of a cookie or promise of some special treat once the child has gotten himself through his shower into his bed.

And notice problems early. He may signal you that he is "heating up to a confrontation" by facial tensing, or acting angry or silly. Check out what's going on with him at these times and back off if he's not ready to talk. Get to know the look of his stress reaction.

7. Give him a good physical and verbal encounter from time to time. The vigorous arm wrestle, the to-the-death game of air hockey at the local video parlor, or the run across the parking lot to get to the car. All these are opportunities for him to show you his power. Don't worry about who wins.

The more he can go all out with you and live to tell about it the more he will feel empowered to trust you and collaborate with you. Let him know what you're made of, because he's made of the same thing and he needs to know this to feel a sense of solidarity within himself.

Help him express the big "No!" by deliberately bantering with him, and keeping your sense of humor while you do it. Encourage him to argue with you. Get to know what he feels passionate about and take the opposing side yourself, making him defend his views. Show him that you can lose an argument and laugh about it. Help him lighten up.

8. Finally, help him *remember* how to comply. In problem situations use "reminder" language to overcome short-term memory problems and increase the chance that he has the information to comply.

Example: To get him to move out of contact when he is yelling or poking others, say, "When you can show me that you have control of your body by stopping your swearing and poking and get to your room, we can talk about what you want."

Daily Workout
Mastering "Non-oppositional" Conversation

Oppositionality is a word that defines an interaction. You can't be oppositional unless someone is trying to get you to do something; you are going to be more likely to resist if you feel bad about yourself or out of control. The following workout is not a discrete event but a description of a style of interaction for managing oppositional communications. The intention is to build your child's sense of his own strength and sense of enjoyment in teaming up with you.

a. Attend to your own state of mind. Know that if you feel negative, or down, he will pick up on your mood and reflect it back to you in his defiance. You have got to have an attitude of "the glass is half full," not "half empty" if you are to succeed. Commonplace as it sounds, you always need to be moving toward a positive outcome. If you don't feel as though you are, do what's necessary to create the feeling.
Don't feed your child's fear of being out of control by getting out of control yourself. Know your stress triggers and have another adult available to support you if possible. He will react best to "matter-of-fact" communications. When you show anger, he will imitate your affect and behavior quickly, in an oppositional manner. An ugly battle can result.

b. Set up your demand with a compliment. Pick something out that he did just a little better and give him a stroke for it: "Hey, kid. I know how hard it is for you to control your anger when you get frustrated. I just saw you wrestle through a mighty frustrating math problem in your homework and you did it without blowing up. Good work!"

c. Make sure to give him a choice. In Chapter Two I discussed how important giving the A.D. child choices is to reducing his stress and building his personal hardiness. Giving choices is even more important in reducing oppositionality. Give him choices that build on his strong sense of inner purpose.
Example: If you want him to finish a project, say, "Would you like ten minutes or fifteen to finish your project?" If you want him to go to the grocery store with you (an activity he dislikes) say, "We need to get some stuff at the store if you want that spaghetti you like for dinner. Is now a good time, or

shall we wait until you've beaten that Nintendo game you're playing?

d. Be calmly but surely persistent. And remember that persistence is also an important aspect of your attitude in this regard. Given the longer learning curves of many Attention Different children, it may take time for him to understand and remember that he can not stall you or wave you off as though he is the little king and you the humble subject. He must learn that sooner or later, he must accommodate your wishes in order to get his goals met.

CHAPTER SEVEN

Overcoming Self-Righteousness and Making Friends

His Own Rules

My son plays chess by his own rules.
Black pawns and bishops run from white.
It's not the game they play in schools.

—Jane Elkington Wahl

In the first chapter, I said that the Attention Different child is caught between two impulses—the impulse to feel alive with a sense of stimulus satisfaction and the desire to feel safe from intrusive stimuli. The power struggle between these two impulses creates a sense of inner chaos and uncertainty about a child's ability to survive the great loss of control over what he feels.

It is this subtle understated, terror that is manifested in the childs lack of flexibility in the judgments he makes of others (his self righteousness) and his ardent assumption that he is never at fault. It is always the other kid who should be blamed for the hassle. It is always the teacher's fault that his homework didn't get done. This stubborn, righteous egotism pushes everybody away from him and leaves him alone.

Here's a typical conversation between one of my ten-year-old Attention Different clients, Randy, and myself during a counseling session:

George: So, your mom said you got in a big hassle with your

friend Geoff at school and had to do detention for it. You want to tell me about it?

Randy: Nothing to say. He's an asshole. He pushed me in front of the other kids. I hit him.

G: He used to be your friend. What happened?

R: Look. The guy's a jerk. He deserved what he got. He tried to cut in front of me in the lunch line. I'm not going to take that. Can we talk about something else?

G: Your mom tells me that you don't have very many friends at school. I thought Geoff was your best friend. Have you tried to talk this over with him?

R: Yea (dejectedly). Mr. Jones (the teacher) got us together and Geoff played along but when it was over he went back to his other friends and now they're all teasing me. They're all a bunch of butts.

There is a temptation to treat the symptom here, to pretend that the child is normal and will benefit from a little lecture on how to relax and keep perspective and let stuff roll off his back. Most A.D. kids, however, will quickly forget both the incident and the lecture and repeat the problematic behavior a dozen times more before the end of the school year. This child is caught in a chronic distress cycle. Getting to eustress means understanding the stressors that fuel the cycle.

Four stressors power the self-righteousness distress cycle

First, there is already an expectation at school that he will *fail*. This is a powerful environmental stressor. Teachers and fellow students have identified him as a troublemaker. He can be taken advantage of by crafty classmates who know how to set him up with a "hit and run" game. The normal child does something to bug the A.D. child and runs. The teacher comes in just as the A.D. child is exploding. All players are in the fight or flight mode and the distress cycle whirls and repeats itself furiously, resulting in bad feelings and further isolation of the A.D. child. Any real defense he had is lost in his loud verbal attack on the other child.

Second, the A.D. child has *underpowered social focus*. Because he is so open to stimulation and has such a difficult time focusing, any demand from his social environment stresses him out. When he has to deal with multiple demands from other kids he gets confused and focuses inward, trying to think his way through the situation. Unfortunately this inner focus cuts him off from awareness of what is going on around him. Consequently, he does not pick up verbal and non-verbal signals from others that warn him to "throttle back" on his behavior.

Unable to coordinate his inner and outer perception, he grabs onto his initial judgment and holds on for dear life. His self-righteousness now has an obsessive feeling to it. It comes out unthinkingly when cued by just being around the other kids.

Third, growing up A.D., he has *not developed social skills*. Knowing how to evaluate interpersonal cues is a learned skill that comes with the ability to assimilate and understand social events. This learning process begins when the child is a toddler and continues throughout his childhood.

If a child has been continually focused on managing his sense of inner chaos, he has not had time to develop the rudimentary social skills to understand nuances of meaning in the verbal and nonverbal language of other people. These are complex, abstract learnings. His perceptual style has resulted in a lack of social skill.

Finally, the child makes things worse by assuming a *fortress mentality*. The child tries to control his sense of inner chaos by assuming a decisional style of either-or. In this wild internal chaos there is no time to listen to the other. It is not perceived as safe to relax. This fortress mentality is a natural human reaction to feeling threatened and out of control. It may be experienced as deeply by the child as it is by the legendary Post Traumatic Stress Disorder (P.T.S.D.) Vietnam veteran who sleeps with a .45 caliber handgun under his pillow.

Given these realities, how do you help your child free himself from the metaphorical "loaded gun" in his consciousness? How do you influence the interaction of his neurology, history, and environment in such a way so that he can put it on safety" and have a life?

Seven Steps To Decrease Environmental Stress and Build Resourcefulness

In order for your child to change, you have to decrease the impact of stressors in his environment. He needs help to develop the personal resources to handle the complexities of social interactions with other children and adults. This process takes time and is fueled by the little successes that you build on to create more success. One step at a time, little successes breed incremental small bursts in self-confidence. The self-righteousness cycle gradually begins to fade. Here are seven important ways to help him develop his social skills:

1. Create awareness among other parents and teachers of your child's perceptual challenges. Make it clear that lectures and consequences will have little effect if the child is stressed out. Teach teachers, bus drivers, and other service staff that your child has a stress management problem related to his attention difference and that he is not acting out or spoiled. Let everyone know you are available to facilitate problem solving and communication.

2. Realize that large classrooms mean more stress and slower social skills learning. Attention Different children have problems learning social skills in large classrooms because these environments are so interpersonally stimulating. Your child's social skills have the best chance of developing in a smaller class— twelve to fifteen children with some one-to-one assistance is a good ratio. If you cannot get him into a smaller class, try to get some "pull out" time for him in a resource room with small groups of other kids and a good teacher. She should have a priority devoted to developing social awareness through group sharing and other activities.

3. Model social skills and willingness to talk in your dealings with other adults in your life, your spouse, and your child. A.D. children are very attuned to parental models and learn from watching how their parents deal with anger and confrontation. If you attack and demonize each other, you load up your child's natural combativeness. The image of you and your spouse rising above an argument to eventually come together gives the child a model of his potential success with other kids and adults in his life. This reality has been a powerful incentive for many of the parents I work with in my counseling practice. They learn and practice adult-adult style assertiveness skills with each other.

4. Ask your child's teachers to use visual and concrete examples to teach him social skills in the classroom setting. For younger children, toy soldiers and other toys can be used to structure the demonstration of the encounter between kids. Older and pre-teen children respond well to stories of how kids solved problems between themselves.

Many A.D. kids have problems integrating information about what the non-verbal cues of other kids mean. At some level they know that a frown means "I am unhappy," but in the moment of their encounter with the other child, the A.D. child does not put this meaning together with the facial expression.

A small social skills group can be very useful to train your child in the interpretation of other kids' "nonverbals." The first thing to go over is what different facial expressions mean. The turned down mouth, furrowed brow, or red face, for example, all signal the presence of the emotion of anger. He must be told this very specifically.

Your child's teacher can help by gentle query of his perception of others when hassles occur. "What does it mean when Johnny clenches his fist, tightens his mouth, and starts yelling at you like that?" Since many A.D. kids do not come by social understanding naturally, once we understand the degree of this challenge, we are in a position to assist them.

5. Strengthen your child's interpersonal perception by setting up intellectual arguments that require him to exercise critical thinking. Force him to make distinctions between a fact or an opinion, and between himself and others. Find out what he feels passionately about and work this subject matter by presenting opposing opinions. Make the opportunity for argument contingent on his ability to respect your opinion. If he is vigorously *for* animal rights and you are arguing the "laboratory researcher" side of the question, the child must argue for his position without calling you an animal murderer for disagreeing with him.

6. Apply the four-step inquiry to a social problem. To help him solve problems, use a four-step question structure involving differentiation of what he 1.) sees, 2.) feels, 3.) imagines, and 4.) wants. Here is an example of how I applied this four-step process with Randy, the boy introduced at the beginning of this chapter. As I led Randy through his problem with the four-step inquiry, he replied:

"I observed Geoff (his friend and adversary) pointing in my direction and laughing and talking to a couple of kids next to him.

"I imagined that he was making fun of me. Mocking me to the other kids. I told him to stop it and he told me to get lost.That's when I pushed him.

"I felt bad about him telling me to get lost and got real angry!

"I want him to like me. He's my best friend. I really feel stuck."

After our discussion, Randy made the decision to ask his friend why he was pointing and laughing. Geoff seemed happy to be asked. "I was telling the other kids about how you looked when we had the snowball fight last weekend and I got one down your pants. I wasn't dissin' you. I thought we were having fun." This cleared up Randy's projection of Geoff's malevolent intention toward him and resulted in the rapid repair of their friendship.

The four-step inquiry presented here is a way for Attention Different children to deliberately separate their fantasies ("I imagine") from what they are really seeing ("I observe"). The tendency to imagine the ill will of others is common in the stress reaction. Our primitive programming seems to readily follow this groove as we enter the fight or flight mode.This is why it is useful to give your child a way to slow down the process—he can make better decisions about how to take care of himself in a given situation.

It is unlikely your child will remember the four-step sequence right away. If you use it, however, to structure your discussions with him around his social problems, it will become easier for him to remember these questions in high stress situations. It is also useful to share this didactic with his teachers so that they may apply it during the classroom's group time or for social skills training.

7. **Teach the "arrow" as a technique for intuitive perception checking.** Attention Different children think in pictures and feelings. Many of them are also highly intuitive; they are able to sense if people like them or not, and make good "gut hunch" decisions.

Train your child's intuition to help him see his position and the other's clearly in a conflict. Ask him to visualize an "arrow suspended in air" between himself and the other person. If the arrow points toward the other, your child's intuition is giving him information that the problem may be with the other, or that that person is in error. If the arrow points back toward your child, he may want to consider that he himself is largely contributing to the problem. If the arrow points both ways, intuition would be saying that both parties are deeply mired in the issue and are both contributing to the problem.

Some children get better intuitive information by visualizing a computer screen with the words "he" or "me" highlighted on it, or with different colors flashing on screen to signify different emotional states the child is experiencing. A high degree of intuitive ability is a well-known characteristic of many Attention Different children. It makes sense to enlist this "hunter's sixth sense" in building the capacity for focus and problem solving.

Daily Workout: Self-Righteousness

a. Identify one positive thing about an adversary. Ask your child to identify one thing about his adversary in the self-righteousness distress cycle that delights him. Keep probing until you get to whatever it is. It might be something that others do not notice, like a gesture or mannerism of a teacher at school, or a particular skill a classmate has—her expertise on the Nintendo, for example. Don't use the information he gives you as an entry to continue an argument. Just encourage him to see that something about the adversary is positive.

b. What am I feeling? Reinforce your child's social skills learning (number 5. above) by asking him to look at your face and guess what you are feeling at the moment. Play with your own facial expression and challenge him to identify specifically what about your face makes him think you are happy, sad, scared, etc. If he has a hard time interpreting your non-verbal behavior, have him focus on discrete elements of your face and ask him to sub-vocalize what he sees: "Her face is red. Her eyes are squinting. Her mouth is drawn down. She looks angry." Or, "Her mouth is drawn up. Her eyes are relaxed. Her whole face looks relaxed. She looks happy."

Keep reviewing this exercise whenever he needs it. It will eventually help him develop his social perception to the point that it will no longer be problematic. Assimilation and accommodation will occur, and along with it permanent change for the positive.

CHAPTER EIGHT

Educating Emotional Wildness

"Here comes Gibbon Boy."
—A mother's description of the look of her A.D. son as he
goes into wild emotionality.

Attention Different children may act emotionally "delayed" or "wild" at times when they are under stress or feel incapable of handling a particular situation. They will be silly, annoying and giddy. This behavior can drive parents up the wall.

A child will act stupid, brainless, annoying, and be unstoppable. He careens around the house, bugging people unmercifully. Teasing them, throwing things around, squeezing the dog too hard. The term "hyperactive" only goes part way in describing this behavior. The term "hyper-annoying" is more appropriate. He seems to seek out whatever action most aggravates those around him and pursues it.

It is important to understand what the child is feeling. The child's consciousness is contaminated by input from his limbic, emotional brain. He does not feel stimulus satisfaction unless the stimulus is delivered loudly, dramatically, even violently. In this emotionally wild place he is unresponsive to the distress being telegraphed by those around him.

Emotional wildness and brain chemistry

Hyperactivity is primarily a result of a low level of dopamine in the frontal lobes combined with an internal sense of kinesthetic pressure. In contrast, emotional wildness is caused by low levels of the neurotransmitter serotonin to inhibitory nerves in the frontal lobes of the brain and in the limbic system, the animal brain. This gives the quality of emotional wildness its animal-like feeling.

Some researchers have suggested that the child's built in action "editor" (a hypothetical brain structure) is not operating. This causes the first behavior in the cue to be the one enacted even though the behavior may be totally inappropriate for the situation.

The wildness distress cycle

Wildness distress cycles often start when the parent is least prepared for them—after some happy time for the child, a visit to the zoo or park, or after a good day of activity. Sometimes they occur in divorced families after the child's visit with the non-custodial parent on Sunday night.

Wildness episodes may not necessarily follow close on the heels of obvious stressors when the child is upset, distraught over rejection by friends, or sick. Many times, they may result from some upset in the child's routine or from "good stress," the kind that follows pleasurable events for the child but is still nonetheless stressful. Any novel challenge or activity generates a certain amount of stress and this will result in neurotransmitter depletion.

Wildness may also come as a "paired association" with predictable events in the child's daily routine. My son Gregory is particularly susceptible to it at nighttime, when he must get himself through a sequence of activities (shower, snack, brush teeth) before bed.

Studying his reaction closely I determined that he is more reactive with me than with his mother at this time. Studying the situation at a deeper level, I realized that I was easier to upset than Joanne and a little less intent on my own purposes with him. He "called up" his "obnoxiousness program" as a direct response to the distress and exhaustion I telegraphed to him on my face. Joanne and I have learned from his behavior and now often trade responsibilities; she helps him more in the evening and I pick up some of the slack in his morning routine.

The parent's reaction is a vital chain in the distress cycle. As I have pointed out elsewhere, Attention Different children are very visual and referent to your emotions. If you are angry, your A.D. child will pick up on your anger and be angry himself. If you look frazzled and out of control, he will reflect this back to you in his behavior. This occurs because of your child's perceptual contamination between what he sees and what he feels—in which one stimulation gets mixed in with another.

At the same time that your child does not hear your *words* (my son Gregory said he hears only "blah, blah, blah" when I scold him), he is taking in unthinkingly, your *emotional* patterns. He observes the tension in your mouth and your face turning red. Suddenly he laughs at you, but now his laugh is tinged with the anger that he has absorbed from you. His taunting has an angry edge that is easy to interpret as pure malevolence, but it is not.

This seeming deliberate cruelty is extremely difficult for many parents to understand and may result in draconian measures to control the behavior. These methods include the use of physical violence (to include corporal punishment), screaming at the top of their lungs, or shaming the child: "You hurt your mother so. You bad boy. Have you no shame? You are on the way to an insane asylum! In fact, I may call tomorrow."

Though violent or emotionally abusive actions may crash through the child's boundaries and halt his behavior momentarily, these measures may also damage the child psychologically. A child isolated, shamed, or hit for his disinhibited behavior may express his anger and shame by self-mutilation or other self-destructive behaviors. He may withdraw into depression, become suicidal, or act out the violence he receives at home against others.

If these patterns continue, the lack of a sense of direction and feeling of hopelessness that underlie all distress cycles will become the rule of the day. Parents will become either more and more punitive or will opt out of trying to control the child altogether. Either option is deadly for family peace and the psychological well-being of the child and parents. What to do?

Take the first step to eustress: calm acceptance

Many parents have not completely accepted their child's neurologic difference and the behavioral limitations that it causes. It is not until he does something really destructive or upsetting that their eyes are opened to the fact of his difference. Shock and anxiety are the first feelings for parents when they see how profound the child's problem is. "My God, my kid is nuts!" They assume that acceptance of his neurology is tantamount to accept- ing him as insane. An understandable but erroneous assumption.

The parent needs to accept the fact that in the heat of emo- tional wildness, her child is neurologically disinhibited but is not crazy. This is not an emotional disturbance, but a perceptual disturbance, a mood state rooted in a biochemical difference that will pass, once the internal or external pressure has lessened.

Acknowledging the neurologic cause of wild behavior is the first step to eustress and positive change. It allows us to take the burden and guilt off ourselves for not being able to easily change his behavior. Our dual task is to manage our own stress and reduce his as much as possible. This too shall pass!

The second step: get to know the challenge that you face

A core feature of personal hardiness and a key to staying healthy under stress is the acceptance of the stressor as a challenge. Emotional wildness in A.D. kids can drive you up against the limit of your self-control. To deal with it you have to embrace it as one of the biggest challenges you will face in your life. Resolve to manage it with persistence and ingenuity.

a. Make it a priority to study how he reacts as he does, when he does. Keep a notebook to record information about stressors, dietary habits, medication dosage, and reactions. Put together a picture of the distress cycles that regularly occur and formulate your ideas about what is going on.

b. Sort out his motivation. Your child's problematic behav- iors are prompted by the positive intention of his gaining either stimulus satisfaction or stimulus safety. Your assess- ment should explore which of these two needs are motivating his particular behavior.

Stimulus *satisfaction* as a motivator. A child seeking stimu- lus satisfaction will attempt to provoke an incendiary reaction from his parents; he craves their dramatic reaction to him. He needs a high "signal volume," his parents yelling at him and losing their temper, to get a sense of stimulation. This child may also demonstrate the aggressive emotional silliness that drives many families up the wall.

Stimulus *safety* **as a motivator.** Obnoxious and wild behaviors also have a safety function for the child. An Attention Different child may provoke a reaction to get a sense of his parents' ability to establish boundaries. This is the child's way of saying, "I'm out of control and scared. Someone has got to be in charge and I choose you!"

The feeling of being over-pressured is common to A.D. kids— a good case of "the sillies" goes a long way to letting off the pressure. Oftentimes the child will appear sated, pleasurably worn out after the experience. Decompression has occurred. Though this trashed his parents' state of mind for the night, this decompression is just what he needed!

Seven Eustress Parenting Strategies To Decrease Emotional Wildness

Accepting the neurologic foundation for your child's wildness gives you the big picture that you need to handle him more adaptively, to know he is not crazy or malevolent. As we have discussed, his behavior is a response to the dictates of his strange brain chemistry and it will pass. It needn't become part of a permanent distress pattern. Here are some ways to nudge it in the right direction.

1. Pay attention to the emergence of the limbic wave. The best time to take any action to manage emotional wildness is as close to the onset of this state of consciousness as possible. Emotional wildness follows a limbic wave pattern similar to the one described in Chapter Three. There is a build-up, a crescendo, and a diminution of energy.

In the build-up phase, the child shows subtle changes in facial expression. His face may take on a waxy grin, and seem "Panlike" or demonic. His sense of humor may seem to have regressed to early Beavis and Butthead. These signals will alert you that the wild limbic wave is building. You then need to decide if it is better to close the distance between you and your child and put more structure on his interactions, or ignore him and let the wave pass.

2. Ignore his silliness as much as possible. Oftentimes just the self-awareness that you are "in it" with him is enough to keep your perspective and not get hooked into giving him a big emotional reaction. Accept the challenge of not getting emotional and relate to him with loving dispassion. Firmly and persistently insist that he comply with your plans. Tell him that you "do not want to play the game" right now.

3. Changing the context may change his behavior. If he seems to follow a daily pattern for the expression of emotional wildness, change the pattern in some way. If hassles happen after school with his sister, keep them apart for a half-hour or so past their normal meeting time. If hassles happen with his dad but not his mom for a particular activity, trade off parent-in-charge responsibilities. Experiment with different ways to nudge the distress cycle into a more positive pattern.

4. Become an expert distracter. A peculiarity of the Attention Different way of being is that these kids often look to their environments for cues as to what to do next. Because they are so immersed in the eternal present they really don't have a firm sense of the flow of things from "this" to "that." Picking a fight with a parent or getting into emotional wildness creates a sense of activity that relieves the sense of anxiety which comes from not knowing what happens next. It may help to distract him with some focus activity that gets him through the transition that he is negotiating.

If you see that he is beginning to heat up to an encounter, begin "talking an image" that appeals to him. Reference any activities during the day that he found enjoyable. Wave a treat under his nose, a cookie or potato chip, and tell him when he completes the activity that you want, he will get more of the reward. Notice how his energy expression changes as you do this and continue to distract him toward your goals if you are getting a positive effect.

5. Draw the line without arguing. Though a child who experiences emotional wildness may not be in full control of himself, or aware of what's going on around him, his parents must be in full control of the situation. Parents who are veterans of this encounter and successful at it share several commonalties of approach:

❖ They do not argue.

❖ They state what they want in positive, cool language.

❖ They insist upon compliance, give the child time to comply, and keep prompting him for compliance.

❖ If the child refuses to comply they may ignore his defiance, they may impose a reasonable consequence, or they may physically control his behavior. Physical control techniques are outlined in Chapter Eleven to use in managing rage.

❖ They seek to de-escalate the stress in the situation and look at their child's behavior as a neurological event, similar to, but not the same as, having a seizure or being intoxicated.

❖ They do not "lose it" themselves.

All of these aspects together describe the eustress approach to managing emotional wildness. Choose your actions and words carefully and move with awareness. This is the "ground of being" necessary for dealing with the considerable stress that emotional wildness will put on you.

6. Give him refuge, not "time out." Attention Different children who are in a hyperannoying state of mind need a place to cool off that is a refuge, not time out. Acceptance of the fact that your child is behaving as he does because of his brain chemistry gives you the perspective you need to select a refuge. The main task is to lower his stress, not to punish him. This is best accomplished in a comfortable, low stress environment.

At school, a refuge may be located in a small room accessible to the student, in a private counseling area, or in some other place both comfortable and private. At home a refuge can be his room or some other dedicated place in the house. In moving him to a refuge, make it clear that you "just want him to be in a calm place long enough to calm down" and that you welcome him back with you when he no longer feels giddy.

7. Track your own non-verbals and understand how they cue his silliness. Look in the mirror at yourself when he is annoying or upsetting you. If your facial expression is tense, take a moment to do a little deep breathing and notice how this relaxes your face. Then return to dealing with him. If you have a certain way of holding tension in your body (shoulders hunched, jaw tight, eyes squinted), take a moment to breathe and relax. Remember that he will follow the picture you give him, so neutralize that tense image. As you cool, so will he. Distress points directly to eustress.

Daily Workout for Emotional Wildness (or anytime it is needed)

Practice of these activities—"quality time" and "alongside time"—strengthens your child by giving him the stimulus satisfaction he craves from you in the form of your full, undivided attention.

Quality time

The quality time you spend with your Attention Different child directly helps him get his emotional wildness under control. The word *quality* in this context means that you give him your full attention, heart to heart, eye to eye. This level of interaction with you gives him the stimulus satisfaction he needs. It also gives you the opportunity to reach him.

When you're in quality time with him, you may touch each other, state mutual preferences and observations, ask personal questions, kid each other, or call attention to each other's foibles. Mutual respect and a sense of humor are primary requirements. Quality time means that you contact each other on the emotional level. This is the domain of "I-Thou" communication; "from my heart to yours." This experience helps fill the child's craving for stimulus satisfaction.

Alongside time

Sometimes a kid doesn't need to be encountered as intensely as may happen in quality time. Some A.D. children don't like eye contact or a heck of a lot of direct "I" contact with their parents. They prefer to play in parallel and have a craving for this kind of interaction. These are the kids who do the same aggravating things time after time and who seem to think that this is how you play with someone.

To satisfy this kid's stimulus craving, you must get into the parallel play mode. Get down on the floor and play a game with him. Tell him a story as you drive somewhere. Mumble things at each other over a bag of chips watching TV. "I love you. Do you know that?" the father says. "I love you too," answers the son. This is stimulus satisfaction!

Because he may not read interpersonal cues clearly it is important to plan activities in which the two of you focus on the activity, not on each other. Board games are great for this, as are outings together. Consider going bowling, biking, or to a ball game.

Observe your child to get a sense of the type of contact that he needs with you. If he discourages eye contact with you and seems to prefer "being in parallel," play this way with him. If he seems to be pushing you to draw you out, then play in this way with him. Give him a wrestle. Give him a sense of who you are.

CHAPTER NINE

Confronting Dangerous, Destructive, and Risky Behavior

"I wanted to astonish the spectators by taking senseless chances and— a strange emotion— I clearly remember that even without any prompting of vanity I really was suddenly overcome by a terrible craving for risk."
—Dostoyevsky, from *The Gambler*

The Attention Different child between the ages of nine and twelve is vulnerable to injury from taking dangerous risks. This A.D. child may possess what researchers now call the recently discovered "novelty-seeking gene" called "D4DR." This gene has a function in the manufacture and absorption of dopamine in the brain. Its presence in the child's makeup signals that the child may have a dopamine imbalance in his brain which gives him a craving for stimulation.

This predilection for novelty-seeking may amplify. Although it is normal for a child to test himself against boundaries, he may push farther into forbidden areas, emerging into risky and dangerous action. Destructive and risky behavior can throw your family into chaos. It is very important to get an understanding of what is motivating this behavior so that you can give him some tools to deal with it.

Two Types of Risky Behavior

The Attention Different child with a predilection for risky behavior may follow two fairly predictable patterns. He may:

a. *Do something impulsively destructive.* Set fires, use knives dangerously, or trash something in his home. He may take this action essentially unaware of the moral right or wrong of the behavior, unconcerned with any consequence or punishment. His thinking brain is turned off. Though this type of behavior is a neurological, not a psychological event, he must still be held accountable for his actions if he is to develop the psychological muscularity to control himself. This being said, it is important also not to mistake his action as an expression of malevolence.

b. *Take inappropriate or dangerous risks,* egged on by friends who know he will accept any dare. Attention Different children often will do dangerous things to "see how it feels." Their needs for stimulus satisfaction is met through dangerous, high action. They jump off high places, ride their bikes with their eyes closed, or do something else stupidly dangerous on a dare.

I find that many A.D. boys rarely turn down an invitation to a fight. Because they are very reactive they may quickly become stuck in anger cycles involving insult and retaliation. They lack the ability to make accurate judgments of the issues in these high stress situations. Fists flying, they are all speed and no control.

The "Iron Fist" distress cycle

Parents sometimes make the false assumption that risky behavior is a marker of a character disorder. This misassumption is reinforced by the "Conduct Disorder" diagnostic category (312.8) in the Diagnostic and Statistical Manual (DSM IV) used by psychiatrists to diagnose their patients. These include behaviors of aggression, destruction of property, deceitfulness, and serious rule violations.

Mislabeling A.D. as Conduct Disorder is to be expected, since the Attention Different child will typically show several of the behaviors included in the four symptom sub-categories noted above for the Conduct Disorder diagnosis. Risky, dangerous, and destructive behavior is also characteristic of kids who have been abused and neglected. "Acting out" the rage that they have experienced is part of the healing process.

But the A.D. child is not behaving this way as re-enactment of trauma, the reason that other kids may get on the wrong track. The A.D. child does these things because of his predilection for disinhibited, unedited, action.

It is a mistake to label this behavior a "character disorder" for children with known attention differences, unless a clear psychological trauma is present that could cause the behavior. Attention Different children have notoriously low self-esteem and are very suggestible. Mislabeling a child puts him at the risk of trying to make himself into a juvenile delinquent out of the belief that he is one.

Never "shame" your child for his behavior

A severe distress cycle can occur if you shame your child for his behavior, or use draconian punishment or consequences in an attempt to control him. These things feed the distress cycle because they cause him to resent you greatly, and do nothing to address the underlying issues or change the situation.

A boy who plays with fire dangerously may be shamed as a "potential pyro" and lose all his privileges for months. A child may be mislabeled "violent" for taking a knife to school to show his friends.

Another A.D. child with the "Bipolar depression" features described in Chapter One may be labeled "conduct disordered." Or he may be labeled "Oppositional Defiant" for resisting any instruction given to him. Misassuming that his behavior is intentional, his parents use corporal punishment on him in steadily increasing severity. Time and again they spank him, first with their hand, then with a wooden spoon. This kind of treatment can create a personality disorder where one did not exist beforehand.

Corporal punishment may traumatize a child who is already over-sensitive to stimulation and it will teach him that it is O.K. to overpower another if you have good reason. This is the last thing you want to teach a kid who already has major problems keeping his hands to himself and accurately perceiving what is going on around him.

The Three Requirements for Eustress Management of Dangerous Behavior

To interrupt the risky behavior distress cycle you must understand what is going on, educate your child in the management of his reaction, and provide consequences that connect him to the community.

1. Develop understanding: keep a journal.

Get to understand the challenge you are facing. Keep a journal of your child's life on a daily basis. Identify his internal stressors, family stressors, and any aspects of his diet, environment, and interactions that you think may be part of the picture. Note any side effects from medication that you observe and when, during the day, he experiences these effects.

Talk to your child about why he did something risky to determine what he was getting out of it. What does it feel like before he does the thing? Does he experience any kind of "antsyness" or agitation? These feelings will occur before the event and can be considered preparatory to it. Help him explore what happens on an emotional and thought process level when he starts feeling agitated.

Ask him if he is aware of any events in his daily life that cause him to move toward risky behavior. These may include low level stressors such as a dare from a friend, boredom, lack of structure or supervision, physical or mental fatigue, or the requirement to accomplish a task he is trying to avoid.

Then talk to him about what he experiences while he is behaving that way. How is it pleasurable for him? Thom Hartmann has suggested that high stimulation activity and risky behavior gives people with A.D.D. a sense of being alive, the quality that I term stimulus satisfaction. It is important to understand the positive outcome he gets from his behavior.

And talk to him about how he feels after the event. Give him the chance to discuss the state of remorse that he may experience. Help him develop awareness of when he is getting into a risky behavior distress cycle. He needs to be aware if he is to successfully interrupt the urge to risky behavior.

2. Educate him in how to control his reactions

Once your child has a good sense of personal awareness of what leads him to risky behavior, he is in position to take action—interrupting the cycle before actually getting into trouble. Sit down with him and help him plan what he needs to do.

a. Help him track the buildup of pressure. Approach the topic of your child's risky behavior in a matter-of-fact tone. Tell him a little about your own childhood—the mistakes you made, the risks you took, and how you make decisions about whether taking a risk is the right thing to do.

Tell him that the agitated feeling he experiences before he does something "dumb" is a good signal to pull back and rethink his plan. Make it clear that you want him to come to you first, when he starts feeling this way.

Create a scale that indicates the strength of this internal feeling with him on a "1" (not likely to initiate dangerous behavior) to a "7" (feel compelled to do something). Ask him to talk to you when pressure reaches a "3." Consider this level of internal pressure to be an indication that some change is in order to avoid the distress cycle.

b. Help him to get moral support early on. To interrupt the stress cycle, your child should have someone whom he can speak with to vent the tension he feels and to get support. Set up a system for him to notify you or another parent or to contact a friend. Other kids with this same problem may be able to provide this kind of support.

c. Educate his behavior around fire and knives. I have often thought that the Attention Different child's fascination with fire and knives confirms writer Thom Hartmann's theory that the children with the A.D.D. diagnosis are "hunters," acting out a style of behavior that had enormous community survival value tens of thousands of years ago. The fire and knife expression of this archetype needs to be explained by the parent to teach the child proper respect for these implements. Create a safe environment for him to experiment with fire, and give him safety rules and extensive explanation about the dangers of fire. A space for your child to experiment could be in the backyard, or with candles on a cookie sheet. Watch him carefully to make sure he is behaving safely. Your local sporting goods store will have a flint fire-starting kit. Work with your child to show him how to use it. Let him tend fires in your household fireplace from time to time and on family camping trips. Teach him respect for fire.

Get him a whittling knife and materials and teach him knife safety. Show him how to use the knife, fingers away from the blade, with the cut always away from the body. Observe him to insure that he is behaving safely. Watch how solemnly he is working with the knife. This is a sign that a powerful and enjoyable learning experience is occurring around this implement.

d. Teach him assertiveness skills. Attention Different children are easy marks for other kids seeking a "fool for a risk." A.D. kids don't edit their actions and usually are social misfits. They are looking for ways to make their mark with others and need special help with assertiveness.

Begin by setting up role-plays of the kinds of situations that he gets into with his peers and practice saying the word "No" with him. Help him devise "scripts" to deal with these situations in which he states his own boundaries politely: "No. You guys go ahead if you want but I'm not into (fill in the blank) today." "No. The last time I did that I got grief for weeks. Not today." Practice with him until he gets a sense of what to say. The assertiveness skills you give him are a lifelong gift!

e. Get him into a high intensity hobby, sport, or artistic endeavor. Risky behavior is a signal that a child needs more intensity in his life, more experience—a way to distinguish himself from other kids. Get him involved in some activity that he finds interesting and requires a focused mind. Many different options are available.

A child may excel at sports, at computers, in a scientific area, in drama, music, in art, or in a martial art such as Aikido. Design and nurture the channel for his creative fire. Remember, he will need to have his interest "jump started" by you. He is so much "in the present" that he has a hard time orienting to long-run activities and he's going to need your help. Talk it up. Give him images.

One of my clients was a twelve-year-old boy with an attraction toward a group of kids who were hanging out on the edge of juvenile delinquency. This boy's parents had the ingenuity to encourage the sport of hockey for their son. This sport gave him the contact stimulation that he was hankering for, that had drawn him toward the junior lawbreakers. Once his star began to rise as an apprentice member of his school's hockey team, he stopped hanging out with the street kid "wanna be" crowd.

3. Provide consequences that affirm his connection to the community.

When a child does something impulsively destructive, it is often difficult to come up with a natural consequence for the act. By the term "natural consequence" I mean a consequence that relates directly to the infraction that illustrates the cause and effect relationship between what a child does and what happens as a result.

How do you make up for the stress that you experience when your Attention Different child punches a hole in your wall in rage? Or perhaps he does something silly and destructive like puncturing your leather couch with his pen knife in an imaginary struggle with a bad guy from a TV cartoon.

How do you sanction him for petty shop lifting, setting fire in a local field, or doing something destructive or irresponsible as a result of a dare from friends? In most cases there is no way that a child can pay for damages. Long-term loss of privileges is an extremely inefficient consequence that just keeps anger up for everyone and does little to address the root causes of the child's irresponsibility.

Your corrective action must help him overcome the isolation from you and others who care about him that occurs as a result of his hurtful behavior. Being isolated in his own self-centered little world of preoccupation with biochemical pressure for action is dangerous for him. He needs a consequence that builds a bridge back to his community and that doesn't shame him.

What the child needs to know and remember every day of his life is that he is not an island. He must understand that his actions have an impact on other's lives, either to hurt or help them. He needs to remember his interdependence with his family and community. He must understand your support for the Golden Rule, " Do unto others as you would have them do unto you."

The primary criterion for an effective consequence for destructive behavior is that the child understands he is interdependent with his family and community. This will prove to be the way out of the distress cycle.

The concept of community service as applied by community justice agencies is useful here. In community service, a child is given some work to do that benefits the community—as an alternative to referral to the legal system. Community service is typically adjudicated for petty infractions like impulsive fire setting or shop lifting and usually involves some kind of manual labor performed for a certain number of hours. At the completion of the community service time, all formal records of the infraction are destroyed.

Use of community service as a consequence for destructive behavior can have long-term benefits for eliminating this problem with Attention Different kids.

The first step is to give the child a context for your decision to have him do community service: "You and we are all part of a community, be it our family, our neighborhood, or the town we live in. When you destroy something that is owned in community by all of us, you must do something to replace what you have taken out." Let this message sink in and argue it a bit with your child if he requires further justification.

The second step is to give him a choice of available community service. Forms of service available include:

❖   Working a certain number of hours at a local food bank, bagging groceries.

❖   Performing necessary tasks for your family's religious or spiritual community.

❖   Working a certain number of hours as a member of a neighborhood clean-up team.

❖   Participating in the repair of damage that he causes— patching the hole in the wall, or cleaning up after the fire. (Sometimes this is a practical alternative, sometimes not.)

❖   Making restitution to injured parties with his labor; five hours of yard work equals one broken window, etc.

❖   Personally apologizing for the damage he did.

When he has completed his service, take some time to talk with him about his experience and re-emphasize why you wanted him to do it. Affirm your commitment to the Golden Rule. Give him a chance to process his feelings and realize that this is a time when what you say to him is very important. Set a solemn tone and talk to him heart to heart without scolding. If you help him resolve the difficulty that he experiences controlling himself through wise and loving counsel this will leave him with a clear feeling of his connection to his community.

Daily Workout: Visualizing New Options To Manage Risky Behavior

Dangerous, destructive, and risky behavior is often related to a child's lack of creativity in coming up with alternative action for getting that all important stimulus satisfaction. New options are now available to structure change and develop muscularity to resist risky behavior. The following exercise is drawn from the powerful bag of psychological change tools labeled "neuro-linguistic programming (N.L.P.) These involve accessing creative resources using mild hypnotic trance.

To set up the context for this Workout, explain to your child about the idea that people tend to have separate bundles of personality traits that you might call "parts." Illustrate these differences by telling him that kids will often show their "friend" part to each other and their "adversary" part to their parents. Depending on the situation, a kid might be kind, gentle, and supportive, or intensely competitive. Tell him about how adults also have parts triggered by the situation they are in: we might show the "Mr. Hyde" aspect of ourselves in our reaction to a traffic jam on the freeway, but as soon as we get to work we are pure "Dr. Jekyll" (out of necessity).

Once he has an understanding of the idea of parts, spend some quality time with your child going through the following short exercise. To begin, ask him to breathe "down to his stomach" and close his eyes.

First, ask him to recall a time when he felt particularly creative in any endeavor. Have him bring to mind an image of what that looked and felt like. It could be a project in art, working with computers or mechanics, playing sports—all are good candidates. Ask him to see it in his "mind's eye" and experience the color, brightness, and feeling that goes with the image. This is his "creative part," a resourceful aspect of himself.

Check to make sure that he has an image in mind. When he's ready, ask him to place it in a "illuminated video frame" on the right side of his inner landscape, around the "two or three o'clock position of the clock face." The creative part can be very useful in helping him come up with new behavioral alternatives to a risky action.

Second, ask him to imagine an image of himself in a risky behavior. When he has an inner picture of it, have him put that on the left side of his visual field and "dim" his illumination of it somewhat.

Third, once he has a good internal image of both states of consciousness, ask the following three questions:

a. "I'd like to speak directly to the creative part of you that you see in your internal field of view. And I would ask that this

part of you signal it hears me by changing its illumination slightly, up or down. Any change will indicate we are in communication. Do you have some change in the illumination of that image?"
Wait for a moment and watch to see if your child nods his head or tells you there has been a slight change in illumination of the frame. Then say:

b. "Thank you, creative part. Now I would ask you to give three other options or choices to the part that does (John's) risky behavior. These options don't have the "unpleasant side effects" of the dangerous conduct. Each of these options should be as *easy, effective, and immediate* as the risky behavior. We don't need to know exactly what these options are but I ask that you let us know that they have been passed along by changing the illumination of the risky behavior image three times."

c. When your child indicates that he has had three changes in illumination, ask if the part of him that runs the unsafe behavior would be willing to use the new behavior choices when "the antsy feeling starts" that signals the start of problem behavior. Ask this part of him to signify, by changing illumination one time.
Once you have the last signal, thank both "the creative part" and "the risky behavior part" for conversing with you. Ask your child to breathe and relax and return to eyes open with a "wiggle of a toe or a finger or some little movement." Don't push for identification of all three options. Often, time is needed to let the experience settle, in order to prepare for new behavior that will not present itself until needed.
Process this exercise a bit by asking your child how he feels, and if there were any surprises in it for him. Surprise is always a sign of new learning and potential change. He may mention some new inspiration at this time. If he does, reflect on it as an aspect of his creativity and tell him you are available to help if he'd like. If nothing new comes to mind, tell him that a change in his perspective is inevitable but may take a few days. Thank him for doing the exercise with you.

"The proof of the pudding is in the eating." You cannot rush the creative process, but don't be surprised to find that your child comes to you in a day or so and tells you he has succeeded in avoiding some risky situation. Calmly compliment him on his work and compliment yourself on helping him successfully deal with his need for stimulus satisfaction.

CHAPTER TEN

Transcending Depression

*"The monster comes and gets me, you see. And he drags me
into his jaws. It is very dark. I am really scared."*
— A nine year-old A.D. boy describing how
depressed mood overtakes him

Depression is a clinical term that many parents and children accept as a kind of psychological death sentence. The parents remember the people in their families who were depressed, and the condition went on for years! They get very anxious when depression emerges in their pre-adolescent child.

Its presence is unmistakable. The child will lack motivation to do anything at home or school and will complain of feeling listless and having low energy. His self-esteem will plummet and school grades drop through the floor. He will assume a pasty complexion. He will have sleep problems and will need to be prompted to eat a decent meal. He may lose friends and become a loner. His most dominant emotion is dysphoric, grouchy anger that can quickly turn to bitter rage.

The depressed child will appear quiet and pensive. He may answer questions in a monotone; his motions seem to lack purpose. You get the feeling that he is pulled back from his contact with you into a place deep inside himself. Parents often experience strong guilt and despair when depression emerges and will question themselves mercilessly to determine what they have done to cause their child's condition.

How stress leads to formation of a depression distress cycle

Depression will usually emerge between the ages of nine and twelve. In my counseling practice, I have seen it afflict as many girls as boys. Many times it is kicked off by a change in schools or by the move of the family from one locality to another, though I sometimes see cases of it that lack any antecedent change or loss. It is often related to the loss of cherished friends or peer groups. The child goes into a funk and in the style of the distress cycle he digs himself in deeper by his isolation and withdrawal from the world.

Boys and girls are particularly susceptible to it between the ages of nine and eleven if their parents divorce or separate. Depression becomes the way that the child telegraphs his distress and grief over his parent's break-up and it's also his strategy for bringing them both back into his life. Because these symptoms are so dramatic and compelling, parents drop their mutual antagonism or dissatisfaction with each other and come together as a "couple" one more time to help their child.

Depression is a well-known result of distress and burnout in both children and adults. It is a natural part of a distress cycle in which too much stress causes low serotonin and dopamine in the brain. This results in both depression and the inability to concentrate, which results in more maladaptive behavior and further distress.

A. Stressor: change of school, divorce, etc.

D. Lower self-esteem and vulnerability to next stressor

B. Drop in serotonin and dopamine

C. Child's energy drops - he becomes listless and irritable

The Depression Distress Cycle

Sorting out different types of depression in the Attention Different child

A kid may become depressed as a result of the experience of failure, as a complication of being obsessional or phobic (irrational fear), from medication overdose, or as part of Bipolar Mood Disorder.

A child may fall into depression as a result of failure experiences related to his A.D. No matter how he tries, he can't seem to control himself and behave like the other kids. His self-esteem takes such a battering that eventually he comes to see himself as an incompetent failure. Through the assimilation and accommodation mechanism, a change in brain chemistry occurs which throws his serotonin levels off and locks in the depressed mood.

Some children also experience obsessions and phobias as a result of lowered serotonin, which can cause low-level depression. The obsessing child is using so much energy to suppress his obsession that he becomes apathetic and listless.

It is important for the parent to check for the presence of obsessionality or phobias by gentle questioning: "How is it for you when you're trying to get to sleep at night? You seem to be staying awake a long time. When I was a kid I used to get 'the worries' when I lay in bed at night. Do you?"

Depression can also be a result of an overdose of stimulant medications. I have most often seen this condition in "A.D.D." diagnosed children with a daily dosage of Ritalin over 45mg. Drug overdose or intolerance is also seen in a tendency to cry easily. As stimulants raise the brain dopamine level the emotional response centers in the cortex and limbic brain are also affected, creating a kind of melancholic emotionality. This effect may also occur as an adverse reaction to anti-depressants such as Prozac.

Bipolar Mood Disorder depression and rage

A child can be genetically predisposed to deep depression. This can manifest itself in the depression seen in children with Bipolar Mood Disorder diagnosis. This depression is remarkable in its severity and may not be linked in any way to trauma in the child's life or his experience of failure. Here are several indicators that Bipolar depression is present:

❖ Depression appears in preschool and (unlike A.D.H.D. related depression) gets worse as the child gets older.

❖ The child experiences a sense of rage at being trapped in the dark depressing mood and projects this rage outward in temper tantrums that may last from a half an hour to two hours. These outbursts are of such ferocity that you could not imitate them even if you tried.

❖ Bipolar temper outbursts are often triggered by the attempt to discipline the child, not (as in other attention differences) by over stimulation or frustration.

❖ Children often have gory and violent nightmares.

❖ In social situations, the child with Bipolar challenges may behave with hostility, unlike other A.D. kids who may seem simply distracted or "socially incompetent" in these situations.

❖ In Bipolar Mood Disorder, the destructiveness of the child is often intentional, unlike that of the A.D.H.D. child who will often break things out of mindlessness or carelessness.

If B.M.D. is suspected, it is important for you to contact a psychiatrist who specializes in the disorder to discuss medication and psychotherapy. Children with this form of depression can become chronically isolated and suicidal. Psychiatric intervention and medication (see below) may be indicated.

Suicide threats

Suicide threats are fairly common among depressed A.D. kids. The feeling of self-recrimination can be powerful after the child does something hurtful to others, but these kids rarely proceed to the planning stage of suicide unless they are experiencing Bipolar Disorder. The internal experience of Bipolar is that of being imprisoned in a "black box" in one's mind. There is the temptation to assume that killing oneself is the only way out. Of course this is fallacious thinking.

Many kids who threaten to kill themselves are reacting to a severe lack of pleasure and excitation in their lives; very little of what goes on around them seems exciting or interesting. Lack of excitation shuts down motivation to do anything and the child may become a hermit in his own home. The result is self-esteem low enough to cause a mention of suicide. This is a genuine cry for help.

Many parents feel helpless dealing with their child's depression even though they recognize it clearly. One mom of a depressed nine-year-old named Bart described her son as "an imploding volcano." You know he's mad at you, he just doesn't say it." A parent may mistakenly blame herself for her child's depression, when in fact it is related to a genetic predisposition in the same way as the other attention different conditions.

The question of medication

Parents vexed with their child's depression have a variety of medications to choose from. All of them have side effects that should be researched carefully with your local library's copy of the *Physician's Drug Reference,* or any number of several other excellent references available, written in layman's terms.

It is important to understand two things: 1. None of the psychoactive medications out today (except the stimulant methylphenidate (Ritalin) have ever been tested on children. 2. It is hard to assess the risks of any particular medication; a drug may be prescribed hundreds of thousands of times before its involvement in injury or death is reported. Side effects are easier to track, but every person is different.

The eustress approach to medication calls for a collaborative relationship between you and your physician. She, or her nurse, should be available to you at all times for consultation about medication. Remember, you are the expert. If your child is experiencing an intolerable side effect or your gut hunch is that the medication is missing the mark, call your doctor and expect her to listen carefully to your opinion before making her recommendation to you for change.

Become an expert on any medication that your child is taking. If you don't understand the medication write-up, consult a medical dictionary or computer on-line information service for clarification.

An extremely important aspect of medication management is parents' use of a medication journal. A spiral notebook with page entries keyed by date works nicely for this purpose. Make sure to mention the time and dosage of the drug's administration. Note side effects and patterns from other days.

The journal gives you a written memory of your child's condition and allows you to track other aspects of his behavior that are important for understanding. It also helps you measure improvement and compare how he reacts to medication, depending on stress. It gives you the information for analyzing how he is when taking the medication and when he is medication-free on "drug holidays."

Medications prescribed for depression

There are several medications that have proven to be effective for treating depression in children and adults. All of these medications have the effect of raising levels of the serotonin in the brain's emotional response centers. These medications include the tricyclics: imipramine (b. Tofranil), desipramine (b. Norpramin), and amiltriptyline (b. Elavil), and the tricyclic-like medications (the selective serotonin reuptake inhibitors, S.S.R.I.'s) fluoxotine (Prozac), setraline (Zolof), paroxitine (Paxil) and the newest S.S.R.I., nefazodone (b. Serzone).

Lithium carbonate has been shown to help children who are diagnosed with Bipolar Mood Disorder. Lithium fortifies natural sodium-based chemicals that are deficient in the brains of people with the disorder. Giving Lithium to the child with Bipolar related problems is similar to giving insulin to a diabetic. It regularizes body function by supplying a biochemical that brings balance to the child's system.

Side effects and misuse of these drugs

I have mentioned that there is little research on the safety of psychotropic medications for children. Though newspaper stories will focus on the tiny percentage of kids who have suffered severe health problems or died from medication, little evidence supports allegations that these drugs are toxic or that they are safe.

Three children have died from heart attacks related to their ingestion of imipramine and desipramine, though it is unclear if proper medical procedures were followed for administration of the medication. Two people have committed suicide while taking Prozac. Thus, physicians will usually not prescribe it if the child shows "vegetative depression" which is demonstrated by extremely low mobility, not getting out of bed, not eating, and suicidal thinking. More detail on these drugs is found in Chapter Twelve, which describes their use for treating obsessions and compulsions, another low serotonin related condition.

You know your child. You know what behaviors are most problematic and which ones are just "a little weird." Medication is only advised if the problem cannot be remedied any other way. This is why it's a good idea to try counseling and other techniques before medication. A child's challenges become most intense when he is stressed; counseling in stress reduction and empowerment of the child will hopefully make medication unnecessary.

Start the healing process by identifying external stressors

A major external stressor for many depressed kids is their parents' idea that the child is damaged and unreachable and that it is the parents' fault. This misconception makes parents feel guilty and leads to them putting a lot of pressure on their child to "buck up and get a life." The child will often feel guilty because he is incapable of following this simplistic prescription.

Because depressed children take a longer time than normals to focus on things, their perceptual style is characterized by a slowed-down cycle of contact between themselves and the rest of the world. This situation is made worse if parents try to hurry up the contact cycle by being too demanding. The child freezes up from the stress—further pushing can cause rage to emerge. This lack of understanding can contribute to the formation of an anger-based distress cycle.

Another major stressor for the child is social isolation. Depressed kids are a drag to be around and will be ceremoniously avoided by other kids. They long to pour their hearts out to a friend, but are incapable of finding anyone who will put up with their dark mood.

The child may be getting through school on the strength of pure grit, but at some point his determination may fray at the edges. He is battling his own neurology without help. When this happens, teachers will often complain that the child is getting "oppositional" and is fighting his school work.

If depression exists on mom and dad's side of the family, the child's situation is worsened. He experiences increased stress having to deal with the depressed and hostile effect of his parents. An anger distress cycle can result which is profoundly upsetting to the family.

Five Essential Keys to Eustress Management of Your Child's Depression

1. **Establish hope by** *reframing* **the feeling of hopelessness.** The first thing that your child needs is *hope*. The second thing he needs is a way to *communicate*, and the third is *motivation*. These qualities must occur in the order listed.

Hope comes when parents are able to escape their own feelings of hopelessness and accept their child's depression as a temporary challenge. Depression is an indication that the child is stuck in a deep rut, which is maintained by his own feelings of being unable to do anything to help himself.

Parents must see the child's depression as an indication that he is not feeling resourceful in the situation and then give him a sense of his own resources by renaming his condition.

Because the word "depression" has such a powerful connotation of despair, it is important to find another word to describe your child's condition: "Intensely inner directed, or introverted" is one option. A "solitary, contemplative child" is another. A "deep thinker who processes information very carefully" is a third possible descriptor. Many variations are possible. The idea is not to deny that the child is depressed but to telegraph to him that he is not damaged, that you accept him and accept your role to help him be more happy.

In my counseling practice I have noticed that so-called depressed children often have ways of controlling their interpersonal interactions with their parents that suit their low energy style. They are good at reading their parents' nonverbal signals and are careful negotiators based on their read. Many have skills in contemplative thinking, mathematics and computers. Most are as desperate to change as their parents and are open to suggestion for doing this.

2. Use reverse psychology to communicate with and influence your depressed child. One good way to establish communication is to use "reverse psychology." Make it a point to give up your attempts to change your child. Tell him you love him, weird as he is and do not want to make him into your "little happy boy." See his laughter at your role reversal toward acceptance as a sign that you are on the right track. This approach turns the great energy that your child has mobilized to keep people away from him to your advantage. It accommodates your child's desire to avoid at all costs being labeled as a "defective."

3. Use scales and ranges to simplify communication and gather information. Once you have rapport, simplify your communication using scales and ranges. Remember, it takes a lot of energy for him to come out and talk, so make it easy by asking him to answer questions that require only a "yes" or "no," or that ask him to pick a point on a range between two extremes.

He may use this range device to give you feedback on his energy level from day to day. Ask him to rate himself on a "1" to "7" range where "1" is equivalent to "The Pits, the Volga Boat Song, living hell," and "7" is equivalent to "Shirley McLaine out on a limb with a 'why-worry-be-happy-its-all -cosmic'" look on her face. Get him giggling by exaggerating the extremes of this mood state. "Mom, I'm a 5 today" is the kind of good news you want to hear, and a starting point for more discussion. Make it easy for him to deliver this message to you.

Move on from a simple "depressed" vs. "euphoric" range to get an idea of what excites him and what turns him off. I call this the "misery" vs. "ecstasy" range. The information you get at this point is essential in structuring his life to get his blood circulating.

You should be able to improve his habitual low energy orientation toward the world.

4. Give perspective by telling him *healing* stories. Use storytelling to relieve the sense of pressure he experiences from the depression and help him move to a more expansive emotional place. Storytelling is effective with depressed kids because it is such an indirect teaching aid. Because they have received so much veiled and overt non-acceptance from adults they are very sensitive to any kind of pushing. Storytelling conveys the wisdom the child needs in a gentle, not pushy fashion.

In my counseling practice, I favor stories drawn from Native American beliefs because there is so much acceptance of things in this world view. I especially like narratives that provide pleasing and calming images of the changing of the seasons:

"Everyone grows in their time and the time waiting to grow, being really still (Fall and Winter) is as important as the Spring. The stillness that a tree is capable of gives it great potential for growth when the time is right. Everything in its own time." Give your child confidence that "this too shall pass."

5. Feed him positive images, thoughts and feelings to create excitement. Your depressed child may desperately want to be out of his funk, but not know how. Fortunately, as an A.D. child he is also very open to suggestion and this openness can be a channel for you to feed him exciting images to draw him out. Make sure to include the feeling and thinking dimension as you assist his imagination with your narrative:

"I can see us all going down to the park to rent a boat for a while. I especially like that first feeling of getting into the boat. Then it's cool to push off and float wherever you want to go. You just think, 'Boy, this is great. What a great day.'"

"Hey, kid you going to hockey practice? You looked great last week. All the kids on your team were talking about how much you contributed in the game. Are you warm enough out there?" (The parent says this knowing it is sure to get a "macho" response: "Of course I'm warm enough, Dad. Do you think I'm a wimp?")

"Look at it this way" (to motivate him to do the dishes). "It's neat just to see them done, sparkling out there in the kitchen and you feeling good about doing something positive. And there'll be ice cream later."

A good time to deliver these kinds of narratives is during "alongside time" (Daily Workout/Chapter Eight), or when he is watching TV, focused on something else. Some parents are more successful if they do not put these comments to their A.D. children directly, but "talk them to the window." Just talking in a relaxed manner seems to work best.

Daily Workout: Exercise, Exercise, Exercise

A large body of stress research shows that depressed people can gain considerable relief by increasing their rate and depth of respiration with mild aerobic exercise. When our lungs are filled with air and our blood with oxygen it is impossible to be depressed. And there is research that shows that any kind of repetitive motion raises the serotonin levels in our brain, thus soothing depression. Make it a point to do some kind of aerobic exercise, be it walking, biking, jump roping or swimming. Let it be part of your child's daily routine and you will begin to see dramatic change. Be careful not to make his exercise too intense as excess exercise has been shown to precipitate manic states in children with Bipolar Mood Disorder. And make sure that his workout is completed an hour or two before bedtime, or he will have a hard time getting to sleep.

Provide the incentive for his daily exercise practice by offering rewards and incentives that have real meaning for him. The best rewards will get him engaged in his environment. They may include outings with dad, going to performances or sports events, or active things like a day at an amusement park or snow-boarding site.

Exercise strengthens the body and is a powerful eustress cycle antidote to your child's depression-related distress. Every day, your child's mood improves just a bit and every improvement strengthens him further for dealing with his special challenge.

CHAPTER ELEVEN

Healing Rage

"I was angry with my friend:
I told my wrath and my wrath did end."
—William Blake

Attention Different Children get angry quickly. Their anger is hot, sometimes expressed with swearing or toilet talk that shocks any adult around them. They may cuss like the Sergeant of Darkness in the movie "Platoon." The situation really becomes difficult when anger turns to rage as the child loses control over his emotional reaction.

Rage may serve a protective or pressure release function

Rage serves two specific purposes for the A.D. child: it protects him from demands from people that upset him (protective rage) and it discharges internal pressure that he experiences (pressure-release rage). In contrast, if he explodes when he is interrupted without warning he protects himself with his rage reaction. This rage says, "Get away from me. Your demand is extremely aggravating to me. I cannot cope with it."

If he explodes suddenly for no apparent reason in the middle of a task he is trying to complete at school, he is probably discharging pressure that has been building up for the last two hours. Remember that he maintains his focus by force of will.

It is important to identify the type of rage a child is experiencing so you can help him deal with the specific stressor that is causing it. If he feels vulnerable, you need to help him feel safe. If he feels over-pressured, help him develop ways to manage his energy and release this pressure himself.

Characteristics of pressure-release rage

A child may experience stimulus pressure from any or all of his internal and external sensory receptors. The external senses include sight, hearing, touch, smell, or taste. The internal senses include cognitive, kinesthetic, emotional, or proprioceptive (muscle feeling) modalities.

The intensity of pressure-release rage depends on the variety and strength of sensory stimulation that a child experiences. If he experiences low level emotional pressure, he may show only short-term anger or momentary bursts of rage that subside quickly. This is characteristic of kids with the "A.D.H.D." diagnosis.

But if he experiences extreme emotional pressure, such as that which is seen in Bipolar Mood Disorder and Tourette Syndrome, his rage may blast out and go on for an hour or more. A big twelve-year-old boy with Bipolar challenges in the midst of a rage can threaten the well-being of everyone in the family.

Pressure-release rage may demonstrate the wild feeling of an animal thrashing at the bars of its cage. In fact this is a good metaphor for what is actually happening as emotional pressure from the child's "animal brain," his limbic system, builds up to overwhelm his consciousness.

Pressure-release rage will often be triggered by attempts to gain the child's compliance with a rule, or enforce some disciplinary sanction. In the heat of the limbic event, he loses all sense of his connection with the adult and devolves into fierce "pushback" against the attempt to restrain his behavior.

Characteristics of protective rage

Protective rage is triggered when the child feels his interior world is being invaded—when his fierce inner-directed concentration is interrupted or when his routine is disturbed. Some A.D. children may experience terror when required to shift focus too rapidly. Their contact rhythm from internal to external figural focus is very slow, and if they are "rushed" they experience the feeling of being lost in "no child's land" with nowhere to go.

Protective rage for the child with poor figure/ground shift ability emerges as a way to defend himself against the feeling of being lost, confused, and disoriented in his environment. Because this child spends so much time inside himself he does not recognize outside stimuli if they have been changed in any way. This causes high anxiety. This kind of rage may happen in familiar surroundings that have changed in some minor way; all the bureau or desk drawers aren't closed or objects have been changed in his room without his participation.

A related variation of protective rage is the rage that occurs when you interrupt his obsessions. Though his obsessionality may not be evident to you, you feel the full force of his anger when you unknowingly interrupt them by requiring him to focus on something else. His frustration at being interrupted, or just from the pressure of the background mental anguish he experiences all day from his obsessions, are sometimes just too much to handle, and he explodes.

The nature of rage determines your appropriate strategy

If your A.D. child experiences protective rage, it makes sense to build routines, safe spaces, and assistance with transitions from one thing to another, so that he has the measure of predictability he requires. He will feel safe with these measures.

On the other hand, if rage is the result of internal pressure, your best bet is to observe your child and get to know his look of being "stressed" before the rage erupts. Use gentle questions to probe the source of distress and attempt to help him shield himself from the aggravating stressor before the pressure builds up. Once pressure builds, he will need constructive ways to release it.

Rage as a limbic brain event

The rage response follows the limbic wave pattern that was described in Chapter Three. The child will often "announce" the beginning of this limbic wave with a change in tension in his face and fist clenching. Rage may explode onto the scene or take several minutes to build to its explosive potential. As the wave proceeds to its crest, the child will run around, swearing, threatening, spitting, or throwing things. Limbic rage diminishes, like a seizure, once energy is discharged. After rage, the child will often express regret or behave despondently.

Whatever the child says in rage rarely expresses his true intention. The rage of Attention Different children, as bad as it sounds and looks, does not carry a sense of psychological malevolence. It does not express psychosis, mania, or hatred. It is a biochemical event that, properly handled, will eventually come more under your child's control. Keeping your own cool in the midst of the great heat your child generates in his rage is essential.

How are rage distress cycles maintained?

Rage distress cycles are maintained by a combination of physical and environmental stressors that set off the reaction and keep it going. Environmental stressors that can initiate the stress cycle include the adult caregiver's attempts to punish the child for running an intentional temper display "to get attention." Other children, good at stealthy hit-and-appear-innocent attacks, may also torment him. They know that his temper reaction will give them good cover to escape once they have provoked him.

Teacher pressure to push a child beyond his capabilities can also begin the distress cycle. The teacher is responding to the pressures on her and has neither the time nor the skill to give him the one-to-one attention that he needs. Environmental conditions at school may also come into play. Crowding, noise, and rapid transitions can drive an Attention Different child around the bend.

If he is at home, a rage cycle may start when he comes down off his mediation, and just wants his own time. This is a bad time to insist that he do anything but "vege out" in a favorite activity. He needs time and space to recharge his batteries.

Once the rage distress cycle is initiated, it usually accelerates rapidly due to the emotional volatility of the situation, until the child is sanctioned, timed out, or in extreme cases, physically restrained. By that time the damage has been done to the harmony of the child's environment. Though he may not remember the incident, the adults around him may carry emotional distress for days.

He may "catch" a temper fit from your disposition

Your Attention Different child may be extremely attuned to your non-verbal behavior. This strange vigilance is hard to understand because this same child will often seem oblivious to the reactions he gets from everybody else. But your child is attuned to you probably as a result of giving your reactions extremely high "signal importance" and he has a resultant inability, as an A.D. child, to screen you out.

He may not want to be this open to you, but he is. When you tighten your brow, darken your gaze, or raise your voice, your child takes in your reaction, claims it and begins putting it out as if it is his own reaction. This can cause a dog-chasing-tail stress cycle that befuddles any remedy—until you realize how expertly your child mirrors your emotional state. Awareness of this "codependent" or, to use the Gestalt term, "confluent" style of relationship can liberate you from the cycle. Follow the ensuing suggestions to rise above the situation so that you do not fuel it with your own anger.

Rage Eustress Strategies

Teaching your A.D. child with a rage problem how to control it is a great gift from him to you. To be successful you must decrease his environmental stress. In order to make it a little easier for him to control himself, build his personal hardiness and his personal emotional muscularity, in order to control his reaction. Here are fifteen important strategies to improve the situation.

1. **Help him through his daily "down" times** when he is tired or going through medication withdrawal. Make sure that his stress is low at these times, that he is not pressed to accomplish tasks such as homework, that he does not over-use the Nintendo

or watch too much TV. Though TV and Nintendo are relaxing in small doses, the intense focus they require can also tire and stress him out to exacerbate the stress leading to temper decontrol.

2. Give him as much control over his schedule and predictability as you can. Though this feature of the eustress approach has been mentioned in Chapters Five (Calming Hyperactivity) and Six (Cooling Oppositionality) it is also relevant here because protective rage is so easily triggered by ambiguity in your child's schedule of events during the day.

Develop transition prompts and warnings: "In five minutes I am going to ask you to close down your project and come to dinner." Then, tell him after the time has passed, "Five minutes are up. Do you need any help closing your project to come to dinner?" If he is totally stuck in his current focus, gently wave a plate of food under his nose and invite him to the table. Children with a protective rage reaction may also have language delays; they often do not understand verbal requests or instructions. To overcome these delays consider showing him a picture of the dinner table or putting a fork in front of him, next to the project he is working on. Try all kinds of ways of getting through to him.

3. Know when to be firm and when to back off. Protective rage, the rage that comes from stress related to transitions, and poor ability to shift focus from one thing to the next, comes from the child's terror of being lost and confused. This kind of rage is best handled by decreasing all environmental stress and backing off from any requirement that you are putting on him.

A pressure-release rage reaction that is triggered by your attempt at discipline or to gain behavioral compliance should be met with a slightly different strategy. First, back off and cool down the situation. Then, restate firmly what you are requiring of him and let him know that you are serious. If the rage cycle begins again, simply cool things down and again, make the strategic withdrawal. When he has his wits about him, restate your requirement and stick to your guns.

Empathize with what he is going through: "It looks like you're really hurting, kid. I'm sorry about that. Let's reconnect when you're in a better place." Get him a glass of water and comfort him in any way that you can. Then return to your demand gently but firmly. Let him know that you mean it.

4. Protect yourself from social embarrassment or serious accident with decisive action. Sometimes rage may emerge in a situation that is dangerous or embarrassing to you—at the checkout counter of your local grocery store or in the car driving down the freeway. At these times it is important to be decisive, quick, and sure in your action. Leave the groceries in the cart and go home. He will learn quickly from your action that this is not a good place to release pent-up pressure.

Stop the car as soon as you can and make him get out. If you're close enough to home, make him walk. If not, let him sit on the curb and cool his heels a bit. This is the only way to cure him of dangerous sideways attacks on you when you are driving.

Sometimes very strong action is required on your part to get his attention. It is important that you not hold back from drawing the line but that you do it non-punitively. To get his attention you may have to stop what you are doing in mid-stream, but, as angry as this makes you, do not lose the learning opportunity by roughing him up or screaming at him. Realize that he is only partially in control and that the path to eustress lies in teaching him more control, not in venting your own stress onto him.

5. Watch for obsessions and compulsions and know that until these phenomena are dealt with, it will be very difficult for the child to self-regulate his emotional response. Though children with obsessions rarely talk about them, they sometimes disclose embarrassment for the "stupid thoughts" they have or they voice concern about being "crazy." Let the child know that having "worries" is natural for everybody, even to the point of not being able to get rid of "silly" thoughts. See Chapter Twelve for a more detailed description of how to help your child manage obsessionality.

6. Do something different. If he is standing, ask him to sit. If possible, ask him to take a drink of water. Give him an old tennis racket and have him beat on an old piece of furniture or work out on a punching bag. If the rage reaction is in its early stages, it can often be interrupted by some little change in routine that gives him five seconds to take a breath and get some control. And teach him how to manage his rage himself. Reduce your child's environmental stress by carefully structuring your parenting approach and his physical environment. This takes you part way to healing. Teaching him how to get a handle on rage when it emerges is necessary if he is to escape the trauma of rage distress cycles in his life.

7. **Help him recognize the emergence of rage in his body by explaining the changes that his body goes through as the limbic wave kicks in.** Talk to him when he is receptive, from your own experience of anger. Tell him what you feel when you get real mad: your jaws get tight, your stomach churns, you feel "hot."

Get him to talk to you about what he is feeling and help him express his sense of pressure. "I feel horrible, like I want to jump out of my own skin," or "My head feels like it's going to burst." If he is able to verbally communicate his feelings, he will be able to extend the length of time that he can hear you as his limbic rage wave begins.

8. **Teach him how to use exercise to discharge the feeling of pressure.** A garage-sale exercycle, jump rope, or punching bag may be an excellent investment in this regard. Exercise not only blows off pent-up pressure, but it releases endorphins, the brain's pleasure neurochemical that directly dampens the impulse to rage. If he is amenable to it and it is not physically punishing for him, give him a moderate number of push-ups as a consequence for rageful outbursts. Though doing push-ups may have an obnoxious para-military connotation, this exercise may be very beneficial if used with compassion. It will develop both physical strengthening and pressure release.

9. **Teach him the "lasso" for keeping more control of his limbic reaction.** This technique, created by Los Angeles-based therapist Jacqueline Small is based on the idea that when people get very angry they tend to dissociate; they leave their bodies or become ungrounded, literally "beside themselves" with rage.

When you notice that he needs the prompt, suggest to him,

that he has a "lasso" in his hand that he can use to catch the part of himself beginning to run around the room and go ballistic. Help him see himself "lassoing" that part, and pulling it back into himself, and taking a deep breath at the same time. This powerful technique for both parents and their Attention Different child is used to regain a feeling of control.

Once rage begins, the best thing to do is decrease stress and remove the child to a low stress environment as quickly as possible. Be careful of *your own* stress reaction or overreaction as you do so. If you have to put "hands" on him, you may get hit, bit, or spit on. Guard against your own anger and resist shaking or hitting your child. These reactions may generally be uncharacteristic of you, but in the intense heat of the moment, long-buried rage from your own life may jump out with surprising speed—you react before you know it.

There is nothing that you as a parent can do other than create physical safety for yourself and the child once the limbic wave has begun. Because this is a period of relative amnesia for the child, any punishment or motivational strategy that you try at this time will be forgotten.

The trick is to recognize the reaction early, before your child's limbic brain is fully involved in powering up the rage. Watch for the telltale signs that things are heating up and gently encounter the child at that time using some of the above techniques.

10. If physical restraint is necessary be gentle and firm. Standing behind him with a firm hold on his hands crossed over his chest, straight-jacket style, is the preferred position. Stay clear of his thrashing head. Be aware of your own anger when you touch him. Do not cause him pain. If you have the impulse to hurt him, back off and get someone else to help.

11. Speak to him in language that he can understand. Use short words and short sentences. When the stress reaction begins, a shut-down of the thinking process occurs in the frontal lobes of the brain. Complex verbal messages will not be understood at this time. This is why it is important not to get into long-winded scolding or instructions when your child is "losing it." "Telegraph" your directives to him and don't argue:

"Please go to your room now."

"Sit down and breathe down to your tummy."

"You are swearing at me. I will talk to you when you stop swearing."

It is easier to remember the importance of brevity if you can recall your own experience of how you hear and understand things when you are under stress. If you are like most of us, you have little tolerance for ambiguity or complexity at these times. Your child is the same way.

12. Remember to breathe. A child's attack may come when you are most vulnerable. Things happen very fast and it is difficult not to react with intense anger. Deep, calm breathing interrupts this stress reaction and gives you time to think about the best way to deal with the situation. Some parents post little dots around the house as reminders to breathe when the going gets tough.

13. Listen to your own self-talk. A parent in this situation will often say things to herself like, "That little s.o.b. has gone too far, now he's going to get it." Sometimes the experience will make the parent feel like she herself is six years old or will remind her of times in her life when she was bullied or violated.

Issues from childhood or a bad day at work may drive the parent toward action that she will regret. A parent should cultivate awareness of stress-induced mind chatter and deliberately change it by saying something like "I'm in charge, he's not. I'm the adult. He's my child and I love him. This isn't going to get me down."

14. Keep consequences specific to the event. Educate him to control himself by implementing a consequence that he can understand. Use time-out or require him to repair or pay for any damage he inflicts. If he breaks something, make him "give back to the community" (see Chapter Nine) by doing volunteer work at the local food bank or some other community work.

15. If you begin losing control, call for back-up from a spouse or a friend and give yourself a time-out. Separate yourself from him. If possible, call a friend. Involve your spouse. It's O.K. to sequester yourself and cry. Deal with it later.

The rage of the Attention Different child is one of the greatest stressors you will face as a parent. If you do lose your temper and the control of your own behavior, talk with him as soon as you can after things calm down. Apologize if you need to. Don't grovel. Tell him what he did to set you off. Share what it's like living with him. Get over the incident and resolve to do things differently in the future.

Rage Daily Workout: Practicing Calm

Rage will often occur when your child gets into certain situations that he "pair associates" with the reaction. Examples include the way a particular teacher talks to him or the way another child teases him on the playground. Here is a way to interrupt the cycle.

First, plan some relaxed time with your child, when he doesn't have pressure on him and is agreeable to doing this exercise. Have him take a couple of breaths "down to his belly" to relax himself.

Then have him close his eyes and imagine some situation that gets him going into a rage pattern. Make it a mild stressor for this first time. Have him picture it and underneath the picture, have him visualize a "bar graph" metered off with a "1" to "7" scale where "1" equals "relaxed" and "7" equals "very enraged." Come to an agreement with him on how much anger he would like to end up putting into the situation; he might say that a "2" or "2.5" is acceptable. This becomes the target level of excitation for him in this setting.

Have him hold the image for ten seconds or so and report to you about referencing the bar graph. Ask him now to "play the image back, like putting the VCR in reverse." Have him tell you when he has gotten to the beginning of the episode in his mind's eye. Now ask him to give you a sense of what number he is on the "rage meter."

Do this exercise a second time. This time, ask him to visualize the setting and, as he notices he is becoming agitated, tell him to "deliberately breathe a little slower." Have him run through the vignette and give you his estimation of his rage index upon completion.

Do this as many times as you need to, breathing and replaying the episode, until he states that his rage reaction is now measured at an acceptable level on the bar graph. Finish your work together by offering him a cool glass of water and the suggestion that he is doing a good job of developing the ability to "cool himself." Tell him you enjoyed working with him, and that you are available at any time to go over the process again as he sees fit.

CHAPTER TWELVE

Meeting the Challenge of Obsessions and Compulsions

"Josh was certain that if he tried to resist these urges some horrible fate—he could never specify exactly what it might be—was sure to follow. He sounded so frightened, as if he had some horribly scary monster-movie-creature in his mind that said, 'If you don't do this right, I'm going to get you."
—Tina—mother of a child with obsessions and compulsions

A child with obsessions and compulsions can drive a family nuts. Obsessions are silly or frightening thoughts that the child can't get out of his mind. As excruciating as his obsessions are, the physical compulsions enacted to relieve the anxiety of the obsession can be even more distressful to the child and his family.

Compulsions are done in obedience to the obsession to give the child a feeling of safety. He may wash his hands incessantly to protect himself from germs, finally having to be dragged bodily out of the bathroom. He may turn the lights on and off hundreds of times an hour "for good luck."

He may require that everything in the house be "exactly so." For example, he may perform counting or checking rituals dozens of times an hour making sure that each drawer is closed exactly right, that everything is in its proper position. He may require two pillows placed in precisely the same way every night or he will not be able to get to sleep. He pesters and fusses with things until everyone begins to feel a little crazy, and oppressed by having to please him all the time. Deep resentment may result.

Phobias, or irrational fears, accompany obsessions and further isolate the child. He may never go outside for fear that his presence will distract the drivers of cars in the street and cause accidents. Or he may be deadly afraid of the germs that will "contaminate" him if he touches anything others have touched. He may feel genuine terror at the prospect of touching paper. This can make things very difficult at school.

Obsessionality is a stone's throw from rage. Because the child's brain is wracked with obsession, he experiences acute anxiety when he is prevented from alleviating the tension of the obsession by doing the compulsion. In fact many children feel that they are in mortal peril if they defy the dictates of the obsession. "If I step on a crack (in the sidewalk) I will break my grandmother's back!" No wonder he rages when he is told to "get those silly thoughts out of your head."

Obsessions and compulsions often accompany other behavioral challenges which include emotional volatility, depression, and hyperactivity. The child's obsessionality may emerge in early childhood and be pretty much a constant feature into the teen years.

Obsessions and compulsions may also seem to bloom out of nowhere as the child enters puberty. If they emerge at this time, they are less likely to be found with other A.D. challenges and will exist as a pure type with the diagnosis of Obsessional Compulsive Disorder. Kids with this kind of "classic O.C.D." may not show any of the hyperactivity or combativeness of other children whose obsessionality is secondary to more severe A.D.H.D. or Tourettic challenges.

Obsessive compulsive activity is related to low levels of the neurotransmitter serotonin in the base brain's basal ganglia area (brain stem area). Low serotonin in this area seems to permit "worry thoughts" to get to consciousness from the brain's vigilance centers. The thoughts that come through have a powerful emotional charge and, repeated hundreds of times an hour, they fix consciousness internally with great power. You get the "fifty-yard stare" when you speak with kids with obsessions who are typically embarrassed that they have them at all. Most are unable to share any aspect of these repetitive cognitions even with those they trust and love. Kept awake at night by incessant gruesome images or mindless computations of how many words begin with certain letters or how many things have a certain weight, theirs is a private hell.

Many parents experience powerful feelings of impotence and discouragement when faced with the challenge of helping their Attention Different child with his obsessions and compulsions. Though they know that his problems have a neuralgic origin, the sheer "Chinese water torture" force of their child's obsessiveness drives them to either fight or flight in short order. Fight occurs as they rage back at him to stop his behavior, knowing that he can't. Flight occurs as they cater to his obsessions, changing their household routines to suit him, walking on egg shells.

The eustress approach: meet the obsession as a challenge

If you take the eustress approach to the situation, you neither capitulate to your child's obsession nor pretend that it doesn't exist. You approach your child's obsessive-compulsive behavior as a challenge to your ingenuity and grit. You are not helpless in the face of it, and have a variety of actions that you may take to turn things around.

You will discover that the path to eustress for your child is marked by little successes that build his resourcefulness to reduce the impact of his obsessionality. As your child experiences each success, he strengthens himself a bit more. Distress becomes eustress as he builds the muscularity of his perceptual apparatus to take charge of his own healing.

Seven Survival Strategies for Parenting Your A.D. Child with Obsessions and Compulsions

1. Empathy, not judgment, is key. Obsessions originate within ancient pre-verbal centers of the brain responsible for protecting the person from harm. Wise parents know that this worry energy is powerfully compelling to their child and do not dismiss it as silly or try to talk him out of it. They know that he is suffering and approach his obsessionality with statements of gentle empathy:

"Looks like you're having a hard time getting to sleep. Are you O.K.?"

"Looks like you're stuck in a 'worry loop' today. Is there anything that I can do to help?"

Never shame your kid for his obsessionality with statements like, "Stop acting nuts! Keep it up and I'm going to send you away." "Stop that or you'll be grounded for a year!" Say, instead: "I am having very hard time today with your obsessions and compulsions. I am really stressed out but we will deal with this together."

2. Give him visual images to contain and carry away his obsessional thoughts. Your child probably does not know how to turn off the repeating mind-loop obsessive thoughts that he gets. You can be of great assistance in this regard by coming up with images that contain and carry away his obsessive visualizations.

When he is relaxed, spend a few moments unobtrusively "pacing" (imitating) his speech inflections and breathing pattern. Research on interpersonal communication shows that this kind of deliberate imitation is essential to forming rapport and trust. A good time to do this is right before he drops off to sleep at night. Get in sync with him through reading a book, talking, singing, or by giving him a little back massage to soothe him. When he is relaxed, lead him through the following exercise:

The Rose, A Visualization

"Imagine that you see in front of you a big yellow rose...Put it in some kind of background that makes it seem real to you...Imagine smelling it, touching it gently. tasting the dew on its petals. As you do, imagine that it begins to open up...Now it is fully open...Now watch it gently close...and with a 'pop' sound, disappear into nothingness.

"Now imagine a beautiful pink rose...(same narrative as above or make up your own).

"Now imagine a beautiful red rose...(same narrative as above to the point of rose opening). Now see the rose in front of you and know that this rose can contain all the mind energy you need to let go of so you can get to sleep. If you have any 'worries,' imagine yourself putting them in the center of the rose. Put all the noise, words, and mind pictures in there...Now see the rose begin to close around the worries and with a 'pop' disappear into nothing...taking all the worries with it."

Coach your child to do this visualization whenever he is bothered by obsessional imagery. Some children prefer other visual vehicles to carry away their obsessions, such as a jet plane or a flushing toilet! Find whatever image works and help your child use it to bring comfort to his mind.

3. Evoke his own mind-calming strategy. Many of the A.D. kids with obsessions that I have worked with have come up with visualizations similar to "The Rose" described above. Others have devised personal rituals and routines to protect themselves from intrusive thoughts. On the whole, these kids tend to be highly creative.

If your child is like many of these kids, he has excellent creative resources for dealing with his obsessionality. To help him develop his own solutions you must be able to talk with him about his obsessions and this requires a deep rapport. You gain this rapport by going slow, pacing, and talking with him in "alongside time," (see Chapter Eight), making yourself available as his consultant. If you are patient and he is suffering, at some point he may risk opening up to you. This is an important opportunity.

Ask him if he would like help dealing with his fears while keeping himself safe. It is important that any suggestions you make are not construed as an attack on the part of him that is running the obsessional pattern. That part is still considered "a friend of the court." Take some time in your conversation to find out what images comfort him or give him a sense of strength and safety. Ask him the last time that he felt really safe and peaceful. Keep searching until you have a set of images and experiences from his life or from other domains (favorite movies, role models, etc.) that seem to give him strength.

Now work with him creatively to select mental imagery he can use to defend himself from intrusive thoughts. One kid might visualize a favorite "power animal" (the kindly bear from the Jungle Book) who "eats" obsessive thoughts. Another child might imagine that he is listening to certain music that banishes fear and the obsession. Still another might choose to create a "sacred space" in his room, a place of meditation used only by him to which he can go to relieve his mind of obsessive worry. In this space are crystals and other objects that purify the negative energy that he feels.

As a psychotherapist I have found that I can trust this process. When I really listen and am there for a child with obsessions, sooner or later he will identify what he needs for healing and it will probably be something that never had occurred to me. Practice patience here and you will be richly rewarded.

4. Use the "stop!" command cued with a wrist band. A old stand-by for helping people with obsessions is to teach them how to sub-vocalize a stop command to their obsessions. First, ask your child to deliberately begin obsessing about something. Pick a fairly minor obsession that he can lose easily. Now, ask him to loudly vocalize the word "Stop!" until he can get the obsession to cease momentarily. As he does so, have him snap a rubber band on his wrist to give a slight kinesthetic jolt as he vocalizes the word. Now, ask him to start the obsession up again and vocalize stop in a little softer voice along with the band snap. Keep repeating this sequence until he is no longer saying the word out loud but is subvocalizing it to himself with the rubber band cue.

Try this method out on several obsessions as time and timing permit. Use a before and after "1" to "7" scale to get information from him on the efficacy of the method. A score of "1" indicates an obsession with negligible force, almost to the point of not being noticed. A "7" on the scale, in contrast, indicates a raging, paralyzing obsession that totally captivates his consciousness. The idea is to calmly but persistently move down the scale with him.

5. Implement Response Exposure and Prevention for major compulsions. The Response Exposure and Prevention (RE&P) approach for treating compulsive behavior (and eliminating the obsessions that lead to compulsion) has been shown to be highly useful for many people who experience compulsions.

RE&P bases its effectiveness on the ability of your child to develop mind "muscularity" to screen out unwanted thoughts. Research has shown that this method can be as powerful as medication (Prozac) in reducing or eliminating obsessionality. This is a major proof of the assimilation and accommodation model, and of the ability of people to heal themselves, to actually change brain structure with a behavioral therapeutic method.

Follow this four-step process:

a. *Gain your child's commitment.* Let him know what is involved. Help him understand how getting past certain obsessions will help him with making friends and having fun in his life. Build in some kind of reward or incentive. It is important that he have something to look forward to.

b. *Do some relaxation exercises with him.* Many such exercises are found throughout this book. Oftentimes use of a visualization like The Rose is a good starter. Help your child self-soothe and manage his anxiety. Many Attention Different children do not know how to relax and so you must provide these skills to support your child's rejuvenation under the stress of the RE&P process.

c. *Note any trigger situations* that might cause emergence of compulsions, and explore the obsessional ideas that prompt the compulsion.

d. *Expose him to the stimulus and help him prevent enactment* of the compulsion on a scheduled basis. Obsessions and compulsions are set off by factors in your child's environment that cue these repetitive loops. Position your child near the stimulus that sets off his compulsion. For hand washing, it may be the kitchen sink or bathroom; for obsessive phobias of things outside, it may be walking around the block. Coach him to avoid doing the compulsion as he is exposed to the stimulus. Agree on how long a period of time you will both be involved in the process each day. It's a good idea not to go longer than an hour; ten or fifteen minutes is fine for the first few days. Eventually he will no longer experience a need to complete the compulsion. Keep a weekly record of your progress using a scale you both set up to measure the intensity of the obsession. Give him daily feedback on his progress, even if it is minute.

e. *Provide rewards for getting through practice sessions.* Give him something to look forward to on a daily basis if possible. Keeping an image of the potential reward in mind goes a long way toward alleviating the anxiety that will occur in this process.

Your job is to gently and compassionately guide your child through the anxiety, even terror, that he experiences facing up to his irrational fears and getting past them.

The RE&P method should only be used once a child has mobilized his personal will to go through with the method. It will not work if he is undermotivated, as the process of facing the things he fears most will generate intense resistance that you must both face bravely.

6. Bring out his "little actor" to build his hardiness. A.D. children with obsessions and compulsions are often talented actors. They love to ham it up and put on costumes. They start early in life, sometimes before the age of four, by making crude stages to present performances that they have designed. Later, they may construct puppet stages and become well-known among their friends for this particular talent.

These kids will often resolve many of the stresses that they face by acting them out. They become naturally expert actors because they have had to pretend to act normal so often when they were feeling so abnormal. Chaos may be going on around them, but their focus, when not obsessing is intent on their theatrical goals. A kind of therapia (combination of therapy and spiritual work) is happening and should be encouraged by parents.

Wise parents will take the child's interest seriously. They will use his dramatic interests as motivators to guide him toward their goals and good intentions for him. One way to do this is to participate in an imaginary play with your child. You give him the chance to express what he is feeling and work through the solutions. A kid may segue from a play theme about the movie "Jurassic Park," suddenly turning serious to talk about the monsters that come to him at night before bedtime in the form of his obsessions. Just roll with this self-revelation and give him a chance to talk.

If your child has serious dramatic interests, help him get into local theatrical productions that do casting calls from time to time. The experience of staying focused on his lines in front of dozens of people will significantly develop his muscularity of focus and a sense of his own resourcefulness. It's great for him to know that he can stay focused when he has to.

7. **Consider medication.** Historically many psychotherapists have clung to the idea that Obsessive Compulsive Disorder (O.C.D.) originates in childhood trauma as a message from the unconscious about the trauma. Then, in the mid-eighties, the drug clomipramine (b.Anafranil) gained FDA approval and became the treatment of choice for the disorder. Its efficacy along with advances in biopsychology has demonstrated that some forms of O.C.D. are a biochemical effect that is probably transmitted genetically.

Medication Available for Treating Obsessions and Compulsions

Here is a short, non-technical listing of the principal medications used for obsessions and compulsions. This discussion builds on that which described drug treatment for depression found in Chapter Ten. See that chapter for discussion of the issue of the safety of medicating kids and possible side effects.

Much of the medication prescribed for depression and for obsessionality has a similar desired outcome: to raise levels of the neurotransmitter serotonin in different parts of the brain.

❖ **Clomipramine (b. Anafranil)**, mentioned above, is prescribed by many physicians for treatment of obsessions, compulsions, phobias, and depression. Like other drugs in the tricyclic category, side effects include gastrointestinal upset, blood pressure effects; (an unpleasant rushing feeling when standing up), and appetite loss.

❖ **Fluoxitine (b. Prozac)** has surpassed Anafranil in the number of prescription written for people with obsessions. Many doctors consider Prozac to be more efficient than Anafranil and it has fewer side effects. It may, however, cause appetite loss, insomnia, agitation, and, in adults, loss of interest in sex.

❖ **Setraline (b. Zoloft)** called "son of Prozac" by some doctors, is a Prozac-like drug that some neurologists feel is a bit cleaner of side effects than Prozac. Because it is fairly new on the scene, there is less knowledge of its interactions than Prozac. Setraline cycles out of the body faster than Prozac, dropping to half levels within a day, compared to about a week for Prozac.

❖ **Paroxitine (b. Paxil)** The PDR warns against use of this medication for people who have a history of mania. It may be slightly more sedating than the other Selective Serotonin Reuptake Inhibitors (SSRI's) listed above. It may be slightly more effective for treating depression and cycles out of the body at the same rate as Zoloft. Withdrawal from Paxil needs to be carefully managed, as some withdrawal symptoms are associated with its use.

❖ **Nefazodone (b. Serzone)** This is the most recently approved serotonin specific drug in the U.S. Initial results indicate that it is as effective as Prozac but does not have that drug's most problematic side-effects—agitation, insomnia, and sexual dysfunction.

The ultimate goal of medication is to terminate the need for medication but all kids are different in how they react to it. Due to natural growth processes, development of individual coping ability, and personal hardiness, many children eventually become less troubled by obsessions and compulsions. The medication may or may not have helped but it can be terminated.

Other kids will have obsessions well into adulthood. These children seem to need the medication all the time to be safely symptom-free. As hard as it is for parents to reconcile themselves to "putting their kids on drugs" the presence of medication is a lifesaver!

It is always a good idea to talk with your physician about cutting back dosage once your child's behavioral crisis is stabilized. She will advise you how to experiment gently with medication levels so that they are least disruptive to your child's life. It is a true joy to hear from parents that their child's physician "has taken him off medication and he's doing great!" This is a rich payoff for all the blood, sweat, and tears they have gone through to bring some comfort to their child.

8. Consider the impact of dietary factors on his obsessionality. Throughout this book, I've pointed out that low brain serotonin is a central aspect of obsessionality and depression. Several of my clients with obsessing kids have told me that they are helped by eating foods high in the natural amino acid tryptophan (TRY). This is the precursor to serotonin, the substance that is processed into serotonin by the body. These foods are included on the following page:

Parents will often pair meals which contain these foods with a good mixed B vitamin that provides both Vitamin B-6 and Niacin. These additional ingredients help the body to make serotonin out of tryptophan.

Medications in the anti-depressant class (above) tend to decrease the amount of Vitamin B-6 in the body. Sugar decreases brain serotonin overall.

Parents who have had success with this diet claim that obsessive challenges will dramatically ease for an hour or two after a meal high in these foods and then will return. Despite the relatively short time that you may experience relief, knowing that certain foods may help your child overcome his obsessionality is important knowledge for the management of your household harmony.

Food   Tryptophan Grams per cup/per lb.

Food	Tryptophan Grams per cup/per lb.
Granola	20 cup
Oat flakes	20 cup
Cottage cheese	40 cup
Wheat germ	40/cup
Avocado	40/ea.
Wild game	115/lb.
Luncheon meat	50/lb.
Turkey	37/lb.
Sausage	30/lb.
Chicken	28/lb.

9. Investigate streptococcal infection as a causative. Some good recent research has shown a link between sudden onset of obsessionality (and the sudden onset of several other attention differences) with the child's exposure to viral, streptococcal infection. These are commonly seen in many childhood diseases involving infection. The body's immune system deals with the virus by hunting it down and destroying cells infected with it. For some reason, the immune system also attacks neurons (nerve cells) in the brain which are responsible for inhibiting obsessionality.

Streptococcus can live for years in a child's throat and sinuses as a low grade infection. Symptoms may improve at dryer times of the year. If your child becomes obsessional suddenly and the obsessionality gets better in the summertime or early fall, it is wise to have him checked out by a physician for an undetected strep infection.

If an infection is discovered and treated with penicillin, make sure to discuss follow up care with your doctor to restore normal functioning of your child's bacterial defenses. Because the antibiotic may have a sterilizing effect, some parents will choose to give their child the natural supplement aciddophilus after treatment with antibiotics.

Daily Workout: Obsessions and Compulsions

Healing space

Your child's battle with obsessionality may be the greatest struggle that he will ever face. He is going to need all of your help and support, as well as a quiet, private place to calm and relax himself. Here he can call up and use the healing images that you give him.

Work together with him to create the kind of personal space that he needs. Help him select objects that are important to him and put them in this space. Tell him that this is a place where he can get some peace and cleanse and refresh his mind.

Encourage him to come here to do breathing and visualization exercises or personal meditations. Make sure that he knows how to do "The Rose" or a similar exercise that contains images involving completion and fading from view. He can use these exercises to cleanse himself of obsessive thoughts when he enters his space.

Burn a little sage or incense and do a welcoming ceremony for the space. Drink some tasty calmative tea like chamomile or a mix like Sleepy Time. Encourage his dramatic edge in the creation of a ceremony.

Working with him to co-create his private, spiritual, healing space gets things off to a great start and is a celebration of his self-healing potential!

PART THREE

Strategies for Changing Family Distress Cycles to Family Eustress Cycles

Introduction to Part Three

Families, like individuals, can deal with challenges that they face from a eustress or a distress perspective.

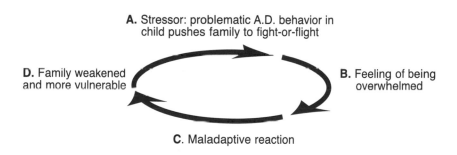

A. Stressor: problematic A.D. behavior in child pushes family to fight-or-flight

D. Family weakened and more vulnerable

B. Feeling of being overwhelmed

C. Maladaptive reaction

Pattern Of A Family Stress Cycle

The distress cycle

Families who live in the distress cycle lack inspiration and information about how to handle their Attention Different child and their feeling of hopelessness. They feel overwhelmed by a merry-go-round of suffering that begins with a particularly stressful behavior their child brings to the family.

Feeling overwhelmed by the stressor (B.), family members react maladaptively (C.). They fight each other for control and attempt to extinguish the A.D. child's behavior through harsh

161

punishment. There is a lot of yelling, anger, physical pushing and controlling, even violence. Or there may be abandonment of the family's dream of living in warmth and love. Parents flee into their own favorite escape modes. They become cut off from each other, watching TV, staying away from home, overworking, or developing intimacies with other adults, where they can find solace from the low intensity nightmare that is "life at my house."

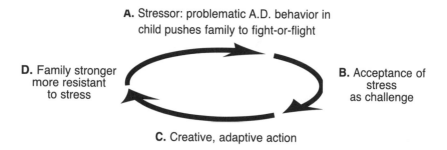

A. Stressor: problematic A.D. behavior in child pushes family to fight-or-flight

D. Family stronger more resistant to stress

B. Acceptance of stress as challenge

C. Creative, adaptive action

The Family Stress Success Pattern

The eustress cycle

Families who choose the eustress pattern embrace the stressor as a challenge (B.) to their creativity. They pull together to open the door to a whole new way of relating.

Living with an Attention Different child is similar to living with someone who has a disability, in that the experience requires family members to find resources in themselves they did not know existed. The experience can be socially isolating and the stress can be great. They must work at developing the gritty determination not to be driven down by the situation which is foundational to eustress.

An important part of being successful on the eustress path is parents' knowledge of the terrain that they will traverse as they learn to manage their child's attention difference. Part Three provides an overview of four of the major patterns I have encountered in my psychotherapy work with families as well as my own experience as the father of a boy diagnosed with severe attention differences of the "Tourette Syndrome" and "A.D.D." variety.

Chapter Thirteen describes the grief cycle that families go through after diagnosis and/or formal recognition of their child's neurologic difference. It is important not to hide your suffering! This is part of the grief process.

Chapter Fourteen is a discussion of how the emergence of behavior problems of the Attention Different child can upset the balance in a relationship and wedge parents apart. This chapter describes the "Uproar" distress cycle, resulting in anger and parental alienation. Following this are nine key pointers for strengthening commitment and restoring vitality to your marriage.

Chapter Fifteen shows parents how to handle tricky aspects of their relationship with their child's school. This chapter provides strategies for making sure that the school does its job and does not attempt to displace their accountability for educating the Attention Different child away from the system and on to parents and the child. Chapter Fifteen is written to empower parents to be successful in implementing changes from the public school system, which sometimes resists with all its might. The bureaucratic as well as the legal dimension is addressed.

In Chapter Sixteen I describe the particular stressors that impact the single parent of an Attention Different child. Stress comes down hard on those that don't have someone to take over when the going gets almost unbearable. This chapter provides a solid set of techniques for single parent self-care and shows how to set up a eustress relationship with your ex that reduces the distress of your child.

In Chapter Seventeen, I explain the stresses that affect families who adopt A.D. kids or who bring an non-A.D. step-parent into the home. Adoption-related stress cycles are awful because adopting "normal" parents have no frame of reference to view the neurologic basis of their child's problematic behavior and therefore label it "intentional." I show how to avoid this trap and several others to develop a eustress feeling in the blended family.

Many Attention Different children grow to be splendid, successful adults, but they don't do this on their own. Their families are the milieu, the culture, that sustains their growth and helps them develop perspective and skill to lead their unusual lives. The practices that are advocated in Part Three enable children and parents to have a great family life despite the stress of the kids' attentional problems.

CHAPTER THIRTEEN

Moving Through the Grief Cycle

"The period following diagnosis is typically a time of guilt and/or blaming, whether it be aimed at oneself, one's spouse, the doctor, the hospital, the environment, or God. As parents try desperately to make sense out of chaos, they must ultimately come to accept that things happen in life that are simply out of their control."

—Lisa Lieberman, MSW, BCD

Emergence of attention differences brings a sense of loss

Most parents of Attention Different children report relief at their child's diagnosis. It is good to know that he is not crazy or that his A.D. behavior is related to some kind of trauma that they do not understand or had overlooked. But diagnosis does not make it any easier to bear the change in a child's personality that either may emerge over years or seem to come out of nowhere, six months later stabilizing into upsetting new patterns. He has become oppositional, obsessional, and totally defiant. He has stopped smiling or only smiles when lost in a state of emotional disinhibition. He rages at you at the drop of a hat.

You cannot hug him anymore. He can't stand it. He has become hypersensitive to everything: noises, smells, the feeling of clothes on his skin. Like a raging little tyrant that really isn't a tyrant at heart, he always seems genuinely regretful for acting the way he does. Then he goes and does it again. Your distress can feel unbearable.

165

And you must face revising your idea of what is possible for him at school. You had envisioned a positive, useful, and fun school experience for him. Now his learning problems, tantrums, and hyperactivity have taken center stage, instead. You are learning a whole new taxonomy of jargon that follows him at school: "I.E.P., "focus of concern," "severe behavior problem, " "least restrictive environment," "due process." You begin feeling that you did not get due process in having to deal with this!

As parents of A.D. children, many of us long for the good old days—sometimes a subtle form of denial can occur that goes on for a year or two after diagnosis. Though we voice an intellectual acceptance of our child's situation, we also cling to the idea that he is basically normal and our parenting strategies continue to be shaped by this image of normalcy. Our old dreams die hard. This is a normal part of the grief process.

Denial maintains the distress cycle

Some parents worry that if "we don't train it out of him now" their child will be an adolescent from hell. They put enormous pressure on themselves and their child in hopes of preventing greater stress later. Given the fact that his problem is neurological, it doesn't make sense to think that he can somehow be molded into normalcy, but since acceptance may be difficult, denial may begin to power an excruciating distress cycle for the whole family.

In some families, the A.D. child is punished quite severely for displays of rage and oppositionality. Parents will use physical punishment, which include spanking him with objects, washing his mouth out with soup, or putting noxious substances on his tongue like pepper or mustard.

Secrecy and keeping up the family image may be very important. "We prefer not to make a big deal of this. He's embarrassed enough already." I have heard this comment many times from parents and it is usually parroted back to me by the child who tries to hide his attention differences from people at school. Unfortunately, this makes things worse. Knowledge, not secrecy is in order.

Knowledge keeps people from making the mistake of assuming that the child is being obnoxious intentionally and it prevents him from being mislabeled "severe behavior problem" ("SBD") or "Conduct Disorder" by the school district. These labels have replaced the old-fashioned term "juvenile delinquent." Once these labels are stuck on your child, the system doesn't have the same responsibility for helping him; he now doesn't have an educational problem, but a *character disorder.*

Denial of the child's attention difference is seen in parents' level of anxiety and suffering. Good parenting solutions, the kind you would use for normal kids, do not, by themselves, improve the situation. These measures cannot compensate for the short-term memory problems, hypersensitivity to stimulation, rage, and learning problems that most Attention Different children have. These make your situation very difficult.

Encounter guilt to get over it. Accepting the fact that your child is different brings up a range of uncomfortable feelings:

Many of us parents experience guilt. We feel guilty for "giving him his problems" because attention differences are genetically transmitted. We feel guilty for "coming down too hard" before we knew that he had a biochemical problem, that is, behavior partially out of his control. We feel guilty for his depression and unhappiness. Feeling this kind of guilt is a part of the grief process. and leads us to the fact that A.D. is a complex problem involving biology, stress, and the personal characteristics of our child. We need to let ourselves off the hook for not seeing it sooner.

And we feel guilty for our own "shadow feelings" around his condition—all the forbidden thoughts we experience in our desperation over the crisis our family has entered. Lisa Lieberman, a clinical social worker from Portland, Oregon and mother of a child with autism, has this to say about these thoughts:

"One of the more isolating aspects of dealing with a child's disability is the experience of forbidden feelings—secret, dark thoughts and seemingly shameful impulses that people feel they dare not reveal. They can take several forms: thinking about suicide; wishing travesty on friends who take their normally developing children for granted; feeling rage boiling just under the surface; wishing, for a brief moment, that their child had died in birth. Such feelings simply need to be expressed. In fact, having a safe place to air forbidden feelings prevents people from taking action they'll regret. Forbidden feelings are, in effect, a way of saying how much the parent in this situation "just wants the pain to stop."

Parents will often voice great relief when they see that their partner also has these forbidden thoughts at times. Sharing the anger, hurt, and desperation is part of the healing process. These dark feelings are an important path to healing. Lieberman points out that the healing process is stymied by the false notions that parents should "buck up and accept it," that they should not be negative and should "think positive."

Five Key Aspects of Hardiness for Parents of the Newly-Diagnosed Child

Letting go of self-imposed perfectionism is the first step in getting on top of the challenge of living with an Attention Different Child. Accepting help from others and learning to take care of yourself emotionally and spiritually is the second step. Here are eight key elements for self-care and hardiness:

1. Don't keep siblings, friends, and neighbors in the dark about your child's attention differences. Let friends and neighbors know a little about him and the challenges that you face as a family. Oftentimes a little explanation goes a long way. Most people want to be understanding and helpful but they need to know that your kid is not some kind of "demon seed" crazy child. Prepare a little write-up that describes your child's specific A.D. challenges that you can give to people for their information.

Encourage discussion of your child's attention differences with his siblings in a family meeting setting. Facilitate heart to heart expression of his feelings and those of his sibs around his attention differences. Talk about how each child is different in how he or she perceives the world and how this difference affects the contributions that each makes. Openness and honesty among sibs is a very important ingredient of family harmony

Let your kids know that everyone needs to pull together more and learn ways to talk with each other. Tell them that there are no "angels" or "devils" in this situation and that every kid has some kind of problem. Share one or two handicaps or challenges that you yourself have faced. Tell your children that you will always love them. Describe the challenges and gifts of each child.

2. Encourage your child to share information about himself at school and require that educators accept it in their program planning. The example of openness and honesty you set at home will be a powerful incentive for your child to disclose his condition at school. The matter-of-fact approach with little elaboration works great for most kids. "Yeah, I'm A.D. (or A.D.D.)" is a simple way for him to explain himself.

If you are really fortunate, your child will enjoy getting into a mentoring role with others about being A.D. or talking in class-room groups with other kids. In any particular classroom there will probably be at least one other child with the same problem. Once one kid starts talking about it, others will open to much greater acceptance.

Teachers will sometimes give lip service to the child's attention differences but then put the same expectations on him as on everyone else in the class. If this happens, let the teacher know that your child has a "health impairment," (educator jargon) and require the school to provide services (see Chapter Fifteen). Your assertiveness in this regard is a powerful cue for acceptance by your child's teacher and his Principal. If you are wishy-washy about your requirements for your child's education, you will be ignored.

Write a letter of explanation to parents of kids in his classroom. If your child's attention differences are sufficiently pronounced in his everyday life, you may want to take the first step to let parents of his classmates know a little about him and you. It always helps to let people know. Here is an example of a letter introducing a child who has Tourette Syndrome to parents of kids in the classroom he is entering.

.   .   .

An Open Letter to Parents

June, 17, 1996
Parent
Mr. John Cleaver's Fourth Grade Class
Kingsgate Junior High

Dear Friend:

We are parents of Gary Simons, who will be starting full time in Mr. Cleaver's class next September and who will be visiting his class several times a week this year. We appreciate having this opportunity to introduce Gary to you as your child's classmate and welcome any questions that you have. Feel free to call us at the number above.

Gary has Tourette Disorder and Attention Deficit Disorder. His Tourette causes him to be loud, and swear or "tic" from time to time. His tics include making a little snorting sound and blinking his eyes. He is taking medication. His educational classification is "health impaired," a term used to describe kids with any kind of physical problem. He is not emotionally disturbed.

Gary is transferring over from John Adams, his school for the last two years. Adams was an important (and very supportive) community for him, and he is going through some transition stress, which will probably make his behavior problematic until he gets adjusted and accepted at Kingsgate JH.

We wanted to write (and will be talking to the P.T.S.A.) to let you know that if Gary swears at or around your child, the best thing for your child to do is to let Gary know that he/she doesn't like swearing, and to pull back from contact for a short time. It may take several times for Gary to understand, but he will. We wanted to write to you because getting past initial impressions can be difficult.

He is also a creative and interesting kid with a love of computers and animals. We are looking forward to his successful experience at Kingsgate and know that open and honest communication between parents is key to this success.

Thank you for taking the time to read this, and feel free to call.

Sincerely,

Jeremy and Linda Simons

3. Don't deny the stress that you are experiencing/share your feelings. Speak it out loudly to those who love you. Let your child know that you will always be there for him but that he is a hard person to live with. You increase your stress by trying to be super mom or super dad. This variation of perfectionism will lead quickly to resentment of your child and your spouse, or to your own depression. Suffering in silence makes suffering worse.

Remember that you are going through a process that is hard wired into human beings for coming to terms with loss. We all get angry, guilty, resentful, confused, even physically sick, in times of grief. As you attempt to adjust to the stress of dealing with your child's attention differences, you need people who can listen to you without giving you advice.

"I didn't sign up for this!" remarked one mother to describe her exhaustion getting her A.D.H.D. son out the door on to the bus every morning. Many parents feel this same sense of unfairness, anger, and resentment. There are no easy answers.

4. Use the "positive negativity" method. Here is a practical way to dump stress and get it off your chest.

The exercise lets a "ranter" (the stressed-out person) dump his negativity to a "listener" whose job it is to listen impassively and keep time. First each person should breathe, relax and "ground," as described in Chapters Four and Five.

The ranter gets to talk for four minutes. During that time, his job is to describe every negative event that occurred in his day. No good news is allowed. The listener listens and as the four-minute limit approaches says, "O.K. Tell me one good thing about your day." It may be something as mundane as getting home in light traffic, but something positive should be mentioned. After the positive comment is made, the roles switch and the listener gets to unload her stress as ranter.

This is the essence of the "talking cure." Getting it off your chest really helps. For the process to work, both people have to be willing to say it all, even if what is stated is not nice or politically incorrect. Let all your anger and bitterness out. You'll feel better immediately.

5. Acknowledge how gender differences impact grieving. Lisa Lieberman points out that men and women experience grief differently in reacting to their child's diagnosis. Women are trained in the care-giving role and oftentimes will be able to direct their grief into the home and school nurturing of their child. They are face to face with the problem every day and often part of a support network.

Fathers have a more difficult time in their grief process because they feel pressure to be strong for their partners and may not be in touch with other fathers with similar problems.

Lieberman quotes a colleague, Ron Baer's statement that "society doesn't value the father's direct involvement with his family." She tells the story of the father of a recently-born Downs Syndrome child that she met in one of her workshops. He said that he felt like "a lone wolf, circling the den, providing protection and resources but never really knowing how to come in for his own comfort."

To balance the picture, the wife is well advised to invite her husband to come in from his self-imposed emotional detachment and become more involved in parenting. The man is well advised to share himself more with his spouse and to seek the company of other men who are fathers of special needs kids. A good resource for fathers to contact other men in their same situation is the National Fathers' Network at (206) 747-4004. This group is made up of men who face similar problems parenting difficult children. This father's support network nurtures the husband and makes the wife's life easier because she no longer has to be the sole source of consolation and understanding.

Lieberman says that the most "resilient" relationships have intimacy. To quote the definition of intimacy provided by therapist Harriet Goldnor Lerner: partners "can be who they are in relationship and allow the other to do the same...neither party silences, sacrifices, or betrays the self, and each party expresses both strength and vulnerability, weakness and competence in a balanced way."

Conclusion: Moving through William Blake's three stages of innocence

The nineteenth-century mystical poet William Blake said that people go through three stages as they deal with adversity in their lives (the grief process). First there is childish innocence. Seeing all good in the world. Then there is cynicism; seeing all bad. Cynicism comes after a wound or trauma.

Blake termed the third phase "higher innocence." This is the attitude of a person who accepts the good with the bad, accepts the contradictions. This is a very hopeful and balanced place to be.

Parents who are successful in coming to terms with the great stress of their child's attention differences have learned how to live in this place of higher innocence. They have given up their illusions and false expectations about their child and see him for who he is: an idiosyncratic, possibly brilliant person with both gifts and problems.

Parents who have gotten to higher innocence reflexively see how their child is "different good" and they celebrate these differences. They stop expecting him to behave normally and accept a certain amount of eccentricity from him—his neurological grouchiness and ill temper, his wildness, possibly his foul mouth on occasions. They don't get hooked by the little things and feel that they have to make a battle of everything or wring their hands about how defective he is.

Parenting an Attention Different child requires you to accept the opposites in your child: his joy and generosity of spirit as well as his mean behavior. Parenting him will also bring out the opposite qualities in you—your bitter anger, short-sightedness, fear, and depressed mood along with your love and dedication. These negative or shadow qualities express the fight or flight dimension of your stress. It is natural for you to experience them. The emergence of these shadow qualities brings you to the heart and soul of a decision for eustress or distress. Distress will happen if you let your stress reaction power a retaliatory or punitive approach to your child or an attack on your spouse. See Chapter Fourteen for a discussion of how this relationship discord occurs. Distress may also occur if you turn your anger in on yourself to create

Eustress begins with your acceptance of your child and yourself as fellow travelers on a strange journey that you only partially control—one full of unplanned events and surprises. Eustress requires that you accept this journey in the spirit of a great challenge, possibly the greatest challenge you will face in your life. This is the spirit of the third stage of innocence and the key to your psychological survival. This is the path that you must choose for yourself and your child.

CHAPTER FOURTEEN

Taming "Uproar" to Revitalize Your Marriage

"Our whole life is centered around him!"
—Mother of an A.D. child

Many parents complain bitterly that they feel that their child's attention difference has become central to everything that happens in their marriage. They want to get out of this situation so badly, and to experience love and excitement in the company of each other for a change. They'd like to be able to relax and have some fun, but they can't, or at least don't see how they can.

The Uproar distress cycle

Uproar is the term that describes a common pattern in families with an A.D. child. It denotes the state of angry chaos that is a consistent feature of the family, along with the alienation of the parents from each other. The initiating stressor is the emergence of the child's attention differences somewhere between the ages of four and ten. The parents are not prepared for this stress. No one could be.

Their child's night terrors, the nighttime horror hallucinations that many Attention Different children begin experiencing around age four were bad enough, but now things have gotten worse. Their son has become hyperactive. He has an incredible temper and a low boiling point. He likes things done just this way or that or else he loses control. There are major problems at school.

Each parent searches for tools to deal with the situation. Constant crisis has put both of them in a state of chronic low-level anxiety. They do not feel in control. Stressed to the maximum, they react with old survival programs, blaming each other for the stress they are experiencing, for how messed up things feel. Fight or flight is the pattern.

The child's attention difference often emerges at a bad time for the parents. Their child is entering the elementary school years just about when his mother had planned on going back to work.

By this time, husband and wife have been in relationship long enough to get through the "honeymoon" period and can see each other's foibles separate from the veil of falling in love. They begin seeing the dark side of each other, the side that comes out under stress—the angry blamer, or the one who withdraws from the pain into work. They mistake these stress reactions for the "real person I married."

The relationship becomes Crisis Central. He stays away a lot. She takes sole responsibility for her son with the school and their angry neighbors. She really pays her dues. He complains about their child's behavior but isn't around to deal with teachers and neighbors. They can't keep a sitter, and become more isolated from other adults.

Now a distressing new aspect of the struggle comes into being and it involves the child coming between his mother and father to make things worse.

Dad comes home from work exhausted. He feels guilty that he isn't doing enough and comes down with a heavy hand on the A.D. child for some infraction. His wife resents this "overreaction" and an argument ensues. He now feels more incompetent, and she more resentful. Although the child lives under his mother's wing, he tries to reject his own dependence on her by giving her a hard time with everything. Everyone is exhausted. The child's growing stress level and internal feeling of distress keep the crisis boiling.

The father feels wedged out of his relationship with his wife and child. As this feeling settles in, the father withdraws more, and intimacy between him and his wife is lost. As the mother and child go into unwelcome alliance against the father, a permanent distress cycle settles in.

Everyone is walking on eggshells. This makes the child more central and more frantically tyrannical. The distress cycle has a life of its own. The child is now pushed by the expectation that he will blow up; he thinks that chaos is all there is. This family is in serious trouble.

From Uproar distress to family eustress

If you are trapped in an Uproar cycle, your primary task is to move this situation off dead center by first taking action to restore intimacy with your spouse.

Uproar ends as you rededicate yourselves to each other and to meeting the challenge that your child's behavior presents to your marriage. It takes courage to let go of the harsh stereotypes of each other that have fueled the stress reaction, but this is the direction in which you must now move. You have shown your spouse your "ugly sides" and he has shown you his. Now it is time to renegotiate your relationship as two imperfect people who also love each other.

To use a term coined by the great psychologist, Carl Jung, the "shadow" of your relationship has been made visible. All those aspects of yourself that you would have preferred not to show to anyone are out in the open. As strange as it seems, this is a gift from your Attention Different child. A.D. kids create so much heat and chaos that polite civility is stripped away, to be replaced by a certain gritty honesty in your relationship.

The real adversary here is not the child's attention difference. It is the feeling that the two of you are helpless to do anything about it. This feeling is antithetical to eustress. Do some honest sharing about what you want from each other and resolve to deal with your child, together. Here are nine keys to success in this endeavor.

Nine Ways to Break the Uproar Distress Cycle

1. First, create space for sharing stress and recharging. You've grown apart and have to make getting to know each other again a priority. Schedule quality time together—Saturday mornings over coffee works for many couples. Go out together every now and then.

Sitters can be a problem, so consider calling up your local Camp Fire Boys and Girls chapter and ask them about their "Special Sitters" program. This is an excellent resource for getting trained teens to watch your Attention Different child while you're out, if he's not too much of a behavior problem. They'll interview you to see if there is a fit.

2. Use the "talking stick." Hassling over the best way to manage your child may bring out your worst communication styles. Many parents will talk over each other, insult each other, sulk, blame, or withdraw into moody silence. Getting clear can be a real challenge. To make sure that you can hear each other, use the "talking stick" technique.

This method borrowed from Native American tradition provides a way to make sure that you and your partner both have a chance to air your views without interruption. The speaker holds an object, the talking stick. As long as he holds the object, he has the floor and is not interrupted. When he is finished with his current stream of thoughts, he gives the talking stick to the other who now has the right to talk without interruption.

Good solutions require the best information possible and this is why it's important for each person to have his or her say uninterrupted. You both have important knowledge to contribute. The talking stick makes sure that communication stays open and two-way.

3. Watch the use of the word "you" in your discussion with each other and try to speak from the "I" position as much as possible. Any sentences that begin "You always" or "You never" will probably result in more hurt. No one likes to be labeled pejoratively. Tell your spouse how you feel without indicting him. "I feel real frustrated and angry right now." "I'm really hurting!" Using "I statements" makes communication between the two of you a safe zone for clearing and problem solving.

4. Decide on how you will handle problems together. One of you should be clearly in charge at all times. If you have a problem with how your A.D. child is being managed by your spouse, call a discreet conference with him out of the range of hearing of your kids.

Air your criticism as your "opinion," and your suggestions as your "preference" for action. See if you can work out an alternative way of dealing with the situation that is more to your liking. Try to stay united in your actions toward your child. This will greatly decrease the stress he experiences which is caused by the antagonism between you and your spouse. As you come together, you may notice a dramatic drop-off in behavior problems of your A.D. child.

5. Recontract your marriage. The two of you have grown apart and accepted roles in your child's life that neither of you wanted. Now it is time to come together and renegotiate your roles. If your husband is taking refuge from his family into work, he needs to consider coming home more. If you feel overworked in your care-giving role at school and home, you need to demand more equal participation and give up your role as the family "rescuer."

Consciously recontracting your relationship can revitalize your lives together and dramatically improve your parenting effectiveness. The role negotiation technique next described will help you do so.

The role negotiation technique

Sometimes it helps to have a way to structure the recontracting process. The "role negotiation" technique is one such structure. It is a vehicle for stating expectations in clear behavioral terms—describing what another does rather than describing character traits or faults—and agreeing on solutions.

Each partner makes a list of "start," "stop," and "keep doing" behaviors for the other. It is important to list things in behavioral terms (what the other person *does*) rather than in adjectival terms (your *opinion* of your spouse's motivation or character). Your spouse may be able to change his behavior in the situation, i.e., he can begin attending your child's school functions. He cannot change his personality, however, to fit your opinion, i.e., your charge that he is "lazy and uninvolved" with your child. Watch your use of adjectives.

Once you have completed the "start," "stop," and "keep doing" narrative for each other, exchange your lists and work out the quid pro quo of your relationship. The main idea is that change is a negotiated process in which you agree to make some change in your behavior in exchange for some alteration from your partner. "You do this; I'll do that." You may want to write down agreements and identify, at least informally, review dates. The figure below shows the format for a role negotiation worksheet.

Role Negotiation worksheet

From: you_____ To: your spouse_____ _____

With regard to (stressful situation),   _____
I want you to:

Start	Stop	Keep Doing

You ask your husband to "start" going to meetings in connection with your son's school and to "stop" ranting at the kids for typical A.D. behaviors like spacing out or not listening.

Your husband asks you to "stop" questioning his parenting approach in front of your son. He wants you to "start" being firmer in your requirements for your child at the dinner table and "stop" giving in to him when he pesters.

You both affirm the "keep doing" behavior of putting a priority on quality time together and make arrangements to have one date a week together, even if it is only a walk around the block.

Remember to be behaviorally specific in coming up with your expectations, and make sure that you devote some attention to the "keep doing" column to express appreciation for each other. This column contains the reasons that you are in a love relationship and is just as important as the start and stop behaviors that you identify.

6. Manage parenting transitions carefully. When one partner comes home after a hard day's work and the kids have been driving the other partner nuts, give the one entering the household time to decompress. Have a quiet conversation or alone time before the change of command. Or, have a fifteen-minute liedown alone in the cool and quiet of your bedroom. This will restore you so that you can pick up some of the chores of parenting from your spouse.

7. Affirm your love for each other frequently. Get in the habit of saying, "I love you." Do this often. Make it a part of the way you are as a family—expressing your affection for each other as it strikes you. There will still be lots of fire in this family crucible. Continue to cool it with love.

8. Do emotional check-ins with each other. "Are you angry?" is a common check-in that is used in our house. Problems get worse when you do not verbally process what is happening on an ongoing basis. When the stress heats up, people have a natural tendency to make assumptions about each other's motivation. Continually check in with each other to short-circuit these hassles.

9. Deal effectively with sibling resentment. Sibling resentment of your Attention Different child can keep the pot stewing even while you are going through a renewal of relationship. This is why it is important to follow eustress parenting strategies in dealing with sib problems. Here are some suggestions:

a. Stay in touch with *all* your kids. Siblings resent their Attention Different brother or sister out of a sense of scarcity of affection. Once a sib gets as much of mom or dad as she wants, she/he will be less demanding and resentful of "what my brother gets away with."

Make sure that each child has enough time with you. Program quality time with all your kids. Your lives are busy; planning for "alongside time" with each of your kids on a regular basis is the only way to stay in touch. Put it on your "do" list. Spending time with your children refreshes your love and keeps you current on all their accomplishments, passions, and current challenges. These things will keep balance in your treatment of your normal and your A.D. children.

b. Use the role negotiation and "talking stick" methods with siblings. Attention Different children like these techniques because they themselves are natural negotiators and recognize a powerful bargaining tool when they see it. Have the kids write down and exchange a "start," "stop," and "keep doing" behavior list for each other and arrive at a quid pro quo that gives both kids a sense of satisfaction. Post written agreements in a family reading area and revisit them as needed.

And the talking stick is a great way to help kids who are chronic interrupters begin to contain their explosive verbal energy, to run it instead of having it run them. Use of this device helps build their ability to listen as well as solve the day-to-day problems that confront them.

c. No "angels" or "devils" allowed. Watch carefully to prevent the formation of this common pattern in your family: The Attention Different child gets all the time and attention and the dysfunctional "devil" label. The normal child gets no attention and the "angel" label. This is short shrift for both kids. Find ways to give both kids quality time and let your angel child know that you see her flaws also. She'll be relieved not to have to carry the halo all the time!

d. Watch out for stealth attacks by your angel child on your Attention Different child. In Chapter Eleven, I described how children at school can get an A.D. child into a temper fit by running "stealth" attacks on the child. Kids with attentional challenges wear their hearts on their sleeves and are an easy mark for other kids seeking to get a temper reaction going. Siblings good at running stealth attacks on the A.D. child will often get the upper hand on him with parents who are not aware of the maneuver.

Get in the habit of observing your children with loving suspicion. When you spy a stealth attack call it and use it as an opening to explore what the angel is not getting in her relationship with you. Don't make the Attention Different child the innocent victim but describe him as a "player" in a game that is beginning to bore and aggravate you. It takes two to tango. Get to know your little dancers and teach them a few new steps!

The look and feel of change

You can tell when an "Attention Different" family has met and turned Uproar around. There is a mutual acceptance of personal foibles, and a sense of humor—even about the attention differences that used to drive the family crazy. There is a lack of perfectionism and a respect for the zaniness that Attention Different kids bring to the mix. A new family identity has formed: "We do not give up on each other!" This family will survive!

CHAPTER FIFTEEN

Meeting the Challenge of School-Caused Distress

"Don't waste my time."
— Rita Walpole Ague, professional legal advocate speaking for her Autistic child to the educational establishment.

A s a parent of a child with attention differences you will find sooner or later that your child is in need of special educational services. Getting results from your school district takes time and planning. But the eventual payoff in program quality is well worth the effort. Dealing with the school district can be extremely distressful to your family if you are not in control of the process. But you needn't be out of control.

To get on top of the situation you need to know three things: (1) what you want for your child, (2) how the law sets up delivery of services, and (3) how the school bureaucracy is motivated to support you or work against you. You have to know what you want and understand how the school district works so that you can influence it.

Know what you want—your knowledge is your power

The first step is to get a clear idea of the results you want. Designing your child's program can seem impossibly technical when faced with the educational jargon put out by school districts and consultants. To get control of the situation, you need to put together a succinct "opening offer," for negotiations. Don't worry too much about technicalities; you will find as you get into the process that decisions are made with a "muddling through" style in which services are continually evaluated and redecided.

Each child has his own needs, but there are some common denominators of success for programs that serve these children.

The most important success ingredients: the right teacher, the right teaching methods

Make sure that you communicate what kind of teacher and teaching approach you want. Most Attention Different children will need some or all of the following qualities in their classroom environments:

❖   A teacher trained in working with A.D. kids who is able to roll with the stress and bounce back with more positive options.

❖   A lot of flexibility for choice but within a very predictable classroom structure and routine. All A.D. kids need to know exactly what they will be doing, when they will be doing it, how to know when the project is finished, and what comes next.

❖   Visual presentation methods. Hands on is best. A.D. children understand explanations with visual language and stories. They often will literally not understand verbal instructions. Pictorial instructional materials are best.

❖   Private two-way signal system (flash cards work well for this) between the teacher and A.D. child for exchange of important information about the need for help or the child's experienced level of tension, frustration, etc. The use of a range for communicating feelings of emotional intensity is important; "1" on the card means "I am calm." A "7" means "I am so frustrated I am about to explode."

❖   Learning materials presented in bite-sized chunks with a lot of leeway on time. A.D. kids typically take twice as long as other kids to complete study projects. If they are interrupted they may "lose the picture" and have to go back to the beginning of the problem solving process. Their powerful minds work slower on the auditory, "central task processing" problems they are given.

Successful teachers will often let the child indicate when he is finished and provide the next activity at that time.

❖ A.D. kids need a lot of help with transitions. Warnings and prompts to the next activity must be delivered reflexively by the teacher.

❖ They need access to a computer (called an "Augmented Writing Device or AWD" in system jargon) to enable completion of writing and math assignments. Problems with small muscle coordination and visual processing make writing difficult. Focusing problems make reading problematic. Providing a computer for a child's use is often the simplest, least expensive way to make sure that his neurology doesn't hobble his potential. The machine is visual, provides instant memory prompts, and the keyboard overcomes visual-motor writing problems.

❖ The ideal A.D. learning program leaves a lot of room for "incidental learning," the kind of learning style most suited to A.D. children; the teacher provides interesting learning opportunities in and out of class and builds study programs around the child's interests. A sharp 11-year-old A.D.'r learns to spell better playing a Scrabble game with his teacher for a privilege than he does from a paper and pencil spelling memorization exercise.

❖ There should be a daily physical education program that provides both individual and team sports opportunities. A child may excel in individual sports such as track, jump roping, gym, or may be inclined toward team sports. Many A.D.'rs are more successful doing individual sports activities because of the complex interpersonal language understanding required in any team support.

❖ The best educational programs for A.D. kids use a collaborative approach to educational planning in which the child is invited to comment on what works best for him, and what he enjoys doing most. This mitigates against ill-advised changes and builds the child's ability to make choices for his own life.

❖ Homework assignments should be kept short. If the work can't be done during the school day, address this problem before accepting hours of make-up homework each night. Parents who take on the school's responsibility to teach run the risk of making their homes into a battleground for unresolved issues at school.

❖ It is important that parents and teachers have a way to communicate daily. Some parents use a written daily notebook or voice mail system. Parents and teachers can support each other and the child if they are able to stay continually in touch on the child's successes and challenges at school.

The right physical environment

❖ Attention Different children are hypersensitive to chaos and noise, but are relaxed by the same bright and happy visual environments found in any classroom.

A good physical classroom environment is filled with colorful projects the kids are working on but is not too visually distracting. It shows lots of wall charts listing rules and steps to follow for completion of activities. A posted daily schedule is present.

❖ There is clearly defined space for the child to move around. Some A.D. kids are assigned two desks that they can use. This gives them a structure within which they can move when they are restless. Desks should not be placed too close to each other.

❖ *Quiet space* in the classroom or building to decompress and reduce stress is also available. This is not a time-out room but a "refuge" that kids can request or teachers suggest. An inexpensive adaptation would be a sound system for this room that permits the kids to listen to music for stress management.

❖ A resource room where a child having problems can be tutored one to one with a teacher or aide should be part of the program. Oftentimes children are "pulled out" to the resource room from their main classroom for a set amount of time each day. Usually there are only a few other kids in the room at one time, which gives the Attention Different child the opportunity to decompress and compose himself.

Three ways to get legal recourse for change

Once you have an idea of the changes that you want, you are in a position to choose a method to plan and implement a change in your child's program. You have three ways to do this: informal accommodations, a "504 Plan," and an Individualized Education Plan or "I.E.P."

Informal accommodations

If your child's attention difference is mild enough that he does not require extensive modification, you may be able to craft accommodations for him informally with his teacher and school counselor.

Though it takes effort for any A.D. child to keep up in a conventional classroom, many children can do so with help from teachers. The most important thing is that the teacher understand and accept your child's attention differences. The best teacher realizes that the A.D. child is not acting as he does to provoke his teacher or to frivolously "act out" some conflict assumed to be a result of bad parenting.

This "A.D. friendly" teacher makes sure that your child has as much time, prompting, and structure as he needs to be a successful learner. She does not allow him to use his A.D. as an excuse, but does understand its impact on problems that come up. She willingly customizes her classroom routine to help your child learn.

Accommodations that she makes may or may not be officially noted for the file, but should be recorded in your child's daily notebook for your reference and the teacher's.

A "504 Plan"

The federal government has established two provisions in U.S. law to provide special education services for Attention Different children. These are Section 504 of the Rehabilitation Act of 1973 (known as a "504 Plan) and Part B of the Individuals with Disabilities Education Act (I.D.E.A.) signed into law in 1993.

A 504 Plan will usually be considered if a child's impairment is moderate. This plan covers accommodations that can be implemented at the school building level and does not normally call in resources, such as provision of an educational aide, administered by the district's special education office. Formal evaluation of the disability is not required. To receive services under a 504 Plan, a child must meet the following two criteria:

a. He is ineligible for services under the I.D.E.A (cannot get an I.E.P.) and,

b. He meets the Act's definition of a person with disabilities: he has a physical or mental impairment that substantially limits a major activity such as learning. Depending on the severity of their condition, children with attention differences such as A.D.D. may or may not fit the definition of the law. Not all children are covered.

The Individualized Education Plan (I.E.P.)

Although A.D.H.D. and related neurological conditions are not separate disability categories under the I.D.E.A., children with diagnosed neurological conditions who require special education and related services can be eligible for services under the "other health impaired" category of Part B of the I.D.E.A. This specifies when "the (condition) is a chronic or acute health problem that results in limited alertness which adversely affects educational performance." Children with A.D.H.D. may also be eligible for services under the "specific learning disability" or "serious emotionally disturbed" categories of the I.D.E.A. when they have these conditions in addition to the A.D.H.D.

Both these laws require schools to make modifications or adaptations for students whose attentional differences result in significant educational impairments. "Special needs" children must be placed in a regular classroom to the maximum extent appropriate (the "least restrictive environment") to their educational needs, with the use of supplementary aids and services if necessary.

Begin by requesting an evaluation of your child's educational needs

Your first step in the process of getting services for your child is to ask, in writing, for an evaluation. This term is taken to mean the total process of gathering and using information to determine if a child has a disability. A variety of testing and observation instruments are used. The public schools are required to pay the cost of the evaluation.

The evaluation is important because it establishes the framework for change planning and sets up the issues that will be addressed in the I.E.P., which may lead to an alternative private or public school placement. The school district may begin the process of evaluation by asking you to sign forms making your child a "focus of concern." You may refuse the evaluation by refusing to sign the focus forms.

If you disagree with the evaluation, you may dispute the district's evaluation findings and retain an independent consultant at your own initial expense. If their consultant recommendations substantiate your contentions, the district may agree to pick up the costs for the second consultation. This is termed an "independent assessment."

If the district refuses to pay for costs of the parents' consultant after she has delivered her findings, the parents may choose to take the district to a due process hearing to recover costs. See below for a description of the due process format. Districts will oftentimes agree to pay the parents' consultant fees to avoid the agony of holding a due process hearing.

The structure of the I.E.P.

The Individualized Education Plan is a written statement of the goals, objectives, and services that will be delivered to assist your child with special educational needs. It should be written succinctly and clearly and show both your child's strengths and learning needs. You have the right to participate in the development of the I.E.P. and can call for changes or rewrite at any time.

A good I.E.P. will proceed from a listing of a general goal to specify measurable objectives with a timeline for realizing these objectives. Federal law requires that it include:

a. statement of the child's present level of performance
b. statement of goals and objectives
c. statement of special education services to be provided
d. statement of the extent to which the child will participate in regular education
e. the date special educational services are to begin and expected ending date

f. criteria for determining if objectives are being met
g. If appropriate, a statement of needed services to transition from school to employment

Example: Individualized Education Plan: Sam Jones

Annual goal: to increase math and problem solving skills to grade level

Short-term objective:	begin date	end date	notes
Given written problem solving examples, Sam will increase his ability to identify which calculation processes to use in 2/3 problems	Sept., 1996	June, 1997	
Given two of three factors, distance, time and speed factors, Sam will be able to correctly calculate the remaining factor	Sept., 1996	June, 1997	

Annual goal: to improve peer relations in the classroom (Sam Jones)

Short-term objective: Sam will be able to respond to verbal cues from peers 3/5 times with one request and sustain the appropriate behavior for 5-10 minutes	begin date Sept., 1996	end date June, 1997	notes
Sam will be able to disengage from grabbing others or taking their belongings with two reminders	Sept., 1996	January 1997	

The I.E.P. should be a "living" plan in the sense that it is continually available for redrafting on the request of either the parents or the school. It is important that the I.E.P. not become a formality, but be the template for measurement of progress. The I.E.P. keeps the district honest by establishing standards that compare your child's progress with other kids in his class. A well-written I.E.P. establishes standards that are measurable enough to keep the district from simply passing your child through without really educating him.

Preparing for the I.E.P. meeting

You can prepare for this meeting by assessing your child's strength and weaknesses through discussion with him, his teacher, school counselor, and through classroom observation. Write down your observations and form a list of priorities that you believe should be included in his plan.

Ask for a copy of all the forms to be used at the meeting that you will be asked to review or sign. Have your questions prepared ahead of time about the forms. Make sure to keep an updated file of all forms, records, and testing reports connected with the I.E.P.

If you believe that the district is not supportive of your educational objectives, bring a resource person with you to the meeting. She may be a representative of a parents' advocacy group (call your local Learning Disabilities Association for a list of such groups). Or she may be your attorney, educational consultant, or a friend who has some understanding of the process.

Rita Walpole Ague (epigram in Chapter opening) suggests that you don't sign anything you have not first read carefully. If you don't have the opportunity to go over the form in sufficient detail make this notation over your signature block: "Signifies Attendance only. Approval pending."

What if you don't like the I.E.P.?

The law requires that you agree to the I.E.P. with your signature before the school district can implement the plan's provisions. You may refuse to sign the I.E.P. thus preventing its implementation. In fact, you must authorize any special education modification made for your child. If you feel that you were rushed through the process, hold off signing and ask for a re-write session. This will give you time to consider I.E.P. contents and write necessary changes.

Placement decisions may also be made based on recommendations in the I.E.P. The law requires delivery of services. If the district does not have these services available, it must provide them with a private school placement.

To influence the school bureaucracy, you must understand its motivation

In the best of all possible worlds, your local school district would be generously funded to provide special education services to every child who needs them. Unfortunately, a great competition for resources exists and parents may not be offered appropriate services. If conflict arises, you must decide if you wish to collaborate with the district or to confront it. Collaboration is always the first step and should be your goal even if you choose to take an adversarial stance to get the district's attention. You will have to work with public school staff one way or the other.

You should make a conscious decision about when you want to confront the district and when you want to collaborate with it. The best attitude is one of *assertive collegiality*. Do not reflexively get your dukes up, but be alert to attempts to cut appropriate services for your child. Make as many friends as possible in the system but don't let your intention for your child be compromised by uncertain assurances from the district.

Don't try to impress them by doing favors. Most parents who are successful in this endeavor will tell you that they learned early on not to "suck up" to the district by agreeing to volunteer duty or by lugging posters around backing the local school levy. You can't get change by simply being nice; you will have to negotiate it.

At some point you may want to get legal and retain an attorney. Rita Walpole Ague suggests that you will know when this time comes if, despite your best efforts, the school continues to waste your child's time with inaction or tired remedies that don't work. This is why it is as important to know the bureaucratic forces that oppose you as it is to know the rules and laws that come to bear on the issue.

Eustress begins with understanding the bureaucratic challenge that you face

If you are like many parents, you will start out with a childlike naiveté toward the school system, believing or wanting to believe that the system is on your side. As you experience the bureaucracy's reaction to your attempts to get services for your child, you will automatically become less trusting and more vigilant of the need to protect your rights. You will learn that though there are loving, intelligent, and caring people throughout the system, parents eventually come up against resistance to change, especially if it is costly to the system.

Many parents take resistance as a bitter surprise and give themselves over to rueful condemnation of the school district without really looking at the tactical advantages that they possess under the law. This is a mistake. Wise parents eventually become less trusting and more tactical. In keeping with the eustress perspective, they embrace the resistance that the system throws at them as a challenge to be understood, met, and transcended. They are able to identify and use the advantages that the law gives them to affirm a new assertiveness in dealing with the system.

Getting appropriate services from your child's school district requires that you understand the power relationships of different actors in the educational system and their motivations. Though this picture may seem "Machiavellian" in that it emphasizes power over caring as motivation, shrinking resources available to schools have pushed them into the position of resisting change unless they cannot afford to resist it. And, parents are the only ones who can create an economic penalty for inaction.

Motivation of major players

First, understand the motivation of all those helping your child get a good education.

Teachers are motivated by the need to keep their class size as small as possible and keep problem children in someone else's class. Given an average national class size in the vicinity of thirty students per room, they are not motivated by the prospect of having to implement a lot of creative services for one or two kids.

Special education directors are motivated by anything that will keep their costs down. They prefer placement of children with behavior problems in central, self-contained special education classrooms. These settings often include kids with severe anger problems related to family trauma and children with severe phys-ical disabilities or learning delays. This, of course, is not an appropriate environment for A.D. kids.

Building principals are motivated by a desire to keep everyone happy—teachers, parents, the district's special education director and the district Superintendent of Schools. They are the ones responsible for delivering services to parents within cost parame-ters established by the district.

School district managers are motivated by a desire to keep state level school system managers off their backs, to keep parents happy, to keep state politicians happy, and to keep costs down. This group tends to be very anxious about anyone rocking the boat and leaking information, as this may alert higher headquar-ters to problems that have not been handled efficiently.

State and Federal school system managers are motivated to solve problems in such a way that they look good to political leadership or the State Superintendent of Schools.

The buck stops with you. A review of the above list of players and their motivations reveals that no one in the system gets special rewards for resolving your issue. You are the main force for change outside the school system. If you are not ac-tively and assertively involved, the issue will keep going around in circles.

You are the only one in the system who could potentially hire an attorney to represent you and the only one who can go to the local school board and complain. As positive as your child's school principal might be, building level staff cannot deliver services until higher headquarters gives the O.K. The buck stops with you.

Collaboration is the first and best choice

The best choice is always collaboration with the school dis-trict to craft a solution that works for everybody. Parents can not afford to let their resentment of the system interfere with their focus on getting results. They should not dissipate their energy in angry recrimination, but channel it with persistence to alert the district to the fact that their child is not receiving appropriate services.

Communicate. First, make sure you foster good communications with your child's teacher and other caregivers at school. Agree to exchange a notebook back and forth. Be sure to have clear information. If hassles are happening on the bus, meet the bus some morning and say hello to the driver.

Look for win-win solutions. Parents often make the mistake of getting so set on a particular option that they lose sight of a gift the situation is handing them. They may, for example, believe that placement in a certain private school is the only course of action that will help their child. In their ferocious insistence on this option they miss the opportunity to discuss placement in another public school run by a principal who has a statewide reputation for educational excellence with Special Education kids.

Gather all available information. Take the time to look around and go a level deeper in your analysis of schools and options. Build relationships with people in the system whom you respect and who can give you information on options you may not have been aware of.

Make sure that you have had a chance to visit and view the school setting that the district is offering when kids are present. Is this a good choice for your child in terms of real educational enrichment or is it a make-do?

Keep your eyes on the prize. The two most important factors for your child's successful educational experience are: a.) supportive building principal and b.) funding O.K'd. by district HQ for delivery of services. Linking up these two factors requires you to listen carefully and cautiously to the options that are presented without letting yourself be sold "a bill of goods."

Negotiate interests not positions. It is important to separate out your list of demands (your *positions*) from the *values* you want to realize in the situation, that is, your interests. A position statement might be, "I want him placed in a private school at district expense." A statement of interest would be, "I want him to like school, and be excited about learning. I want to see his ability to think critically developed." People often get conceptually high grounded on their different positions. "This is my position. That is yours." No common ground is seen. In contrast, when you negotiate interests you ask the question "Why?" or "What do you get?" from a certain position. Your *interest* is to place him in a happy, interesting learning environment. It is also in the school's interest to educate your child. Negotiating interests opens up new options that are foreclosed by position taking.

All parents who enter into discussion with their child's school to get special services for him share a common disadvantage. Most all of us spent our childhoods in school subject to the authority of teachers and administrators. Next to our parents, no one else had more authority over us. This experience creates ambivalence in us in our dealings with the school; we feel powerful urgency to help our child but we sometimes find it difficult to retain our own authority in the face of opposition from school administrators.

Seven Strategies of Resistance and Distress

To keep costs down, the school district instinctively uses a set of strategies that challenge the parents' ability to gain services and allocation of resources. These strategies are part of the organization's culture and the way it defends itself and keeps control.

Distress Strategy 1: "It's the parents' fault."

Children with attention differences often slip behind in their schoolwork because of their neurologic impairments in the areas of short-term memory, "auditory processing" (understanding words spoken to them), and their ability to stay on task. The school's reaction may be to deny the neurologic basis for the problem and try to remedy it by heaping on the homework, detentions, and trips to the principal's office.

When parents suggest that their child needs special services, the school may react by implying that the child needs to learn better homework habits and social skills from his parents. School officials may also imply that stress in the home could be leading to the child's "acting out" at school. Or parents may be blamed for turning the child against the school.

Distress Strategy 2: "Believe us. We're the professionals."

School districts must establish the need for providing special accommodations for a child with appropriate testing of his capabilities and limitations. The type of special accommodations that are recommended depends on the testing psychologists' evaluation of test results.

Sometimes its hard to be assertive in decision making with the district. Many parents have found themselves in large meetings attended by psychologists, psychiatrists, educational consultants, special education specialists, and the child's teacher(s). Before the meeting the assembled group (minus the parents) had decided on the meeting outcome and everyone seemed to push in unison for that outcome.

Once the meeting got under way, it was clear that the parents' concerns did not matter all that much. Many times solutions arrived at are simply the most cost effective approach for the district and not suited to the needs of the child. Such an impressive array of technical jargon may be used so that the parents' don't have the opportunity to state their side–their interests get lost in the shuffle.

Parents may exhaust themselves wading through these meetings only to end up feeling further negotiations are futile and agree to the district's plan. Given their inability to change this situation and an uncertainty about their own goals, many parents eventually drop out altogether and take their child out of the public school system. Others leave him in year after year knowing that he is being passed through with a poor education.

Distress Strategy 3: "It's the child's fault."

Despite medical diagnosis to the contrary, the school staff will often cling to the idea that the Attention Different child is behaving as he does to get attention or out of a sense of "false entitlement." This term translates into "spoiled child" and is a double slam directed at both parents and the child.

A child may have a temper problem caused by continual frustration at being required to complete task work that is beyond his ability. His classroom distress is caused by his teacher's assumption that he is behaving intentionally to thwart her. She wants to get him out of her class and actively lobbies her principal to help her. She may make a few accommodations, but nothing significant enough to really make a difference. She has twenty-nine other kids to deal with.

The teacher's power is seen in her inaction. Doing nothing makes the situation worse and parents more frantic. Eventually they may opt to homeschool the child or seek a private school for him. Getting their son educated becomes their problem, not the school district's.

The teacher may suggest that the child's behavior seems "intentional" thus taking the problem out of her domain (to devise creative educational strategies) and putting it in the domain of therapists or the parents to solve the child's psychological problem. Blaming the child is strong fuel for the distress cycle as it puts pressure on him to deny that he is in any way different from other kids. Being Attention Different becomes a liability. He becomes defensive and even more uncooperative.

Distress Strategy 4: "Who do you think you are?"

"Why should your child get special attention when all these other kids have needs too? What makes your case so different?" This tactic is reflexively used by some school bureaucrats to energize the parents' sense of shame for asking for anything for their child. It may never be stated straight out but it is an undercurrent in discussion when it comes to dividing up resources.

Distress Strategy 5: Stonewalling.

Stonewalling, or the practice of delaying decision on a child's school program, can drive parents nuts and dry up their resources. This is a common tactic for gaining compliance in labor negotiations. It gives power to the party that has the resources to hold out longer than an opponent. The economic life of many families requires some certainty about school plans for all their kids. Having to take time off to deal with a child who is not in school can be very punishing. A school district may hold off evaluating a request for action until the last minute, thus forcing the parents to accept a sub-optimum solution. In a typical case, the local district may delay beginning the evaluation process (to support a placement decision) until August, a month before school starts.

Testing and evaluation typically takes from two to six weeks. By the time testing is finished and an option is presented, the parents are desperate for resolution. Their child has already missed the all important start-up of the first two weeks of the school year and now faces coming into a class that has already formed social cliques. This puts enormous pressure on parents to give up their fight for a higher quality option and take what they are offered just to get their child in school.

Distress Strategy 6: Gambling with professional costs.

Under U.S. law, school districts may be directed to reimburse parents for costs they incur in the pursuit of appropriate services for their child, to include attorney's fees, if the parents prevail at the due process hearing. This means that if parents are unsatisfied with the program the school district is offering they can attempt to prove at a hearing that the district is wrong in its decision. Due process hearings are expensive undertakings for all concerned.

If at the hearing the administrative judge rules for the parents, all costs will be picked up by the district. If the judge rules for the district, the parents may be stuck with legal costs as well as costs for testing and professional evaluation.

Thus, middle-class parents are forced into playing a game of high stakes poker with school districts without the resources and financial staying power that the districts have. The decision to seek a due process hearing must be made very carefully. Once scheduled it is unwise to frivolously cancel the hearing (playing "chicken" with the district) because this may anger the hearings judge whose schedule is already overcrowded.

Distress Strategy 7: D.D., S.B.D., or Out.

State law governs the delivery of educational services, and each state is different. This is true in regard to how an Attention

Different child may be classified. Parents have a say in the category that the district uses to classify their child. Most often, the child will be in special education because of hyperactivity in the classroom, behavior problems, or inability to keep up. Though each state uses different terms, parents should make sure that their child is classified "health impaired," or is said to have a "communication disorder."

Schools, in the attempt to realize economy in the delivery of services often will put children with attention differences in self-contained classrooms with kids who are classified as "developmentally delayed" or "D.D." Though there may be exceptions, this is an inappropriate environment for most A.D. children. Many of these kids are above average in I.Q. Slowing their pace of learning to that of kids who are measured with lower I.Q.'s creates boredom. Boredom is a stressor and stress will lead to problematic behavior for your Attention Different child.

Putting A.D. kids in with children classified as "severe behavior problems" or "S.B.D." is even a worse mistake. Children in the S.B.D. category are usually so classified because they have demonstrated violent behavior and have severe emotional problems. Many of these kids come from abusive home environments. They are angry and easily provoked. The A.D. child with poor interpersonal skills is ripe for abuse in this situation. This option should be challenged as inappropriate straight out. The law requires that a child be educated in the "least restrictive environment." An A.D. child in S.B.D. is in a highly restrictive, and possible dangerous, environment.

School districts will sometimes say that S.B.D. is their best offer. A review of the educational setting frequently reveals that this option is so inadequate that a letter from the parents' attorney contesting the district's placement decision is in order. The district, obeying its bureaucratic imperative, will try to get away with the least costly option and sadly, may simply ignore the fact that its action is hurtful to the child. When this happens, parents must be willing to stand up and go the distance legally. This may involve hiring their own consultant who, in concert with the parents' attorney, will require compliance under the law.

Taking a More Adversarial Stance: Five Steps to Gain Services for Your Child

If your school district is not open to collaboration, or talks a good game but never gives up on its preferred option, you may choose an adversarial stance. Choosing this approach displays your power in such a way that the district knows you are committed to getting a change in your child's education. Your goal is to enter into collaborative discussion with the district, but it may be necessary to take a political or legal stance first to get the system's attention.

Step 1: Know your power as a citizen and be assertive.

You may not realize that you are just a phone call away from decision makers at any level in the educational system. You are just days away from the next meeting of the school board. Your power lies in your willingness to expand the arena of discussion of your child's case until the situation develops momentum for change.

Educational administrators and politicians are busy people with busy agendas. Once you put your issue on their agenda they have a responsibility to do something. They incur this responsibility when they answer your phone call. And they all have a stake in calming the situation and looking good in the outcome.

To get more information on your child's educational rights, contact the National Information Center of Children and Youth with Disabilities (NICHY) at 1-800-695-0285.

Assertiveness Tips

❖ *Remember to be on the alert* that your own childhood school experience may diminish your assertiveness with the district. Stay in your power by getting your facts together. Conference with your attorney if you must. Then tell the district what you want. Don't be afraid to disagree. Your child's success is on the line. In fact, it may pay to be a bit stubborn and inflexible at first. Be aware that you are dealing with people who have had a lot of experience negotiating minimum options for parents. Let them know you mean business.

❖ Hold the district to time-for-decision standards; ten days is the time established in many administrative processes for decision. Don't tolerate excuses such as, "I'll get to it in August, I'm on vacation." Ask whom the administrator has delegated decisional authority to and deal with that person. Make it a habit to politely ask who will be getting back, by when, with a decision. And persistently follow up with phone calls, weekly, if you must.

❖ *Put it in writing.* After meetings with administrative staff, send the ranking person who was at the meeting a letter that politely and tersely sums up decisions; include copies that can be distributed to all concerned.

❖ Talk to those who have the authority to solve your problem. Don't waste your time browbeating your child's teacher. She is all-important for success in your program but has very little formal power. You need to target the decision makers who are most probably at the district's central office. Your success at the district level may yield resources that will make your child's teacher's job easier. Collaboration with her at all phases of your change planning is essential.

Step 2: Educate the educators.

A major factor in the school district's resistance to your request for services is its ignorance about the impact of your child's attention difference on his educational needs. There is always a tendency to doubt the parents' contention that additional services are needed and therefore it makes sense to recruit as many people on your side as possible.

Attention Different children rarely fit precise clinical categories. A child may have only special learning needs (dyslexia, visual-motor problems, language comprehension and expression, problem solving delays) or he may have these impairments, plus behavior problems. Some Attention Different kids' suffer from obsessions and compulsions. Some may crave predictability and routine so intensely that they go off the wall when their routine is upset.

You yourself must first understand your child's idiosyncratic perceptual style, his strengths and vulnerabilities, and then articulate this neurologic profile to the district. Identify what classroom accommodations are necessary. No one knows your child as you do, and no one is in the position to observe him as closely as you are.

Since an ongoing educational campaign is required, you must budget time to deliver your message. Teachers, principals, district psychologists, Special Education directors, and system managers must get to know your case. Remember, you realize gain by expanding the issue throughout the bureaucracy and support community. To the degree that you are isolated, you will lose.

Step 3: Hire an attorney and consultant whom you trust.

What to look for in an attorney. If need be, you may want to retain an attorney to represent you to the district. Given the bureaucratic and cost-conscious culture of the school district, a short letter from an attorney on her letterhead identifying educational services desired sends the message that parents are willing to go the distance to get due process. This can have a powerful effect. I like Rita Walpole Ague's suggestion that you get the name of several prospective attorneys by asking the district to give you the names of those lawyers who prevailed against the district in due process hearings. This query also alerts the district to the fact that you mean business.

If you get your attorney from another source make sure that she has a specialty in "educational law" or "disability law" and interview her to see if she is a good choice to represent you. Though legal help can be pricey on the front end (as much or more as an hour appointment with a psychiatrist), it can be well worth the cost in the long run..

The attorney can help you understand about what you can hope to gain and what it will cost you. She can advise you of the gamble you take in hiring her. Her fees will only be paid by the district if you prevail over the district, though you may not necessarily have to prevail at a formal hearing. In many states attorney costs will be picked up by the district if it decides for administrative convenience to reverse itself and make the changes that parents require.

A good attorney will have knowledge of the organization she is dealing with, the personalities involved, and, of course, the rules, regulations, and laws that impact the situation. She will be able to state your position politely and knowledgeably in such a way that the district understands that it has to make your wishes a priority.

Federal education law requires that schools make a "reasonable accommodation" to provide a "free and appropriate education" to children with special needs in the "least restrictive environment." School districts may overstate the cost of an accommodation or understate their ability to make one. As previously mentioned, they may attempt to warehouse the A.D. child with kids with severe emotional problems (thus violating the "least restrictive environment" rule). Your attorney will help you decide what you can reasonably demand from the district and what might be considered unreasonable to a hearings judge.

Your attorney will also help you structure your argument so that you avoid the burden of proof in your dealings with the district. If, for example, the district has been providing special education services, and terminates those services, it must prove that it has a better option for delivering educational services to your child. It must bear costs for testing and evaluation and, if you disagree, must prove its action is legitimate to a hearings judge in a due process hearing. Your attorney will make sure that these costs are not shifted on to you.

What to look for in a consultant. If you are dissatisfied with the services that your Attention Different child is receiving you may eventually need to hire an educational consultant. She will study your child's learning needs and make a recommendation for an appropriate placement (an "independent assessment"). Educational consultants usually hold a Master's degree or Ph.D. in Special Education or Neurodiagnostics (psychological and educational testing).

To locate a consultant, look in your Yellow Pages for "educational consultants" or contact your local Learning Disabilities Association information and referral line. Their national headquarters can be contacted at (412) 341-1515. Your consultant may also be an expert witness that you could call on to testify in a due process hearing. For that reason it is a good idea for parents to ask their attorney for recommendations of education consultants that she has worked with.

You should also query potential consultants on the amount of work that they have done for the district. Oftentimes districts will hire local consultants to represent them at the hearing, and the consultant may experience a conflict of interest representing parents who are contesting a district decision.

Step 4: Structure and present your option.

Your attorney will improve your leverage by giving you advice that strengthens your case and by representing you at I.E.P. related meetings, and placement proceedings. She will help you devise an approach at each stage of the process: evaluation (with consultant costs), writing of the I.E.P., and decisions involving program and placement. She will also help you decide when and if to go for due process.

If you do not choose to retain an attorney, make sure that you have an advocate who knows the law, the forms, the process, and can help you make decisions about the program that is offered. This person can be of tremendous assistance at every step of the way from the I.E.P. to the due process hearing if one should be necessary. Your local Learning Disabilities Association can provide you with the number of volunteer and for-fee parent advocacy groups in your area.

Step 5: Be ready to go to "due process."

The due process hearing is an administrative and judicial proceeding that either the school or the parents can request to resolve issues for service delivery. Due process is the end of informal or collegial negotiation—it is the trial. Decisions made here may result in allocation of major resources on behalf of your child's education.

The due process hearing is conducted by an administrative judge, with the parents and district represented by lawyers. The judge applies relevant educational law and makes a decision. Districts do not like to "go to hearing" if they have the burden of proof. Hearings typically cost in the vicinity of $10,000 a day to the District if it has the burden of proof, for it must bring in its own specialists at salary and pay the fees of educational consultants that it uses.

"Going to due process" can be nasty and very expensive but this must be an option that you accept as a best alternative to a negotiated settlement of your issue. If you pull back from this possibility you are gravely weakening your position.

The district as a political bureaucracy is like a huge donkey that will only pay attention if it knows you are willing to use a big stick to get its attention. Don't even mention due process unless you are close to choosing this option, but if it is necessary, don't hesitate to pick up the stick. Do whatever you have to do to come up with initial legal fees (remember, you can be sure of reimbursement only if you win) to power up your threat. Be ready to compromise to avoid the hearing but don't drop your guard or give up too easily. This may be your opportunity to craft a program for your child that will guide him for the rest of his time in school.

Conclusion: Know your strength but don't flaunt it.

By U.S. law, your local public school system is required to provide a free and appropriate education in the least restrictive environment to any special needs child who attends it. The law is on your side. This is your basic advantage.

Sometimes it is difficult to move the district's bureaucracy to action, but sooner or later, if you persist, it will have to make reasonable accommodation. Your attitude of assertive, non-combative confidence is the *eustress* attitude in action and is the key to your success. You must let the district know that you are totally serious and stand behind your convictions. You must also be ready to thank them for making even small changes, one step at a time.

Don't flaunt your power. Years back, I was wrestling the issue of placement of my own son with the local school district. I was on the phone with my attorney holding forth about the legal action I wanted to take against the district that had caused our family so much grief with its endless inaction.

My attorney, a master in the field of education law, cautioned me to keep my cool. He said he would not waste his time representing me if I had an ax to grind. Our subsequent experience building an educational environment for our son, collaboratively, substantiated the validity of his philosophy. Collaboration with sure focus on the interests for your child is by far and away your optimum choice.

CHAPTER SIXTEEN

Mastering the Stressors of Single Parenting

"If I tell my boss one more time that I've got to leave to get my son from school, he'll fire me. This stress is excruciating! I feel like I'm going to throw up."
— Single mother of a twelve-year-old A.D. boy

Single parenting an Attention Different child tempers you like fire and water temper steel. The experience changes you, forever.

Sometimes a child's attention difference can be profound—behavioral problems, obsessions, compulsions, and depression are all wrapped into one small body. Having to face this challenge and also have a life puts a massive drain on your personal energy. The high level of stress you face must be balanced by deliberate hardiness in your lifestyle. And hardiness begins with understanding the stressors that you face.

The Major Stressors of Single Parenting

As a single parent, you and your child face a particular set of stressors that must be encountered directly to mitigate their impact on his behavior and your peace of mind.

Your child is stressed by having to *change households*. Transitions stress the Attention Different child because he is required to shift focus more rapidly than he is able to. Just as he was getting accustomed to one household environment and what was required of him, the entire context shifts to another household system. These situations may occur:

❖ You may medicate him when he's in your home, but your ex-spouse doesn't like the medication and doesn't give it to your child. The abrupt cessation of medication causes distressing fluctuations in your child's behavior and feeling.

❖ You may be strict, your ex may be lenient.

❖ Your ex has remarried. A new wife and other non-A.D. children are in his household. The new wife doesn't understand or support the idea that your child is Attention Different, and considers him a malevolent little pest. Your child's relationship with his dad has taken a back seat to dad's other relationships. This is a cruel and powerful stressor.

If the child's experience is consistently positive in the other household, transition stress is considerably lessened. But there is really no way of getting around the fact that the parents may have split up because of their difference. Stress is built into their intention to stay in their child's life. It is part of the challenge to be reckoned with.

You are isolated by your child's wild behavior. The emotional delays, temper problems, and nasty oppositionality of an A.D. child can become a daunting barrier between you and other adults in social and relationship situations. You may take your child to the movies but you don't go to events with a lot of people and stimulation. You don't socialize much at get-togethers with people from work or in your neighborhood because you have to stay "tactical"—on the alert for signs your child is about to act up.

Starting a new relationship can be especially problematic. You may invite a friend over for dinner and find that after a couple of hours around you that he has lost interest in getting together with you again. Sometimes mutual attraction may be powerful enough to begin a relationship. The Honeymoon Stage is a powerful stress euphoric. But eventually the veneer wears off and the potential new step-dad or step-mom begins asserting his or her idea how to handle things. Oftentimes the newcomer's opinion is uninformed and this means big stress for all concerned.

One thing is for sure. Being stress-hardy means you must have people in your life who care about you and people whom you can give your caring to. The challenge of isolation is one to face head on.

A friendless child seeks to make you his best buddy. A.D. children often do not have many friends. Their biggest problems in this area lie in the difficulty they have reading interpersonal cues and in their emotional lability. The custodial parent is put in the position of being both caregiver and chief buddy.

It's lovely to be accepted as a friend by your child, but when his behavior isolates you from other adults, having to meet his social needs can take on a bitter feeling. You feel guilty because you're not doing more. You find that you experience great relief when he has a friend over, finally enjoying himself with someone his own age. For a while you are free from the imperative to do something with him that may bore you to tears.

You must fill his need for the other gender parent. Men and women, fathers and mothers, give their children different things at different times in the child's life. Children are open to these gifts and seem to call for them at specific times.

Mother gives the child a sense of his being welcomed in the world and loved. Father's gifts are most important as the child grows away from his mother in late childhood. The father welcomes his children to the world at this time and gives them a sense of their potential in it. Girls model their mother's behavior and are affirmed as good by their fathers. Boys model their father's behavior and are affirmed as good by their mothers.

As a single parent, you may be aware of the fact that sometimes your child puts demands on you that you know should go to the other gender. Single moms often say that they miss the male bass voice in discipline situations with their child: "He always listens to his dad, but he gives me hell!" And single dads cannot supply the "arms of the goddess" around their children— the bone deep sense of belonging and lovability that kids get from their moms.

These gifts build the child's self-esteem. Attention Different children are vulnerable to low self-esteem because of repeated failure experience caused by their attention difference. They desperately need the gifts of wisdom and example of each parent and will fight for the parent's attention by "acting out." Though this kind of behavior is not exclusive to A.D. children, the A.D. child's predilection to get caught in a situation and not have the awareness to rise above it can make the situation much worse.

As the single mom of a pre-adolescent boy, you may get all of his anger, his father may get none. This is a common pattern. Your are his mother, he lives with you and gives you most of his rage from dusk till dawn. When he is visiting his father on weekends or longer trips, he is a perfect angel. Some fathers do indeed scare their sons into repressing problematic behaviors. But many seem to control the situation (from mothers' accounts) with their "tone of voice."

Two factors account for this phenomenon. First, Dad wears the halo because he does not deal with the issue of school-week discipline. He gets his child during "laughter time" and this makes a big difference in the child's mood. Second, boys need their fathers to supply an imprint for gender development. The boy is loathe to alienate the person, his dad, who will provide him a map of next steps.

Your task in this situation is to get through to your son that eventually he must come to terms with his loss and stop taking it out on you. As your son grows into young manhood and finds the male mentoring that he requires he will lighten up on you, but considerable grief and suffering often comes before this event.

You must try to balance your job with your parenting responsibilities. Having to work part or full-time and parent an A.D. kid presents special challenges. It is hard to depend on him going to school every day because he may wake up with a stomach ache. Or, if he is depressed, he may cry like a baby being forced through his routine and out the door to the bus.

Schools will often call you to come get your child because of some problem that they can't or won't handle. Having to take time off to get him and take him home can sour your relationship with your employer. Being a single parent, you have no one to spell you and have less control over your work-parenting time. This lack of control can be very distressing.

The requirement to take time off to get your child from school may provide a useful impetus for you to assertively approach your school district to develop an appropriate learning program for your child, one that will keep him in school all day. The district is in business to teach every kid, whatever his or her learning problem or attentional style, and you should not be required to take this responsibility on yourself.

The Six Habits of Stress-Hardy Single Parents

1. **Find someone to share your burdens and joys.** The keystone of stress hardiness is the ability to give and receive love and affection. I am not talking here of romantic love. I'm talking more about the love that people feel in deep friendship—that involves caring for, respecting, and knowing the other. Stress-hardy single parents deliberately bring this emotion into their lives. This is especially important for the isolation-prone parent of the A.D. child.

Seek others who might have an understanding of the stress that you face every day. A good way to start is to attend meetings of organizations in your area that serve parents of kids like yours. These include Ch.A.D.D. (Children and Adults With Attention Deficit Disorder) at (305) 587-3700, or the national Tourette Syndrome Association at (718) 224-2999. Fathers may wish to contact a local chapter of the National Father's Network (mentioned in Chapter Thirteen), an organization of fathers of children with disabilities at (206) 747-4004.

Look for potential friends. Open yourself to the possibility of getting to know someone without there being a romantic agenda. Seek to involve yourself in nurturing communities of people who share your interests and joys in life. You will derive great relief from just having someone to talk with. Let friendship find you.

2. **Nourish yourself spiritually.** The kind of powerful stress that single-parenting an A.D. child causes forces you to look at the spiritual, "big picture," aspect of your life. Give yourself time and space to find a way to nourish your sense of inner peace, to make

meaning of it all. The spiritual dimension is expressed by any-thing you do that you *love*. It might be expressed in art, or helping others, or in dedication to integrity and excellence in your job.

Many find spiritual contact outdoors. I remember sitting in awe at the base of Arapaho Mountain in the Colorado Rockies some years back. The whole place seemed to vibrate with the life of the mountain— tremendously old, totally indifferent to me and yet totally connected to me. The tears of joy I experienced were an expression of the spiritual dimension.

Seek this kind of "peak experience" in your own life. Try to get some time on a local hiking trail with other adults if you can. Consider taking your child camping if this experience can be positive for both of you and not just add to your stress.

You may also find spiritual nourishment in religious worship. Involvement in church activities can give a single parent a com-munity as well as a place of peace.

Many parents do not believe that they deserve to get their spiritual needs met. They consider this too much of a luxury that others get but that they do not. Evidence from stress research argues against this reluctance to develop a spiritual side. Research shows that the most stress-hardy people find a way to experience inner peace on a daily basis.

3. Work out transition traditions with your ex. Create a specific sequence of activities that surrounds transitions with your ex. Use all your clout and influence to make sure that hand-over times occur at predictable intervals. When your child comes into your home, seek to create a positive mood at the start and gently remind him that the way you do things are different from your ex. At the end of his visit, take him through a wind-down ritual; go for a pastry and decaf latte with him. Have a few minutes of quality time with him.

Your A.D. child is led by the images and feelings you create in the space between you. It makes sense to deliberately evoke positive feelings at transition times. Positive feelings cause release of endorphins in the brain which leads to great reduction of all the challenges associated with being A.D. Create this good feeling at transitions, the time of greatest stress for A.D. children.

4. Develop impeccable communications with your ex. The single most important thing that you can do to reduce stress on yourself and your child is to have the best communications possible with your ex. Imaginative strategies are needed to get past the animosity that can remain after divorce or separation.

The first thing for you to do is get clear on what you want from your communications. Do you need to be right about the situation? Are you angry and seeking justice for yourself? Do you feel that you need to control the communication for some reason? Or do you want to create a positive communication environment? Though the first three outcomes may be entirely justified, the only one that counts for stress reduction is the creation of a positive climate for communications.

Follow These Steps to Excellence In Your Communications with Your Ex:

a. Come to terms with your anger. The breakup of a marriage is hard on both parents and it is natural to feel angry, but don't let this feeling get in the way of your communication effectiveness. Keep a journal and write out the things you are angry about. Give full voice to the resentment that you feel. If your anger is alerting you to give attention to something, make a note for follow-up. If there is nothing to be done, write it down—then do something to let the anger go that does not involve getting into an argument with your ex.

Use personal ritual. The great psychologist Carl Jung said that we can heal ourselves and achieve peace through ritual as well as we can through action. The unconscious responds to both physical action and symbolic action (ritual).

Nurture symbolic closure of angry unfinished business with your ex by developing your own anger release ritual. You could write a letter and never send it, or tear it up and throw the pieces out to sea or into a comforting fire. You could take something that represented the joy and the suffering you experienced in relationship and make these things part of your own "letting go" meditation. You could write his name on the bottom of your shoes and enjoy the knowledge that you are walking all over him all day! If you exercise, you can imagine that with each pull on the weight machine you are sending him further out of your life.

Do something that gives voice to all the unfinished feelings of resentment and then achieve closure and let go in the most appropriate way. Do not stress yourself and your child out by expressing old resentments directly to your ex. There is no way that this kind of expression will move you to healing or resolution; it will just make things worse.

b. Know what you want from each communication and articulate yourself assertively. Keep communications on track and don't allow yourself to be distracted by side trips, old resentments, jibes, or attempts to knock you off center. If your ex baits you, tries to control the conversation, or is outright hostile, listen to him without interrupting. When he is done, restate your idea of what he was trying to tell you. Don't push for conclusion of the task you both are working on until enough feeling has been expressed to get on with the task.

c. Come to an agreement with your ex on custodial specifics around your child's A.D. limitations. Both of you must agree on how your child's attention differences impact his behavior and on what you must both do to help him. Too much disagreement about medication, parenting approaches, the lenient vs. strict dimension, and the intentionality or non-intentionality of behavior can cause much stress, especially when transitioning the child from one parent to the other.

It may be difficult to get your ex to accept the role of biochemistry in your child's behavioral challenges. Make it a priority to talk with her as many times as you have to, to educate her about the real limitations that he faces because of his attention differences. Use examples from your own experience or others and encourage her communication with your child's neurologist.

And, try to set up an arrangement in which you and your ex

share equitably in expenses connected with raising your child. This kind of arrangement may remove the need to have one or the other partner pay alimony or child support. Cultivate trust around money and establish financial record-keeping procedures that make clear your responsibility and that of your ex on an ongoing basis. Money hassles can create big resentment, but this needn't be the case if you make ongoing management of this dimension a top priority.

d. Be prepared to defuse anger through apology; see your own part. The words "I'm sorry" may stick in your throat on occasion but sometimes these words can be magic to diffuse a nasty hostility cycle. Saying you're sorry not only unfreezes communication logjams but helps you see the issue from the other's side. In most cases there are a number of things both you and he are "guilty of" in terms of maintaining disharmony in the relationship. Saying you're sorry doesn't mean you accept domination by the other or his control of the situation. It just means that you own your part and do not mean to make his life more uncomfortable.

e. Don't complain about your ex to your child. Though you may be tempted to complain about your ex to your child it is a good idea to resist the temptation. You may paint yourself into a corner if you do this because you are forcing your child to take sides. He may attempt to deal with this pressure by withdrawing from the both of you. Or your child may take sides against your ex with the kind of single-minded ferocity that is typical of A.D. children. Either outcome makes management of the situation more difficult for you.

5. If you are a single mom parenting a son, seek male mentors for him. If you are parenting a daughter as a single dad, seek to bring her into contact with strong female teachers. Encourage your kids to participate in athletics or special interest groups at school that put them in contact with coaches and trainers of their own gender whom you respect.

If you are a single mom of a son, make it a priority to get him in classes at school which are taught by men you respect. If you are a single dad of a daughter, encourage mentor relationships in her interest areas. It is essential for your kids to have other nurturing adults in their lives who can give them a different perspective on things than your own. These others help your pre-adolescent child to begin the transition from childhood to young adulthood.

Boys and girls in late childhood often seek "initiatory" experiences to mark their transition to puberty and their teen years. One way of providing this important marker of change is to enroll your child in an outdoors program that deliberately draws out the child's strength and affirms him as a young adult. Several programs for pre-teens are available in the Seattle, Washington area. through an organization called The Institute of Cultural Awareness. The Institute may be contacted at (206) 486-5164. Outward Bound is another nationally recognized outdoors program that provides opportunities for boys and girls to "test their mettle" and get a sense of themselves as powerful, competent, young adults.

A.D. kids have a natural tendency to be extremely self-centered. This self-centeredness is greatly mitigated by nourishing relationships with other adults who are free from the oppositionality hassles that naturally exist between you and your child. Since other adult mentors will provide a different perspective than you do, they fulfill the function of inviting your child into the world! This invitation is required for the development of your child's sense of belonging in the world, his self-confidence, and self-esteem.

6. Forgive yourself and let in delight every now and then. There is no getting around the fact that divorce hurts kids, and A.D. kids are especially hurt because of the loss of consistency and sense of permanence in their family. You may have taken on intense guilt because of what your child has experienced as a result of your divorce. Your non-custodial ex may not experience this powerful sense of guilt because he does not have to witness your child's depression and anger on a day-to-day basis.

No one gets through life without suffering. This won't be the last time your child has to deal with emotional trauma. Your gift to him is to show him how to handle his grief and sense of loss in such a way that he is strengthened for the challenges that will be thrown to him in his life. You must give him boundaries and the example of your grit as well as unconditional love. It will be difficult to do these things, however, if you are consumed with guilt. Eustress begins when you break through guilt to find compassion and acceptance for yourself.

Nourish yourself by letting in *delight* now and then. Just forgiving yourself gets you two thirds of the way there. As you forgive yourself, you are able to notice the little sensory delights around you—the play of sunlight on the wall, the sensations of a hot bath with candlelight and music. Don't deprive yourself. You deserve to celebrate your accomplishment as a single parent of a very challenging child!

CHAPTER SEVENTEEN

Dealing with the Blended Family Blues

Haiku

Cherish every tile—
plain, broken, iridescent—
that makes the mosaic.

—Joanne Barrie Lynn, 1992

Blended families, those with adopted Attention Different kids or with step-parents of A.D. kids in the home, are subject to the stress that occurs when people with different inherited perceptual styles are required to make a life together as a family.

The attentional style of "normal" families results in fairly efficient problem solving. People take the time to look at the facts, assimilate relevant information, and take action based on the new information. Family members listen to each other fairly well. Things are far from perfect, but family members usually get along and support each other.

Patterns of *attention differences* may also characterize a family. There is a large body of research to substantiate the genetic transmission of conditions like A.D.H.D., depression, Obsessive Compulsive Disorder, Tourette Syndrome, and Bipolar Mood Disorder. The family genograms of A.D. kids will show parents, grandparents, and great-grandparents with the same A.D. perceptual style and challenges.

People who grow up in Attention Different families have a

greater acceptance of behavior challenges related to "being A.D." They have endured the stress of being culturally marginalized for some "weirdness" and are oftentimes better able to meet the challenge and roll with the stress when an Attention Difference emerges in a child.

Normal people don't have this background for tolerance. When an A.D. child is adopted by a normal family, communication problems can be severe. The adopting family has no frame of reference for understanding the child's neurologic differences and the challenges inherent in them: the extreme emotional states, oppostionality, obssessionality, and depression. The child's behavior is assumed to be an intentional affront to the parents and their control.

And problems occur when a normal step-parent joins a family who have attention differences in their blood line. The step-parent may be a God-given gift to the child who badly needs a mentor, but big problems can occur if differences in perceptual style are not taken into account in their relationship. The child may turn on the step-parent in angry encounter and refuse his discipline. The step-parent may be surprised that he is not supported by the child's biologic parent, herself A.D. Mutual re-education is needed.

A child's Attention Different genetic heritage is not a sentence of death on family harmony but an invitation to explore the challenge and develop eustress skills for dealing with it.

Are more A.D. kids adopted than normals?

My experience as a therapist with A.D. blended families indicates a higher than normal percentage of adoptees are Attention Different kids. There are several reasons for this phenomenon.

First, undiagnosed attentional problems in biologic parents may lead them to have unwanted children early in their lives. The A.D. young adult parents are drawn to each other as a source of fun and sexual enjoyment but they may not have well-developed family planning skills. Biologic mothers and fathers may also experience problems related to substance abuse which is seen in the lives of many A.D. people. The lack of predictability and intolerance for stress that accompanies addiction moves the parent to give up the child for adoption. This is a reasonable and loving course of action, given the chaotic state of the parents' lives.

Older adopted children may get into the system as a result of abuse or other severe stress in the home related to the parents and child's attention differences. Sad to say, some parents give up their children for adoption because they know that they cannot handle the child themselves. They have lost all measure of control except physical violence.

The child adopted after his first or second birthday can be much more problematic than a younger adoptee who experienced a primary bonding experience with adopting parents. Adopting the older A.D. child is a crucible experience for the adopting parents—they must deal with the after-effects of psychological trauma as well as the child's attentional peculiarities.

Adoptive Parents of an Attention Different Child Face Five Major Challenges

First challenge: acknowledge the differences between you and your child. The first challenge that adopting normal parents face is to come to terms with *differences between themselves and their A.D. child.* These differences are seen in several important areas.

a. Perception. The A.D. child has a strong tendency to hypervigilence, hyperfocus (gets stuck), or hypofocus (spaces out). He literally does not see what is going on around him. He is "hard wired" to have big problems taking direction when he is under stress. Adoptive parents may mistake this neurologic predisposition for a lack of concern for their wishes or oppositionality.

b. Problem solving. The A.D. child is stimulus overloaded and is not able to make the figure-ground shifts required for efficient problem solving. He may try to cover up this problem by displaying obstinacy. In reality he needs a lot more time and assistance to work things through than normal kids. He is not being deliberately stubborn or oppositional.

c. Motivation. The A.D. child is so present-moment centered because he has to be. It is very difficult for him to hold a time line that incorporates past memories and future plans in his world view. This perceptual dynamic coupled with his low self-esteem greatly inhibits his forward thinking, his goal directedness, and his motivation. Adopting parents may mistake his lack of conventional motivation for laziness. He is not lazy but he does lack the internal context for "looking forward" to things. This prevents him taking the initiative to do things in his life.

Parents with normal perceptual styles may misunderstand the motivational system of the A.D. child and use the wrong incentives with him. One child might be hyper energetic, extroverted, the typical "A.D.H.D." type. This child will be powerfully motivated by an offer of a visit to the local go-cart track or wild ride amusement park and powerfully unmotivated by the threat of punishment.

A more retiring "A.D.D." child who is a bit phobic and naturally obsessive may be very sensitive to any kind of punishment. This child's parents must be careful that they do not lose him altogether as he withdraws into anger at himself, and into depression. In either situation, understanding the A.D. child's motivation is difficult for adoptive parents with a normal perceptual style. They do not have a meaning for appreciating all the stresses of being Attention Different.

d. Stress management ability. Most normal adults and children are able to rebound from stressors and rise above the fight or flight reaction if they have to. Attention Different children often flare up in anger or space out because they are simply less neurologically equipped to handle any requirement put on them. The adoptive parent will often say, "He's bullying me with his anger." In reality, the child is not being deliberately malevolent or upsetting. His stress defense is just biochemically underpowered.

Second challenge: understand his communication style. The A.D. child may have a hard time understanding long strings of spoken instructions and guidance. He "spaces out" five seconds into his parents' anguished pleas for change. Because of his neurologically based language processing problems (the attachment of meaning to words), he does not understand what is required of him.

Though some A.D. kids may deliberately turn off listening to adults around them, many simply do not understand what is being said to them. I have described my own son Gregory's admission to me—he sometimes hears the things I say to him like the dog character in the Gary Larsen "Far Side" cartoon, hearing only "blah, blah, blah, blah," as the humans speak to him.

The situation is made worse as the normal parents incessantly lecture the child in an effort to reason things through. The A.D. child's understanding is garbled at the level of perception; he hasn't even gotten to the place of making a reasoned consideration of the points in argument. To cover up his terrifying lack of bearing in the situation, the child will get loud and argumentative, thus contributing to the distress cycle.

Third challenge: accept biochemical influences on your child's mood. Your child's moodiness is probably not your fault. Normal parents will often experience guilt because their adopted A.D. child "looks depressed" and "unhappy." They will go to great extremes to get a smile out of him even to the point of teasing the child mercilessly for his lack of humor. The child may be suffering from depression related to biochemical factors. The parents do not realize this because they have no ready frame of reference for understanding that this is not their fault.

Fourth challenge: develop accurate expectations for your A.D. and non-A.D. kids. An adopted child with attention differences in a family of normals may be required to meet the same standards as his normal siblings. This can be excruciating for the A.D. child and his siblings. A deep distress cycle happens with the parents' repeated failures to get the same results that they do with their normal children.

The sibs are torn between their love for the adopted child, their knowledge of his attention difference, and their anger at him for causing such chaos or unhappiness in their family. And they may also feel guilty because they continually enjoy the positive attention of the parents without having to do much to earn it.

Fifth challenge: escape the guilt and resentment cycle. Many adopting families did not know that they were getting a child with attention differences. Though it is never admitted, family members may be angry that their expectations of having a normal child, grateful for his adoption, were not met. Parents may not admit this anger, and feel guilty for experiencing it, but it is a reality in their relationship with their child every minute of every day.

The parents' guilt and resentment may become a fixed pattern in adopting families and result in harsh treatment of children. The presumption that the child's behavior is intentionally mean becomes accepted wisdom. Corporal punishment to include spanking with objects and deprivation of all amenities for the child become ways that parents exert influence. A mood of surliness, insistence on absolute obedience, and boredom settles into the family.

The child's self-esteem plunges and severe behavior problems occur as a result—only to be met by more harsh punishment. Though parents may be able to maintain control in the pre-teen years, the emergence of puberty will largely terminate their influence in the situation and real suffering for all will begin as the child runs afoul of the law. This deep distress cycle must be reversed.

Four Basic Distress Patterns

Differences in perceptual style can also be highly problematic for normal step-parents of A.D. children. Unlike the biologic parent, who may herself have an attention difference or come from a family of Attention Different people, the normal step-parent is faced with bewildering new complexities in his relationship with his step-child. He does not have the data base or family history to understand what is going on. Problems occur in four basic distress patterns:

1. Guilt and resentment wedge parents apart. Resentment is often a major dynamic in step-parenting families. A step-parent may resent the disharmony that the Attention Different child brings to his relationship with the child's biological parent. If an ex-spouse is in the picture who is mishandling his/her relationship with the child, the child may bring home more anger and stress to his custodial home. The custodial step-parent feels helpless to make things better. He is tempted to flee the scene into some activity out of the home.

2. Differences in parenting philosophy may "triangulate" the step-parent out.

Distress also happens if the child's biological parents are more lenient and accepting of the child's attention differences than the normal step-parent because either one or both natural parents are A.D. themselves. In this case, the step-parent can be pushed out of the triangle formed by the child and his biological parents.

The child suffers because he gets different messages from his A.D. custodial mom and normal step-dad. To resolve this dilemma, the child may forcefully accept the value system of the A.D. ex-spouse, thus driving a wedge between himself and his step-parent. "My dad (the biological father) knows how to deal with me. You don't!" he yells at his step-father as he runs out of the house in anger and sadness.

3. The relationship between the son and his step-father is problematic. I pointed out in the last chapter that as a boy approaches the age of twelve, he is biologically primed to look to his father and other males for a model of manhood. If the father is out of the home, the boy may develop a deep longing for the father's modeling, companionship, and advice. This longing is based on more than loneliness for the other parent; it is also based on the fact that the boy requires a blueprint for becoming a man that only a mature male can provide. This requirement for maturation is a cross-cultural phenomenon seen in both A.D. and normal children.

If the father is not available to teach the boy, the boy may seek an understanding of manhood from his friends (who know little more than he) or he may flee into depression or angry acting-out. Depression or conduct problems that emerge at this time are best understood as acts of love that the boy makes to his father and his own growth requirements. These extreme actions say: "See me. Hear me. Help me learn what it is to be a man. If you will not pay attention to me, I will force you to with my wild behavior."

A step-dad can provide the boy's need for gender modeling if he has not opted out of a relationship with the boy because of the attention differences. The step-father must understand that the boy's behavior is a combination of his Attention Different neurology and the biochemical and psychological changes a boy goes through as he approaches puberty. The successful step-dad does not let the step-son's surliness get in the way of his relationship. He is in it for the duration and lets his son know this!

4. Pre-adolescent A.D. girls and the "wicked step-mother" problem. The mother-daughter bond gives the child a blueprint for womanhood. Though the daughter will most probably never relate to her step-mom with the same natural intimacy that she does to her biological mother, her relationship with her step-mother can be a powerful add-on to her life and provide important lessons for being in the world.

But sometimes the girl becomes alienated from her step-mom the same way that the boy does from his step-dad. An Attention Different girl with a perceptual style that causes strong oppositionality and temper problems has special difficulty approaching adolescence. She is naturally inclined to take up the sword against the woman who has taken her mother's place in her father's life—her "wicked step-mother." Special care must be taken to prevent permanent establishment of this energy in a distress cycle. The step-mother may have to cross swords occasionally with the girl, but must always have her eye on re-establishment of a loving relationship.

As aggravating as the pre-teen girl is to her step-mother, she needs her step-mom to teach her how to handle her predilection for high stimulation as much as the A.D. boy needs his step-father to provide the same lessons.

Pre-teen A.D. boys may express their "high stim" preferences in aggressive and impulsive behavior. The pre-teen Attention Different girl faces a different challenge. She must develop the assertiveness skills and sense of self-esteem necessary to prevent her from being victimized by others who would use her willingness to take high stim risks to manipulate her.

If the girl's biological mother is A.D. herself, the non-A.D. step-mother may be an "angel in disguise" to the daughter. She can teach the girl survival skills that the girl's natural mother may not yet have mastered herself. Novelty-seeking behavior, compulsivity, and dangerous living preferences are often seen in A.D. adults. The pre-teen girl does not need lessons in how to live her life this way. She needs gender modeling from a woman whose "No!" is as firm as her "Yes!" The normal step-mom is often the one who can best provide this training.

Five Essential Aspects of Eustress Parenting in Blended Families with A.D. Kids

Adoption-related Issues

1. Develop awareness of the difference between behavior problems caused by psychological factors and behavior related to being born A.D. Children may experience adoption-related psychological distress if they were adopted later in childhood out of foster care and have a longing memory for the biologic parents. Psychotherapy is definitely in order if separation from the birth parent was traumatic. The child will signal his distress with depression, withdrawal, or a tendency to act out his feelings of abandonment and rage in destructive ways.

Gently query the child about his feelings and keep a journal in which you describe your perceptions of his feeling states. Explore counseling as an option to deal with unfinished issues around his adoption. The fact is that in most situations involving problem behavior, distress caused by the initial adoption experience is much less of a factor than distress related to the child's inherited Attention Different predisposition. "Could he do it if he had to?" is an important question for parents to ask. If the answer comes back "No. He couldn't do it if his life depended on it," there is a good case to be made for neurology, not psychology, as a causative.

Once this distinction is made, you are ready to put your energy and attention on the kind of remedial help that your child needs. This will involve both lowering his stress and your stress and learning ways to compensate for the challenges presented by his attentional style.

2. Treat the issue of his adoption with tender loving care. Adopting parents can also cause problems by sharing their knowledge of the biologic parents with a negative tone: "No wonder you act like you do, your mother was a teen-age drug addict!" This kind of talk is like a shot to the heart of the child's self-esteem. It can make his behavioral problems much worse. "These (adopting parents) are not my people," he will declare to himself. "I am like my mother. Her life is my life. Her fate is my fate."

Wise parents will share the circumstances of their child's adoption in a matter-of-fact way and will spare him specific details until he is ready, willing, and able to contact his natural parents himself. The vast majority of children react well to this philosophy.

3. For step-parents, accept your child's longing for the non-custodial parent and don't blame yourself. Attention Different children experience more stress than other kids with a divorce because their coping skills and emotional control tend to be less developed than those of normal kids. Your child may turn on you, his step-parent, with ferocity or may dissolve into heart-wrenching depression. You may be the best thing that ever happened to him, but you may have to wait for quite a while to get his acceptance. You may be sorely tested in the meantime.

Don't blame yourself or assume that the child's non-custodial parent is inflaming the situation. Take care of your relationship with your spouse and make yourself available as a "consultant" to your step-child. As a consultant, you may provide emotional support and problem solving on your child's request but do not push for communications if you are not asked for help. Discuss your feelings of loneliness, sadness, or frustration with him if the opportunity opens up for heart-to-heart communication.

Most Attention Different children eventually come to accept their step-parents and seek the parents' counsel as they approach adolescence. The child is naturally moved to seek the wisdom of an adult role model of his own gender. As a step-parent you position yourself to be accepted by your step-child by giving him your love, acceptance, and firm guidance.

Issues for All Blended Families

4. Identify and accept the differences between how you see the world and how your A.D. child sees things. This is an essential condition for eustress. Normal parents have no way of naturally understanding their A.D. child's perceptual style; they have not walked in his shoes. Use the questions found in Chapter One to explore your child's inner experience. Get in the habit of asking questions like, "What is happening for you as you do 'x'?" or "What are you feeling right now?" "What do you want?" and "What do you imagine is going on?" "What do you see is happening here?"

These kinds of questions give you the data base you need for understanding him. Please notice the avoidance of questions beginning with the word "Why" in this set. Asking your child "why" he does something requires him to analyze himself. It puts him on the spot for coming up with a solution for his dysfunctional behavior. This kind of question does not open doors for better understanding.

Get a sense of your child's internal experience of the world—you will soon see what you need to do to reduce his stress and build his strength.

5. Create an embracing *family story line*. Family members define themselves as a unit by the stories that they tell about each other. A child gets a reputation for some aspect of his character related in these stories that highlight his talents and challenges. "He's always been like that," are words that will be used to describe a child or "We're that kind of family," may be said to identify an inclusive trait of the entire nuclear family.

A.D. kids who come into a family in early childhood rather than infancy as a result of adoption, or who join a home headed by a step-parent may not have a sense of this story line. Either they are seen as "baggage" that came with one of the parents, or parenting the child is so stressful that there hasn't been time to notice his positive aspects and really welcome him. He has become a "problem to be solved," part of the ongoing crisis.

Savvy parents deliberately create a story line by the use of a family history, photo album, or video record. These records serve as a way to say, "You are one of us. We welcome you and embrace you. We accept your challenges and thank you for your gifts!" Give him a sense of rootedness and predictability in his life and he will put down roots and grow up to do you proud!

Conclusion: Creating Community to Contain Our Kids' "Wyrd" Gifts

"It's the weird part of people that makes unusual contributions to life."

— Michael Mead

I began this book by describing my meeting with the mother of three Attention Different children who used the metaphor of a garden with many different kinds of plants to describe her family. This lovely metaphor conveyed her acceptance and love for her children as they are—strange challenges and powerful gifts. I remember her telling me how all varieties of plants grow in the garden. In nature, all varieties are part of the natural balance. This one provides shade to the others. That one holds soil. This one attracts seed-carrying bugs. All are necessary for the survival of the whole biosystem.

You and I are the ones who parent the strangest little plants in the garden. Culture would make all children corn stalks in a row, but some plants are hardier than this and have a job to do on the windswept outskirts of the garden. This is where our kids live. Those who enjoy the symmetry of corn fields define our kids as "weird" and we all know what that label means: dysfunctional, crazy, repugnant, different.

But strong cross-cultural wisdom argues the opposite view: that our A.D. children are a precious resource, an enormous cultural asset. "Weird" is an asset, not a deficit. Mythologist Michael Meade says in his book, *Men and The Water of Life*, that fairy tales and myths going back thousands of years inform us that in times of crisis those who have "weird" qualities will emerge to help us through great change. This is why, Meade tells us, the ancient Celts also give the word "wyrd" the meaning, "destiny."

It makes sense that at this time in our evolution when all the conventional answers seem to be failing that we would see the emergence of so many Attention Different kids with their strange abilities and excesses of character. Just as A.D. kids have "little anarchist" temperament challenges, they also possess rare gifts in their weirdness—we need them as a culture to renew ourselves and avoid stagnation.

Many Attention Different children are able to apply radically different perspectives to problems and come out with radically different solutions. I have pointed out throughout this book how *passionate* and *creative* and *innovative* A.D. kids can be. We need this kind of breakthrough vision to get us through the turbulent times ahead.

We are clearly at a time of crisis. The world's population growth is dangerously high. Resources are depleting. Our economic system is going through traumatic change. Pollution and war are at an all-time high.

We have seen how other probable A.D.'rs in history have changed world culture in remarkable ways—people like Mozart, who may have had Tourette Syndrome, Samuel Johnson, who may have been Obsessive Compulsive, or Thomas Edison and Picasso, likely Attention "Deficit" candidates. These men brought direct gifts to all of us from their "wyrd" natures.

Following on Meade's thesis, could it be that the emergence of so many kids with A.D. diagnoses these days is part of nature's self-healing process? Could it be that they are harbingers of the profound changes that the ecosystem is experiencing and will experience? Are they the special allies that are needed to revision what is required for our survival? Could it be that mythological wisdom is resonating with ecological wisdom here?

And new models for education are needed if culture is to realize the gifts that its Wyrd children bring. The key to the successful education of Attention Different children is to contain and educate *both* their creativity and their wildness. This process starts with the educational system's acknowledgment that these kids cannot and should not be "civilized" to the behavioral standards of normals. Their gifts must be developed with full acceptance and valuing of who they are.

New teaching methods are needed that begin with an assessment of the positive differences that the A.D. child brings to the mix, and the acceptance of his incidental learning style. He learns by doing *interesting* things. Our A.D. kids like to work on real things in the real world. They like to get their hands in and their minds around problems that have some personal meaning to them. They are notoriously unable to sit there and do paper and pencil exercises all day. They should not be made to do these things!

We are moving through the electronic age at a rapid pace. The old methods of industrial society are obsolete: the desks in a row, the quiet scratching of pencils on innumerable pieces of paper, the idea that if you obey the rules and do these things you will have a good job eventually and a good life. All this has changed. Pathfinders are needed. The educational system should start nurturing our kids' resourcefulness and stop suppressing them with Ritalin and behavior modification.

An African proverb says, "It takes a whole village to raise a child." My wife, Joanne Barrie Lynn, and I learned that we ourselves had to build our own community by educating friends, the media, and the local schools ourselves. And, as we have done this, we have enjoyed the community gathering around us, embracing our son Gregory.

Things change so fast. Only a few years ago Gregory seemed lost, slipping through the cracks in our local school district's educational system. He had been in a private school which did not help him and so we turned in desperation back to our local neighborhood school. We were pleased to find there a building principal, Mr. Lou Cenname, and a teacher, Mr. David St. Antoine, masters of their craft both, who accepted Gregory and began building a program for him. This has not been an easy task for them, for the school is located in a conservative community where the reflexive swearing and temper of a child with Tourette Syndrome is not welcome.

But they, we, and Gregory have succeeded because we did not give up on our relationship and kept our eyes on the prize, Gregory's achievement in school. This would not have happened if Lou and David had not accepted him as he is, wyrdness and all. David's genius has been in his ability to roll with Gregory's A.D. predilections and design the educational process around it. They spend a lot of time on the Internet researching real issues: the U.S. forfeiture laws, the issue of animal rights. Gregory is a genius on the computer and, like most A.D. kids has a powerful underdog sympathy; he takes the side of outsiders and the less fortunate. David folds these interests into his lesson plans with marvelous results and he is not put off by Gregory's occasional temper outbursts. He rolls with these challenges and either lets them go or uses them in the lesson plan to help Gregory develop greater empathy.

We don't know what role Gregory will choose as an adult, but he is already getting mighty good preparation for whatever it is. David follows the warp and weft of Gregory's interest. He knows how to evoke the wyrd and run with it!

Joanne and I (she more than I), have spent a lot of time working with Gregory's school to set up the right environment for Lou and David's efforts to succeed. It has felt good to be in a truly collaborative mood with the district, a state of affairs which I thought impossible to attain five years ago. When I think of *why* we are enjoying this exceptionally positive experience it becomes clear to me that Lou has put together a community that treats Gregory with respectful acceptance and in which being untrustworthy is unthinkable.

We put Lou's requirements for respect and trustworthiness on ourselves and require the same of Gregory. At twelve he is thriving. Every kid deserves this kind of education. It happened for us and it is possible for you!

Looking back I see that the most important dimension of all has been our success in achieving a community of school and friends who *accept* Gregory and value his "wyrd" nature. We earned this regard by standing up for ourselves and Gregory, and by articulating his situation to so many people that excluding us was unthinkable! So I close on this note of encouragement: do not let yourself be excluded and pushed aside. Know that eustress begins in earnest with your assertiveness on the one hand, and willingness to accept community when it is offered to you on the other.

To help your child weather the storms within his gifted and idiosyncratic personality you must be standing on the firm ground of your own emotional health. Take control of your life in order to give him the control that he requires. Know that you are on a hero's journey and that the wild plant you are nourishing is growing tall and straight and has a place in this world!

PART FOUR

Appendix

Author's Introduction to Dr. Walter Crinnion

Just before I read Dr. Walter Crinnion's following article for the first time, I came across a short parent-written case study in the innovative publication *Latitudes,* a special interest news magazine that covers the topic of exploring alternative treatments for Attention Deficit Disorder, Hyperactivity, and Tourette Syndrome.[1]

In this short article the parents described how nutritional and environmental allergy treatments were used to help their son. Before treatment his parents described him as a boy with many of the behavior problems highlighted in this book: not listening, sullenness, aggression, verbal outbursts, and general unhappiness. The results of treatment for their child were remarkable. His mother described it as "unbelievable." Their son became "more responsive, gentle, and attentive." His relationships improved considerably and a sense of sanity was restored to their family.

You may want to consider this kind of therapy for your child, but it is hard to sort out the facts on just what alternative approaches have been shown to be effective. Good research back-up is what you need. It turns out that there *is* some pretty good research on the specific foods and food combinations that have been shown to cause problematic behavior in Attention Different children.

In this regard we are fortunate to have Dr. Crinnion's perspective. As one of the pre-eminent Naturopathic authorities in the area of environmental toxicity, he gives us a good overview of what the research on diet and behavior says and what it omits.

For more information on Naturopathic methods you may call the American Association of Naturopathic Physicians at 206-323-7610.

1. Interview: "An Attention Disorder? A Case Study," *Latitudes,* Introductory Issue, (1993) published at 1120 Royal Beach Blvd., #283, Royal Palm Beach, Fla. 33411.

Nutritional Alternatives to Ritalin– Treating the Causes as Well as the Symptoms

by Walter J. Crinnion, N.D.

"I am not meaning to belittle medication, but if all you have is a hammer, everything starts to look like a nail."
— A physician reflecting on the over-prescription of Ritalin

Between 1990 and 1994 the number of prescriptions written in this country for the three main stimulants used for attention-deficit hyperactive disorder (Ritalin, Dexedrine, and Cylert) tripled. In fact Ritalin's popularity led to a shortage of the drug last year. In response, the Drug Enforcement Administration actually increased the Ritalin production quota for Ciba-Geigy to four times the allotment of four years previous. That is a lot of Ritalin! The question about this increased use is whether or not it is beneficial, and the availability of any alternatives.

Unfortunately, many physicians are using Ritalin as a diagnostic tool to assess for the presence of ADHD. In a recent survey of 1,000 pediatricians from across the U.S., 70% reported using Ritalin as a way to diagnose this problem. The pediatricians surveyed stated that time constraints were a major reason for doing this, as it could take several hours to do a thorough workup, and many patients would be unable to afford it.

One big trouble with using these stimulants for diagnosis is that some individuals who do not have ADHD will have improved attention and concentration with such medications. This, of course, will give the impression that they have this disorder. In addition, between 20% and 30% of ADHD patients do not improve with Ritalin, Dexedrine, or Cylert! With that in mind it is obvious that using Ritalin diagnostically will leave some without ADHD with an improper diagnosis of having this disorder, and some who have it without help! In addition, it leaves all of those with the problem far short of a cure. The problem has not been fixed, but a temporary improvement in some cases is granted.

While doing a symptomatic "cure" may take the pressure off parents right now, it does not yield long-term benefits. As a gardener I have found it much more beneficial to take the time required to pull the dandelion root up (getting to the cause) rather than pulling the leaves off of it and hoping that it will go away (treating the symptoms).

Unfortunately, research has not yet pinpointed the actual cause or causes of ADHD so it is impossible at this point to treat it with precision. But some interesting alternative treatments show promise.

Those doing research into ADHD have found that a high percentage of adults (50%) and of children (70%) with ADHD have a generalized resistance to their own Thyroid hormones. This condition is thought to be genetic, but no causative mechanisms for it have been found, and no treatment presented.

Another very interesting finding is that boys with ADHD have lower levels of two oils (fatty acids) in their bodies, than boys without ADHD. While they all have the same amount of oils in their diet, those with ADHD are unable to properly take those oil building blocks and make the substances they need. One of the deficient oils is found plentifully in fish (salmon oil) and could possibly be added through diet. These deficiencies were most noted in boys who had some classic symptoms of Essential Fatty Acid (EFA)[2] deficiency: thirst, eczema, and asthma. Unfortunately,

2. Essential Fatty Acids (EFA) refer to the oils or fats that are absolutely needed by the body to maintain health and that must be acquired through the diet. This is normally accomplished by using cold-pressed flax, safflower or sunflower seed oil, and the fish oils in the diet. Your body also requires Essential Amino Acids from proteins, but has no Essential Carbohydrate requirement!

supplementation with oils high in the EFAs (Evening Primrose) has failed to improve the symptoms of ADHD in two studies. The boys' bodies were just unable to make what they needed.

While there appear to be some genetic components to ADHD that are not yet fully clear, including the Thyroid hormone resistance, numerous studies have looked at the effect of diet on these individuals. While the EFA study showed a problem in properly metabolizing the oils, most studies have looked at other aspects of the diet.

In 1973 Feingold published his book, *Why Is Your Child Hyperactive?* Here he stated his theory about preservatives, dyes, and salicylates in food being the cause of this problem. While the preservatives and dyes are artificial and deliberately added, the salicylates are naturally occurring compounds in the foods themselves. Some salicylates are found in other plants and are extracted for various pharmaceutical uses. One example of a common salicylate is aspirin, which was originally extracted from white willow bark.

With his diet Feingold claimed to get 70% improvement for his hyperactive patients. To the credit of Feingold, both the public and the scientific communities responded. The public developed Feingold associations throughout the country, with literature and dietary help for thousands. In addition, between 1976 and 1988 eleven scientific studies were published in the medical literature, trying to reproduce his results. Six of the studies removed only artificial colors from the diet, four more studies removed both artificial colors and salicylates, and one study removed all synthetic additives. Only three of the studies showed positive" results (two with removal of artificial color and one with artificial color and salicylates). A positive result meant that there was some noticeable improvement in the test subjects, and in two of these three positive studies the difference was noted at school.

It is interesting to note that the Feingold diets tested in the medical literature were not actually Feingold diets. The Feingold diet eliminated artificial dyes (colors), preservatives and salicylates. Unfortunately the medical/scientific community doesn't do well with multiple factors. They prefer to "test just one thing," and then find if that one item is the culprit or not. Unfortunately, many conditions have multiple factors causing them; eliminating only one of the causes rarely gives adequate relief.

Following this theory of hunting for a single causative agent, a study was published in the *New England Journal of Medicine*.[3] In this study 48 children, who were described by their parents as "being sensitive to sugar," were rotated through three different diets each lasting three weeks. One diet was high in sugar, the next in aspartame, and the third in saccharin. They found no difference in behavior or mental ability between the three groups. This study made headlines, but you will note that they never had the children on a diet without any sweeteners! My bet is that the results of this study did not alter the parents' rules on giving their children sugar.

The *Journal* study results contradicted an earlier study which looked at children with and without ADD.[4] This study found that children with ADD did in fact have increased problems with inattention after the sugar was given. The problems with inattention were not increased in the group of children without ADD.

One obvious conclusion is that children with ADD *react* to items that other children do not; in this case it was sugar. So, while this leaves the sugar controversy at a stalemate (one study showing sugar causes attention problems in some, the other study showing no increase in attention problems), it does show that studies which eliminate only one or a few items from the childrens diet do not seem to give consistent results. On the other hand, studies that look at removing multiple foods from the diet have given consistent results.

The idea that foods can cause mental or neurologic responses is not new. Back in 1905 an Australian physician by the name of Francis Hare published a book entitled *Food Factor in Disease*. In his book he included case histories showing that foods could bring on cases of psychoses, seizures, headaches, joint pains, and

3. Wolraich, et al. Effects of diets high in sucrose or aspartame on the behavior and cognitive performance of children. *New England Journal of Medicine* (NEJM) 1994, Feb. 3, 330(5), p355-6.

4. Wender and Solanto, Effects of sugar on aggressive and inattentive behavior in children with ADD. *Pediatrics*, Nov. 1991, 88(5), p960-6.

even alcoholism. In 1922, W.R. Shannon published an article in the American Journal of Disorders in Children[5], showing that learning and behavior could be influenced by diet. In 1947, Theron Randolph published an article in the Journal of Pediatrics showing that food reactions caused fatigue, irritability, and behavior problems in children.[6] In addition, the removal of allergic foods" from the diets of children has also shown improvements in more hard core neurologic problems to include EEG[7] abnormalities[8] and elimination of seizure activity in children with epilepsy.[9]

So far, three published studies and one unpublished study have looked at removing multiple food allergens from the diets of children with ADD/ADHD. All have shown dramatic improvement in those subjects tested, and is by far the most promising of the alternative therapies.

The first of these studies to be published was done by Joseph Egger from the Childrens University Hospital in Munich, Germany.[10] In this study he looked at 76 children who were socially handicapped" by their behavior with overactivity and inattention. They were put on a diet with very few allergens (oligoantigenic)— lamb, chicken, potatoes, rice, bananas, apples, cabbage, sprouts, cauliflower, broccoli, cucumbers, carrots, etc. While on the diet, 62 improved (81.5%) and a normal range of behavior was

5. Shannon, WR, Neuropathic manifestation in infants and children as a result of anaphylactic reactions to food contained in their diet. *Am J Dis Child*, 1922, 24:89-94.

6. Randolph, TR. Allergy as a causative factor in fatigue, irritability and behavior problems in children. *J Ped*. 1947;331:560-72.

7. EEG or electroencephalograph is a test that measures the electrical brain waves in an individual.

8. Kittler, Baldwin, *Ann Allergy* 1970;28:203-6.

9. Egger, J, et al. Oligoantigenic diet treatment of children with epilepsy and migraine. *J Ped* 1989;114:51-8.

10. Egger, J. et al. Controlled trial of oligoantigenic treatment in the hyperkinetic syndrome. *Lancet,* March 9, 1995, i:940-45.

achieved in 21 of these (28%). Of the 76 children, 28 were then put through a protocol in which the foods were reintroduced along with placebos.

The placebo follow-up study found that symptoms returned with certain foods, but not with the placebos. The most reactive foods were: colors and preservatives (79%) [good work Feingold!], soy (73%), cows milk (64%), chocolate (59%), grapes (50%), wheat (49%), with 42 more foods reacting to fewer than 50% of the children for a total of 48 reactive foods.

The next study to be published was done by Bonnie Kaplan[11] in which she looked at 24 boys with ADHD. She had them on a diet free of artificial colors, flavors, and preservatives like Feingold, but also excluded chocolate, MSG, caffeine and any substance that the family thought was a problem. I was actually very impressed that she decided to listen to the families in this matter, and eliminate items they were sure caused their child problems. Such listening seems rare indeed in the medical world and is always refreshing to find. With these dietary changes, the parents reported a reliable improvement in the behavior of 54% of the children.

In the third study, 26 children with ADHD were put on a diet free of dairy, wheat, corn, yeast, soy, citrus, chocolate, peanuts and artificial colors and preservatives.[12] Within two weeks 73% showed improvement. Interestingly enough, over 75% of those who did respond well to the diet had a history of allergic problems. These problems included asthma, eczema (both of these were also listed as EFA deficiency symptoms previously!), seasonal runny nose (hay fever), and hives.

The final study, presently unpublished by this author, looked at 19 consecutive patients with ADHD in a private Naturopathic practice over the span of three years. These children were all tested for food reactions and were recommended to be on a diet free of the foods which came up positive in testing. The foods that showed up

11. Kaplan BJ., et al. Dietary Replacement in Preschool aged hyperactive boys. *Pediatrics* 1989;83:7-17.

12. Boris, M and Mandel FS. Foods and additives are common causes of the attention deficit hyperactive disorder in childen. *Annals of Allergy,* 1994, 72:462- 68.

as reactive for 50% or more of the childen were: wheat, cane sugar, chocolate, dairy (milk and cheese), apples (one of the foods used in Eggers study for the elimination diet!), and peanuts. The biggest problem with this type of dietary therapy is the child's willing compliance, and as a result 21% did not go on a diet free of these foods. Of those that did 86% *reported improvement.*

In summary, when dietary measures are implemented the improvement shown in medical studies ranges from 54-86%. In addition to our improvement in behavior and attention many of these children noted improvements in many other physical areas: bedwetting, sleep disturbances, headaches, stomach aches, anger outbursts, seizures, sinus problems, bad breath, and stamina. These may be thought of as positive side effects of this treatment. One parent actually called and thanked me saying, I have a different son now, I no longer dread getting up in the morning!" These beneficial side effects are generally not reported with the use of Ritalin.

As mentioned before, the toughest part of the dietary proto-col is keeping the diet clear of the offender foods. Unfortunately, many of the offending foods are the ones most preferred by kids (what a person craves they are often allergic to) and easiest to prepare. If both children and parents are willing to make the extra effort, however, the benefit is substantial.

Fortunately, there is also a new rapid desensitization proce-dure that can knock out a bad reaction to foods with a relatively minor elimination period of only one day. While this method has not yet been assessed for the treatment of ADHD, it appears promising.[13]

It is interesting to note that the majority of the diets that worked well for ADHD children were free of sugars. In addition to its adverse neurologic reaction, sugar also robs the body of calcium. Calcium is a natural relaxant to the muscles and nerves, as are magnesium and the B vitamins. Any dietary protocol for ADHD should include a good supplement of these calming nutrients.

There are also some calming herbs from both the western

13. Referral number for Nambudripad Allergy Elimination Technique (NAET) for rapid desensitization: 714-523-0800.

herbal tradition and the Ayurvedic tradition that may be beneficial. One such Ayurvedic herbal combination called Mentat does have some intriguing studies to back up its use. These studies, done in India, show an increased attention in children who were using it. While the children were not specifically screened for ADHD, the benefit may be just as great, if not greater, for those who do have it.

While the makers of Ritalin are cranking more out daily, some very viable alternatives may exist for yourself or your family members. If you are interested in such an alternative, diet therapy, supplementation, and herbal treatment may reduce the need for Ritalin or eliminate it entirely. If you would like to explore these possibilities, I would recommend that you contact a licensed Naturopathic Physician near you.

Dr. Walter Crinnion received his undergraduate degree in biology from the University of San Francisco in 1975. He received his N.D. (Doctor of Naturopathic Medicine) from Bastyr University in Seattle, Washington in 1982. Since then he has been in private practice in Bellevue, Washington at the Northwest Healing Arts Center, which he founded.

In 1987 he opened the country's most comprehensive cleansing program for treating environmental toxicity. He has been a faculty member at Bastyr University since 1989 teaching Clinical Ecology (food and environmental allergies), Geriatrics, and Environmental Medicine. He is also adjunct faculty at the Southwest College of Naturopathic Medicine in Scottsdale, Arizona where he teaches Environmental Medicine. He is a frequent speaker on the topic of Environmental medicine, allergies, and other chronic health problems, at medical conferences across the country.

Chapter Notes and Bibliography

Chapter One

Ornstein, Robert, *The Roots of Self,* Harper Collins, San Francisco, 1993, (page 192).

American Psychiatric Association, *Diagnostic Criteria from DSM IV,* Washington, D.C., 1994.

Callow, P., *Vincent Van Gogh, A Life,* Ivan Dee, Chicago, 1993.

Cohen, A.J., and Leckman, J.F. "Sensory Phenomena Associated with Gilles de la Tourette's Syndrome," *Journal of Clinical Psychiatry,* 53:9, September, 1992 pp. 319-23.

Grandin, Temple, *Thinking in Pictures,* Doubleday, New York, 1995.

Gruber, Howard and J.J. Voneche, Eds., *The Essential Piaget,* Basic Books, New York, 1977.

Hallowell, Edward and Ratey, John, J., *Driven to Distraction*, Pantheon Books, New York, 1994. Provides an overview of salient research behind the theory that sensory hypersensitivity causes A.D.D. (p. 282).

Perls, Frederick, Hefferline, Ralph, Goodman, Paul, *Gestalt Therapy,* Delta, New York, 1951.

Sacks, Oliver, *An Anthropologist on Mars*, Knopf, New York, 1995.

Vincent, Bartlett, M.D. "Some Notes On Distinguishing Attention Deficit Disorder (ADD) from Bipolar Mood Disorder (BMD)" 1996, incorporating ideas of Chas.W. Popper, M.D., Harvard University Medical School.

Chapter Two

(epigram) Sacks, Oliver, from "Losses" in *The Man Who Mistook His Wife For A Hat*, John Curley, Co., South Yarmouth, MA, 1986 (p6).

Comings, David E., *Tourette Syndrome and Human Behavior*, Duarte, California, Hope Press, 1990.

Gardner, Howard, *Multiple Intelligences, The Theory in Practice*, Harper Collins, New York, 1993.

Gardner, Howard, *Frames of Mind: The Theory of Multiple Intelligences*, Basic Books, Inc., New York, 1985.

Pines, Maya, "Psychological Hardiness," (an overview of the Kobasa/Maddi hardiness research), *Psychology Today*, December, 1980.

Selye, Hans, M.D., *The Stress of Life*, McGraw-Hill, 1978. Introduces the eustress and distress concepts. p. 74.

Chapter Three

(epigram) Deepak, Chopra, *Ageless Body, Timeless Mind*, Harmony Books, New York, 1993 p.193.

Comings, David E., *Tourette Syndrome and Human Behavior*, Duarte, California, Hope Press, 1990. Provides an excellent overview of limbic brain interaction in stress and behavioral disinhibition (pp. 321-332).

Selye, Hans, *Stress Without Distress*, Philadelphia, Lippincott, 1974.

Chapter Four

(epigram) Lilly, John C., "From Dolphins To LSD--A Conversation with John Lilly," by Sam Keen, *Psychology Today*, December, 1971.

Keen, Sam, "The Spiritual Journey: Twelve Rules of the Road, *Natural Health*, November, December, 1992.

Lynn, George, "Self-Care Skills for Parenting Attention Different Children," *The Missing Piece*, Olympia, WA (newsletter of the Learning Disabilities Association of Washington), Spring, 1994.

Lynn, George "Tips for Parenting Your Attention Different Child," *The Missing Piece*, Olympia, WA (newsletter of the Learning Disabilities Association of Washington), Fall, 1993.

Pellitier, Kenneth, *Healthy People in Unhealthy Places, Delecorte, New*

York, 1984. Identifies factors present in the lifestyles of stress-hardy people.

Chapter Five

Armstrong, Thomas, *The Myth of the A.D.D. Child*, Dutton, New York, 1996.

Brooks, Mona, *Drawing with Children*, Jeremy Tarcher, Los Angeles, 1986.

Comings, David E., *Tourette Syndrome and Human Behavior*, Duarte, California, Hope Press, 1990. Provides research showing relationship between frontal lobe dopamine and serotonin levels and hyperactivity (p.400).

Copeland, M.E., *The Depression Workbook*, New Harbinger Publications, N.Y., 1992. Describes how over-strenuous exercise has been shown to exacerbate manic stage effects in people with Bipolar Mood Disorder.

Chopra, Deepak, *Ageless Body, Timeless Mind*, Harmony Books, New York, 1993.

Hartmann, Thom, *Attention Deficit Disorder: A Different Perspective*, Underwood-Miller, Lancaster, PA, 1993.

Communication with Thom Hartmann, 1995, via CompuServe, on the link between T.V. viewing and hyperactivity in children.

Rapp, D.J., and Bamberg, D., *The Impossible Child*, Practical Allergy Research Foundation, 1986.

Sacks, Oliver, "A Neurologist's Notebook," *The New Yorker*, March, 1992 pp. 85-95. His famous essay on the Tourettic physician from Alberta, Canada.

Awareness "shuttling" is an exercise drawn from Gestalt Therapy. See *Gestalt Therapy Now*, Fagan, J. and Shepherd, IL, Eds., Harper, New York, 1970.

Siegel, Bernie, *Peace, Love, and Healing*, Harper Perennial, New York, 1989.

Stevens, John O., *Awareness*, Real People Press, Moab, Utah, 1971. Also contains a good set of awareness training and shuttling exercises.

The idea of a daily planner notebook was communicated to the author by John Whitehead, a Seattle, Washington based educational consultant who designs learning structures for children with severe attention differences (Autistic, A.D.H.D.).

Chapter Six

(epigram) Hallowell, Edward and Ratey, John, J., *Driven to Distraction*, Pantheon Books, New York, 1994. p. 129. Provides good description of "The Big Struggle," a phenomenon in which antagonisms of A.D.D. children become set as habit patterns.

Grinder J., and Bandler, R., *TRANCE-formations,* Moab, Utah, Real People Press, 1981. Shows how to use negative language structure to overcome chronic oppositionality.

Lynn, George, "Ten Principles for Avoiding the A.D.D. Oppostionality Trap," Olympia area *Learning Disabilities Association Newsletter,* Olympia, WA, Winter, 1996.

Chapter Seven

(epigram) The first stanza of a poem, "His Own Rules," by Jane Elkington Wahl, *Mothering,* Summer, 1991.

"The Arrow" perception-checking visual was taught to the author by Ann and Jim Armstrong at a seminar on the development of intuitive ability held at Cold Mountain Institute, Vancouver, B.C., March, 1978.

The "four-step inquiry" is a standard feature of interpersonal communications training which is especially relevant for children with stress-related communication problems.

Chapter Eight

"Standing Outside The Fire," Garth Brooks and Jenny Yates, Pearl Records, 1995.

Baron-Cohen, S., M.D. and associates: "Can Children With Gilles de la Tourette syndrome edit their intentions?" *Psychological Medicine,* Vol. 24, sec 29-40, 1994.

Chapter Nine

(epigram) Fydor Dostoyevsky, *The Gambler,* W.W. Norton, New York, 1981.

American Psychiatric Association, *Diagnostic Criteria from DSM IV,* Washington, D.C., 1994.

Andreas, Connirae and Steve, *Heart of the Mind*, Real People Press, Moab, Utah, 1989. The Andreas's are well-known writers in the area of Neuro-Linguistic-Programming (NLP) and the inspiration behind the Daily Workout for this chapter.

Associated Press release, January 1, 1996, "Gene Said to Touch Personality." Describes discovery of the D4DR gene associated with "novelty seeking" as an inherited characteristic.

Comings, David E., *Tourette Syndrome and Human Behavior*, Duarte, California, Hope Press, 1990. Provides research showing relationship between frontal lobe dopamine and serotonin levels and risky behavior (p.240).

Davis, M., and Robbins, E., *The Relaxation and Stress Reduction Workbook*, New Harbinger Publications, New York, 1995. Provides easy-to-understand-and-apply assertiveness techniques.

The idea of pursuing stimulation to get a sense of being alive was communicated to me by author Thom Hartmann via CompuServe concerning his work in progress, *Leaping Into Life,* January, 1994.

Chapter Ten

Vincent, Bartlett, M.D. "Some Notes on Distinguishing Attention Deficit Disorder (ADD) from Bipolar Mood Disorder (BMD)" 1996 incorporating ideas of Chas.W. Popper, M.D., Harvard University Medical School.

Comings, David E., *Tourette Syndrome and Human Behavior*, Duarte, California, Hope Press, 1990. Provides research showing relationship between serotonin imbalance in the brain and depression. pp. 429-436.

Copeland, M.E., *The Depression Workbook*, New Harbinger Publications, N.Y., 1992. An excellent research-based workbook for children and adults with depression and Bipolar Mood Disorder.

DeLong, R.G., and Dwyer, J.T., "Correlation of Family History with Specific Autistic Subgroups: Asperger's Syndrome and Bipolar Affective Disorder," *Journal of Autism and Developmental Disorders*, February, 1994. Provides description of how protective rage (Asperger's) differs from rage with a Bipolar origin.

"A report links an antidepressant drug to the deaths of children," Daniel Goleman in *The New York Times*, December 15, 1993, Vol. 143, p. B-9.

Hallowell, Edward and Ratey, John, J., *Driven to Distraction*, Pantheon Books, New York, 1994. Provides an excellent description of depression as a side-effect of A.D.H.D. to include overview of Bipolar Mood Disorder (Chapter Six).

Norden, M.J., *Beyond Prozac*, Regan (Harper-Collins), New York, 1995. Dr. Norden, a researcher from the University of Washington, provides an excellent overview of the new medications for depression and a description of the tie-in between exercise and elevated serotonin levels.

Physician's Desk Reference, Medical Economics Co., Oradell, NJ., 1996.

Physician's Drug Reference, Mosby Year Books, Inc., St. Louis, Mo. 1996.

"Prozac said to spur idea of suicide," Michael Waldholz, *The Wall St. Journal*, July 18, 1990, p. B1.

Chapter Eleven

(epigram) Blake, William, "A Poison Tree," from *Rag and Bone Shop of the Heart*, Robert Bly, James Hillman, and Michael Meade, editors. Harper Collins, New York, 1992 p.302.

Castenada, Carlos, *Tales of Power*, Simon and Schuster, New York, 1974.

Lynn, George, "Self-Care Skills for Parenting Attention Different Children," *The Missing Piece*, Olympia, WA (newsletter of the Learning Disabilities Association of Washington), Spring, 1994.

Small, Jacqueline, *Transformers, Therapists of the Future*, DeVorss, Marina del Rey, CA, 1984.

Weisinger, Hendrie, *Dr. Weisinger's Anger Workout Book*, Volcano Press, San Francisco, 1981.

Werbach, M., *Nutritional Influences In Illness*, Keats Publishing, New Canaan, CT, 1987. Shows tie-in between diets high in magnesium and tryptophan and serotonin levels; key factors in both depression and obsessionality.

Williams, Donna, *Nobody Nowhere*, Avon Books, New York, 1992. Williams, a brilliantly self-aware autistic woman provides a good understanding of *terror-based rage*, as a distinguishing characteristic of the Autistic attention difference.

Chapter Twelve

(epigram) Dolnice, Edward, "Trapped in A Web of Senseless Rituals," *Health* magazine, September, 1994, p. 80.

Baer, Lee, *Getting Control*, New York, Plume Books, 1990. Provides an excellent description of the Response Exposure and Prevention method for overcoming compulsive behavior.

Baxter, Lewis and Associates, "Caudate Glucose Metabolic Rate Changes with Both Drug and Behavior Therapy for Obsessive Compulsive Disorder," *Archives of General Psychiatry*, September, 1992.

Cox, Brian J. and Associates, "Clomipramine, Fluoxetine, and Behavior Therapy in the Treatment of Obsessive-Compulsive Disorder: A Meta-Analysis," *Journal of Behavioral Therapy and Experimental Psychiatry*, Vol. 24, no. 2, pp. 149-163, 1993.

Goodman, W.K., and associates, "Pharmacology of Obsessive Compulsive Disorder," *Journal of Clinical Psychiatry*, 53:4, April, 1992.

Norden, M.J., *Beyond Prozac*, Regan (Harper-Collins), New York, 1995.

Swedo, S.E. and Leonard, H.L., "Speculations on Antineuronal Antibody-Mediated Neuropsychiatric Disorders of Childhood," *Pediatrics*, Vol. 93, No. 2, February, 1994.

Werbach, M., *Nutritional Influences In Illness*, Keats Publishing, New Canaan, CT, 1987. Shows tie-in between diets high in magnesium and tryptophan and serotonin levels; key factors in both depression and obsessionality.

Chapter Thirteen

Baer, Ron, *Supporting Fathers of Special Needs Children to Claim Their Own Fatherhood,* unpublished dissertation, University of Mass, 1994.

Johnson, Robert A., *Owning Your Own Shadow*, Harper, San Francisco, 1991. pp.-64-65. Johnson, a first-class Jung scholar provides a good description of how shadow qualities manifest in relationships.

Lieberman, Lisa, M.S.W, L.C.S.W., "There's No Time for Us As A Couple: Maintaining Your Relationship When Your Child Has Autism," presentation paper at the "Best Of The Northwest," conference presented by the American Society of Autism, Seattle, WA, March 2, 1996.

Lerner, Harriet Goldhor, Ph.D., *The Dance of Intimacy, A Women's Guide to Courageous Acts of Change in Key Relationships,* Harper and Row, New York, 1989 p.3.

Markowitz, Laura, "After The Trauma," *Family Therapy Networker*, November/December, 1991, pp. 30-37. Provides a description of William Blake's model of the three stages of innocence.

Ryan, R.S. and Travis, J.W., *The Wellness Workbook*, Ten Speed Press, Berkeley, CA, 1981. The Positive Negativity method is derived from an exercise titled "Working with feelings," p. 131.

Chapter Fourteen

The term "Uproar" was first coined by Dr. Eric Berne in his seminal book, *Games People Play*, Castle Books, New York, 1964.

The Role Negotiation technique was originally developed by Dr. Roger Harrison for use with organization decision teams. Author cite: *Group Facilitator's Handbook*, University Associates, LaJolla, California, 1974.

Chapter Fifteen

(epigram) Rita Walpole Ague, "Legal Assistance and Raising A Child With Autism," Advocate, Newsletter of the Autism Society of America, Nov-Dec, 1995.p. 20.

Armstrong, Thomas, *The Myth of the A.D.D. Child,* Dutton, New York, 1996.

"Attention Deficit Disorder: Adding Up The Facts," Published by the Division of Innovation and Development, Office of Special Education and Rehabilitative Services, U.S. Department of Education.

The Federal Register, "Assistance to States for the Education of Children with Disabilities Program and Preschool Grants for Children With Disabilities: Final Rule," September 29, 1992, 34 CFR parts 300,301.

Fisher, Roger and Ury, William, *Getting To Yes,* Penguin Books, New York, 1981. Provides negotiation strategy and shows importance of identifying your educational values and interests for your child.

Gerlach, Elizabeth, *Autism Treatment Guide*, Four Leaf Press, Eugene, Oregon, 1996, p26.

Gordon, Michael, *A.D.H.D./Hyperactivity: A Consumer's Guide,* GSI Publications, DeWitt, N.Y., 1991.

Hallowell, Edward and Ratey, John, J., *Answers to Distraction,* Pantheon Books, New York, 1994.

"Questions Often Asked about Special Education Services," pamphlet published by the National Information Center for Children and Youth with Disabilities," 1993. (NICHY). A good guide for beginning the I.E.P. or 504 process.

Chapter Sixteen

Jarema, William, *Fathering The Next Generation*, Crossroads Press, New York, 1994. Provides excellent description of "positive" and "toxic" fathering practices for boys in single-parent and two-parent families.

Lynn, George "Raising Fire-Spirited Boys," *The New Times*, Seattle, Washington, April, 1995.

Meade, Michael, *Men and the Water of Life*, Harper San Francisco, 1993.

Chapter Seventeen

Comings, David E., *Tourette Syndrome and Human Behavior*, Duarte, California, Hope Press, 1990. Shows how attention differences are communicated in the intergenerational cultures of families.

Minuchin, Salvador, *Family Kaleidoscope*, Harvard University Press, 1984.

Nichols, W., *Treating People in Families*, Guiliford Press, N.Y., 1996.

Stress and The Family, readings, Vol. I, McCubbin H., and Figley, C., Editors, Bruner-Mazel, New York, 1983. Provides good understanding of how patterns of distress are communicated in families.

Conclusion

(epigram) Meade, Michael, *Men and the Water of Life*, Harper San Francisco, 1993, p.387.

Anderson, N.C., "Creativity In Mental Illness," *American Journal of Psychiatry*, 144:; 1288-1292 provides research on the connection between creativity and attention differences. See also *Tourette Syndrome and Human Behavior*, p 300 for a discussion of how people with attention differences often choose career paths to law and politics.

Lynn, George, "Wild Boy," *Family Therapy Networker*, May, June, 1995. pp. 52-62

Lynn, George, "Wyrd Kids and Planetary Survival," *Seattle Men Magazine*, June, 1994.

About the Author

George Lynn is a Certified Mental Health Counselor and writer with a practice located in Bellevue, Washington. He has taught counseling and group psychology at the University of Puget Sound and Antioch University.

His innovative techniques for working with children with attention differences have been featured on National Public Radio, the *Family Therapy Networker* magazine, and the CompuServe ADD Forum.

George lives in the Seattle area with his wife, poet Joanne Barrie Lynn and son, Gregory Barrie Lynn, a bright 12-year-old who is diagnosed with Tourette Syndrome.

Index

A

adoption, 225, 228, 231-232, 234
Ague, Rita Walpole, 194-195, 206
Aikido, 76, 115
alcoholism, 248
American Association of Naturopathic Physicians, 243
American Psychiatric Association, 8
amiltriptyline, 126
amino acid tryptophan (TRY), 155
amnesia, 141
amygdala, 48
Anafranil, 153-154
Armstrong, Thomas, 72-73
artificial colors, 246, 249
artificial dyes, 246
aspartame, 247
Asperger's Disorder, 16
aspirin, 246
asthma, 245, 249
Augmented Writing Device (AWD), 187
Autism, 15-17, 167
Ayurvedic, 251

B

bad breath, 250
basal ganglia, 146
bedwetting, 250

Bernie Siegel, 79
Bipolar, 76
Bipolar depression, 111
Bipolar Mood Disorder (B.M.D.), xiii, xx, 8, 13-15, 17, 23-24, 123-124, 126, 131, 134, 223
blended families, 223-224, 231, 233
blood sugar, 41
Brooks, Mona, 81

C

caffeine, 249
calcium, 250
cerebral cortex, 67
Ch.A.D.D., 215
chocolate, 249-250
Chopra, Deepak, 79
Ciba-Geigy, 244
clomipramine, 153-154
compulsions, 145-148, 151-155, 157, 205, 211
CompuServe, 56
Conduct Disorder, 110-111, 167
cortex, 48, 123
Crinnion, Walter, xviii, 243-244, 252
Cylert, 244-245

D

D4DR, 109
dairy, 249-250

depression, 11, 13-15, 23, 56,
    101, 121-128, 130-131, 146,
    153-155, 167, 171, 173, 211,
    220, 223-224, 226-227, 229,
    231-232
desipramine, 126-127
Dexedrine, 244-245
Diagnostic and Statistical Man-
    ual (DSM IV), 8-9, 110
divorce, 232
dopamine, 67-68, 72, 75, 99,
    122-123
Downs Syndrome, 172
dyslexia, 205

E

eczema, 245, 249
EEG, 248
Egger, Joseph, 248, 250
Elavil, 126
epilepsy, 248
Essential Fatty Acid (EFA), 245-
    246, 249
Evening Primrose, 246
exercise, 59, 61
expression, 205
external senses, 134

F

Feingold, 246, 249
flash cards, 186
fluoxotine, 126, 154
Frontal lobes, 67-68, 72, 75, 99-
    100

G

General Adaptation Syndrome
    (G.A.S.), 47
Gestalt, 137
grapes, 249

H

Hallowell, Edward M., 83, 86
Hare, Francis, 247
Hartmann, Thom, 19, 68, 112,
    114
headaches, 247, 250

I

imipramine, 126-127
Individualized Education Plan
    (I.E.P.), 188-191, 193-194,
    208
Individuals with Disabilities Ed-
    ucation Act (I.D.E.A.), 189-
    190
insomnia, 154
Institute of Cultural Awareness,
    220

J

joint pains, 247
Jung, Carl, 177, 217

K

Kaplan, Bonnie, 249
Karate, 76
Keen, Sam, 57, 64
Kobasa, Suzanne, 32

L

language comprehension, 205
Learning Disabilities Association, 194, 207-208
Lerner, Harriet Goldnor, 172
Lieberman, Lisa, 167-168, 171-172
limbic brain, 47-49, 123, 135, 141
limbic rage, 49, 136, 140
limbic reaction, 140
limbic system, 49-50, 100
limbic wave, 49-50, 103-104, 135, 140-141
Lithium, 126

M

Maddi, Salvatore, 32
Meade, Michael, 236
medication, 123-127
meditate, 60
milk, 249-250
motor cortex, 48
MSG, 249

N

National Father's Network, 172, 215
National Information Center of Children and Youth with Disabilities (NICHY), 204
Nefazodone, 154
Neurodiagnostics, 207

Neurolinguistic Programming (NLP), x, 118
neurotransmitter, 68, 72, 100, 146, 154
Niacin, 155
Norpramin, 126

O

obsessions, 145-155, 157, 205, 211, 226
Obsessive Compulsive Disorder (O.C.D.), 146-147, 223, 236, 151, 153
Outward Bound, 220

P

paroxitine, 126, 154
Paxil, 126, 154
phobias, 146, 152, 154
Physician's Drug Reference, 125
Post Traumatic Stress Disorder (P.T.S.D.), 93
preservatives, 246, 249
Prozac, 123, 126-127, 151, 154
psychoses, 247
psychosis, 136

R

Randolph, Theron, 248
Rehabilitation Act of 1973, 189
Response Exposure and Prevention (RE&P), 151-152
Ritalin, xvi-xvii, 123, 125, 237, 244-245, 250-251

S

S.S.R.I., 126
saccharin, 247
Sacks, Oliver, 72
salicylate, 246
salicylates, 246
seizures, 247, 250
Selective Serotonin Reuptake Inhibitors (SSRI's), 154
Selye, Hans, xiv, 29, 32, 43, 46, 58, 60
serotonin, 68, 72, 75, 100, 122-123, 126-127, 131, 146, 154-155
Serzone, 154
setraline, 126, 154
severe behavior problems (S.B.D.), 166-167, 202-203
sex, 154
sexual dysfunction, 154
Shannon, W.R., 248
sinus problems, 250
sleep disturbances, 250
Small, Jacqueline, 140
sodium, 126
stamina, 250
sugar, 155, 247, 250
synaptic pool, 68

T

Tai Chi, 76

thalamus, 48
The General Adaptation Syndrome, (GAS) 29-31
thirst, 245
Tofranil, 126
Tourette Syndrome (T.S.), xiv, 5, 8, 12-15, 17, 24, 31, 39, 55, 72, 134, 146, 163, 169, 223, 236, 238, 243
Tourette Syndrome Association, 215
tricyclic, 126
tryptophan, 155

V

violent behavior, 203
visual-motor problems, 205
vitamin B, 250
vitamin B-6, 155

W

Wellness Model, 29, 32
wheat, 249-250

Y

Yoga, 60

Z

Zoloft, 126, 154